Immunobiology of Human Milk:

How Breastfeeding Protects Babies

Immunobiology of Human Milk:

How Breastfeeding Protects Babies

Prof. Lars A. Hanson, M.D., Ph.D., F.R.C.P.C.H. (Hon)
Professor Emeritus, Clinical Immunology, Pediatrician
Göteborg University
Göteborg
Sweden

Immunobiology of Human Milk:

How Breastfeeding Protects Babies

Pharmasoft Publishing
1712 N. Forest St.
Amarillo, TX 79106

(806)376-9900
(800)378-1317

Library of Congress Control Number: 2004105834

ISBN 0-9729583-0-4

Contents

Acknowledgments vii

How To Read And Understand This Book ix

Common Abbreviations xi

1. The Newborn Meets A World Full Of Microbes 13
   - The intestinal colonization of the neonate 16
   - Bacterial colonization of the newborn in different countries 20
   - Neonatal colonization and breastfeeding 20
   - Effects of antibiotic treatment on the infant's gut microflora 21
   - Risk of infections at delivery and in the neonatal period 21
   - Intestinal microbes make the immune system of the infant grow 22
   - Probiotic bacteria 22

2. The Components Of Host Defense 27
   - **Innate immune defense mechanisms** 27
     - The phagocytes 30
     - The cytokines 32
   - **The adaptive immune system** 34
     - Antigen presentation 34
     - T lymphocytes, the thymus, and cell-mediated immunity 35
     - Antibody production 39
     - Secretory IgA (SIgA) - the main antibodies on mucosal membranes and in human milk 41
   - **Vaccination** 43
     - Mistakes by the immune system: autoimmune and allergic diseases 44

3. Host Defense Of The Growing Baby **47**
The immunology of pregnancy **47**
The innate defense mechanisms **49**
Defense in the fetus 49
Mechanical and chemical defense factors 49
Biochemical defense factors **50**
The phagocytes 52
Macrophages and monocytes 53
NK cells 54
Antigen-presenting cells 54
The adaptive immune system **55**
The thymus 55
T lymphocytes 56
B lymphocytes 56
The mucosal defense system 57
Small for gestational age (SGA) and intrauterine growth retardation (IUGR) **61**
The effects of vaccinations on infants, young children, and pregnant mothers **61**

4. Mother's Defense Of The Fetus Via The Placenta **71**

5. Mother's Defense Of The Offspring Via The Milk **77**
Components of human milk with immunobiological activities **77**
Antibodies 77
Lactoferrin 83
Alfa-Lactalbumin 86
Lysozyme 87
Carbohydrate components 88
Lipids and milk fat globules 90
Nucleotides 91
Defensins 92
Cytokines 92
Hormones and growth factors 95
Anti-secretory factor 98

Anti-inflammatory components 99
Soluble CD14 and soluble Toll-Like Receptor 101
Leucocytes in milk 102
Neutrophils *103*
Macrophages *103*
Lymphocytes *103*

6. Breastfeeding And Protection Against Disease 123
Breastfeeding and infant mortality 124
Breastfeeding and protection against infections 129
Protection against diarrhea 129
Protection against respiratory tract infections 133
Protection against neonatal septicemia 136
Protection against urinary tract infections 136
Protection against necrotizing enterocolitis (NEC) 138
Protection against other infections 139
Long-term effects of breastfeeding 139
Breastfeeding and vaccinations 139
Long-term protection against infections 142
Breastfeeding and allergy 144
About allergic diseases *144*
Breastfeeding and allergy: food allergy in infancy and early childhood *146*
Milk factors possibly involved in protection against, or development of allergy in the child *146*
The Hygiene hypothesis of allergy development *147*
Review of studies investigating whether breastfeeding protects against various forms of allergic diseases *150*
Nutrients, breastfeeding, and allergic diseases *154*
Breastfeeding, autoimmune, and other inflammatory diseases 157
Breastfeeding, obesity, and other metabolic conditions 159
Breastfeeding and tumors 162
Mechanisms behind possible long term effects of breastfeeding 164

7. Infectious Agents In Milk **195**
Bacteria **195**
Mastitis **196**
Viruses **197**
HIV- 1 and 2 197
Human T cell leukemia virus (HTLV) 202
Cytomegalovirus 203
Hepatitis viruses 205
Rubella and other viruses 205
Parasites **206**

8. Concluding Remarks **213**
The mother, the baby, and science 213
White and black swans 215
How useful is breastfeeding - what can we tell the parents? 216

Glossary **219**

Index **235**

Acknowledgments

In 1955, my studies of milk proteins, especially immunoglobulins, started as my PhD work in the Department of Medical Chemistry and continued in the Department of Bacteriology at Göteborg University, Sweden, in parallel with my medical studies. That is when I found that the main antibody in human milk, later called secretory IgA, was different from the antibodies in blood. As I became a pediatrician, I continued with more clinically oriented studies of human milk and breastfeeding. Later, I was awarded a personal Professorship by the Swedish Government so I had optimal possibilities for the combination of research and clinical activities as head of a Department of Clinical Immunology at Göteborg University. My research on human milk and its effects evolved to include many studies in developing countries like Pakistan and Guatemala.

During the early period, I saw a decline in breastfeeding. Subsequently, as the expansion of our knowledge and understanding of this field grew, I witnessed the slow increase in the prevalence of breastfeeding. I have through the decades been involved in spreading our growing knowledge of why breastfeeding is such a remarkable mode of transferring from the mother not only optimal nutrients, but also a specially adapted defense to her baby. The fact that human milk contains numerous active components, many even with long term effects, makes these efforts easier.

In my work in poor countries, one function of breastfeeding among the many was very striking: the contraceptive effect. That fact made me approach the Holy Father in Rome suggesting that the Vatican promote breastfeeding because at the population level it is such a remarkably effective natural contraceptive with so many additional advantageous capacities. The Pope did, after two meetings five years apart, deliver such a message.

The purpose of this book is to provide a scientific basis for how breastfeeding favors the short and long term health of the baby. It covers a large area of research.

I have had great help and support from many friends and colleagues while working on this book which, in a way, is my scientific testament. Ia Adlerberth provided support for Chapter 1. Kristin Svensson also reviewed chapter 1 and provided helpful comments. Esbjörn Telemo was very constructive in criticizing Chapter 2. Anders Fasth reviewed Chapter 3. Chapter 6 was reviewed by Ann-Marie Widström, Genevieve Becker, and Carol Campbell. Shakila Zaman gave me statistical advice. The hardest task of all was undertaken by Wendy Oddy who read the entire manuscript and provided very helpful comments.

My hope is that this summary of a complex but fascinating field of knowledge will be of help to those who work with mothers, babies, and breastfeeding.

Dr. Lars Hanson

How To Read And Understand This Book

Human milk contains a large number of components which help support and protect the infant via a number of advanced and complex biological mechanisms. To fully understand the role of breastfeeding, it is necessary to know how the newborn and infant meet a world full of microbes and how the baby develops its own tiny defense mechanisms in response to them. It is important that the mother's immune system assists the baby by sending protective components through the placenta and, especially, through her milk. To give the reader up-to-date information on the functional role of breastfeeding, this book will cover the following.

The book begins with a description of the sterility of the baby at delivery and how it needs to be colonized with a normal bacterial flora. This flora is not a threat but rather helps to protect the baby against many potentially dangerous bacteria by competing with them for space and nutrients. These "good" bacteria are most efficiently obtained from the mother's stool. This is why the baby, like all other mammals, is delivered next to the mother's anus. After delivery, there will normally be a transfer of mostly harmless bacteria from the baby's surroundings, especially from the mother and family.

At delivery, the baby's immune system is very small; although, quite complete. It expands in response to exposure to newly acquired bacteria. It will take quite some time before the baby has the full capacity to defend itself. To appreciate the remarkable complexity and the many capacities of host defense, it is described in some detail for both the fetus, its' mother, and the growing infant.

While the baby's defense system is maturing, the baby needs help from its' mother. This help comes via the placenta and the mother's milk. During pregnancy, antibodies called immunoglobulin G (IgG) from the mother's blood are transported via the placenta to the fetus. The fetus will have a full set of its mother's IgG antibodies by birth. These antibodies protect the baby's tissues and blood.

However, most infections reach the baby via the mucosal membranes in the respiratory and gastrointestinal tracts. Mother's milk provides many protective factors to defend those sites. During the last several years, we have learned that human milk provides bioactively adapted, efficient protection of the mucosal membranes through a number of mechanisms which do not cause inflammation. The rule for host defense in tissues and blood is that complex mechanisms are initiated to efficiently stop the infection. Unfortunately, these defense mechanisms cause tissue inflammation because many white blood cells are brought to the infected site. The white blood cells produce a number of bioactive substances. These active substances induce the symptoms of infection - fever, tenderness, pain, tiredness, loss of appetite, etc. They also cause tissue destruction and increased consumption of energy.

In contrast, maternal milk provides a number of components which defend efficiently without inducing inflammation, symptoms of infection, tissue damage, or loss of energy. It is obvious that human milk provides defense specifically adapted to the newly born, rapidly growing baby. A newborn needs to use all available energy from food for growth, not for fighting infections. We now know that human milk contains a number of signals from the mother to her offspring that actively direct many functions in the baby including build up of host defense mechanisms. These protective effects last long after breastfeeding is terminated and include enhanced protection against certain forms of infections, enhancement of some vaccine responses, possible protection against obesity, and prevention of symptomatic celiac disease.

Thanks to the Internet and other sources, today's parents are better informed. Sometimes, they ask questions about the immunological properties of breastmilk that may be difficult for some health care providers to answer. Much of the research on breastmilk immunology has been done in the last several years and information on the complexity of the defense mechanisms in breastmilk is growing rapidly. This book reviews and interprets recent literature. To simplify the reading of the text, small boxes with concentrated facts are included in the text and each section is followed by a concluding summary giving you the essence and an interpretation of the data presented. After reading the book, you may agree with the saying: "Still confused, but at a higher level."

Common Abbreviations

AF	Anti-secretory factor
APCs	Antigen-presenting cells
cm	Centimeter
CMV	Cytomegalovirus
g	Gram
GBS	Group B Streptococci
G-CSF	Granulocyte Colony-Stimulating Factor
GM-CSF	Granulocyte-Macrophage Colony-Stimulating Factor
HAMLET	Human α-lactalbumin made lethal to tumor cells
HLA	Human Leucocyte Antigen
IFN−γ	Interferon-γ
IgA	Immunoglobulin A
IgG	Immunoglobulin G
IgM	Immunoglobulin M
IL-1β	Interleukin -1β
IL-6	Interleukin -6
kg	Kilogram
l	Liter
LIF	Leukemia Inhibiting Factor
LPS	Lipopolysaccharide
NEC	Necrotizing Enterocolitis
NK cells	Natural killer cells
SC	Secretory Component
TGF-β	Transforming Growth Factor-β
TLRs	Toll-like receptors
TNF-α	Tumor Necrosis Factor-α
Treg	Regulatory T lymphocytes

1 The Newborn Meets A World Full Of Microbes

At delivery, the infant is sterile and enters a world full of bacteria. It is important to realize that we normally carry various forms of bacteria at many sites on and in our body. These bacteria are needed for a normal life. It takes time for bacterial colonization of the baby's skin and some mucosal membranes, like in the gut, to be completed.

We normally have bacteria on our skin, in our oral cavity, nose, upper respiratory tract, gut, a few centimeters up our urinary tract, and in the lower genital tract of the female (Table 1).

Table 1

❖ **Bacteria are normally present on or in:**	
➢ Skin	➢ Small bowel, mainly lower part
➢ Oral cavity	➢ Large bowel
➢ Nose	➢ Anus
➢ Upper respiratory tract	➢ A few centimeters up the urinary tract

The substantial numbers of bacteria we usually have in different sites is shown in Figure 1. It demonstrates that the number of bacterial cells we carry is much higher than the number of human cells in our body.

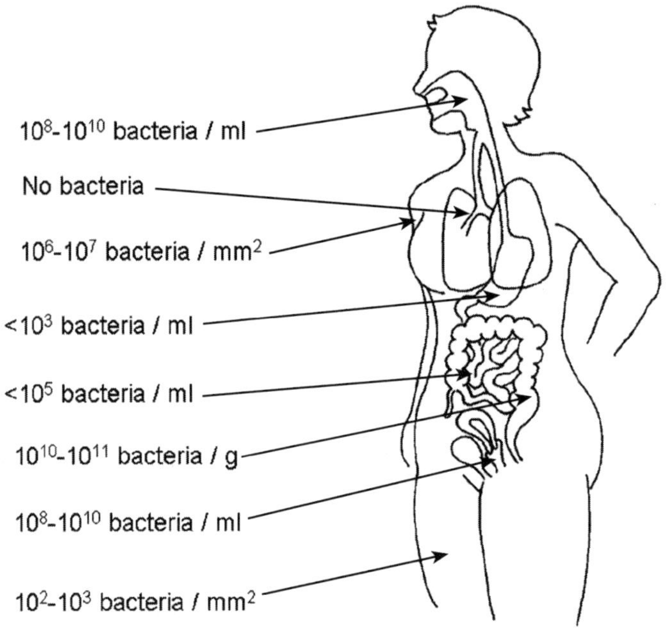

Figure 1. The number of bacteria normally carried at different sites in the body. (This figure was kindly provided by Dr. Ia Adlerberth).

Human babies, like all mammals, are delivered next to the mother's anus. This insures exposure to bacteria which may be advantageous to the baby. An adult carries approximately 1 kilogram of bacteria in the gut, mainly in the large bowel (colon). More than 99.9% of these are *anaerobic* meaning that they cannot survive in the presence of oxygen (Table 2). They consist of some 400 different species many of which are ill defined and do not even have a name. Anaerobic bacteria are totally harmless under normal circumstances. By competing for space and nutrients, they limit the number of aerobic or facultative anaerobic bacteria which tolerate oxygen (Table 2). Aerobic bacteria are normal members of the intestinal microflora, but they are not completely harmless and may cause infections if they spread to other parts of the body.

Table 2

Examples of Bacteria Normally Colonizing The Infant's Gastrointestinal Tract		
Aerobic and facultative anaerobic bacteria thrive best in the presence of oxygen and include some potentially pathogenic bacteria.		
	Gram staining*	Pathogenicity
Enterobacteriaceae family		
Escherichia coli	Gram negative	high
Klebsiella	Gram negative	high
Enterobacter	Gram negative	high
Enterococcus family (enterococci)		
Enterococcus faecalis	Gram positive	low
Enterococcus faecium	Gram positive	low
Staphylococcus family		
Staphylococcus aureus	Gram positive	very high
Staphylococcus epidermidis	Gram positive	low
Streptococcus family		
Group B (GBS)	Gram positive	high
Anaerobic bacteria do not thrive or thrive less well in the presence of oxygen. Most, but not all, are totally harmless.		
Bifidobacterium	Gram positive	low
Bacteroides	Gram negative	varies
Lactobacillus	Gram positive	low
Clostridium	Gram positive	varies

* Gram staining is used to characterize bacteria.
Bacteria that turn blue with Gram stain are Gram positive.
Bacteria that turn red are Gram negative.

The intestinal colonization of the neonate

The newborn's gut does not provide a strictly oxygen-free, or anaerobic, milieu so a neonate has much higher numbers of aerobic bacteria in their guts than an older baby or an adult (Figure 2).[1] When these bacteria reach very high numbers, there is an increased risk that they will pass through the intestinal mucosa. This "translocation" may result in an infection such as septicemia - a bacterial infection of the blood. Neonates with septicemia have a high mortality rate. Another result of translocation may be meningitis - a very serious infection of the membranes around the brain. Therefore, it is very important that anaerobic bacteria become established in the infant's gut and compete with the aerobic bacteria to limit their numbers (Figure 2). This capacity of the normal microflora to compete with new settlers is called "colonization resistance" and is a form of natural defense.[1]

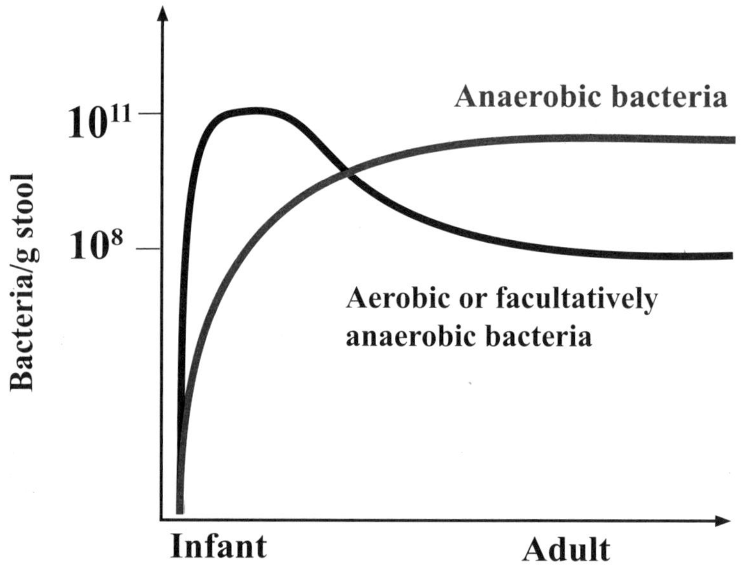

Figure 2. This figure shows the high numbers of aerobic and facultative anaerobic bacteria in the gut in early life. Among them are potentially pathogenic bacteria which may cause septicemia and meningitis. Their numbers are reduced by competition with the increasing numbers of non-pathogenic strict anaerobes. This decreases the risk of infections. (This figure was kindly provided by Dr. Ia Adlerberth).

Among the most common facultative anaerobic bacteria in the gut are *Escherichia coli (E. coli)* which belong to the *Enterobacteriaceae* family (Table 2). They are typically found in human and animal feces. *E. coli* previously appeared in the gut of the neonate during the first few days of life. Recent Swedish studies suggest that it may take some months before *E. coli* can be found in the stools of infants indicating that the spread of fecal bacteria from mothers and other individuals to the infant is presently very limited.[2, 3] *E. coli* are examples of microbes which are harmless in their normal environment in the colon, but in other sites, like the blood or urinary tracts, may cause an infection. Bacteria can have special characteristics, called *virulence factors*, which add to their capacity to cause such an infection. This is true for *E. coli* which can cover themselves with polysaccharide capsules for protection against the attacks of the body's defense forces. They can carry structures on their surface called adhesins, or pili, which make them able to attach to the mucosal epithelium in the gut or the urinary tract. This attachment may be the first step in causing an infection (Figure 3).

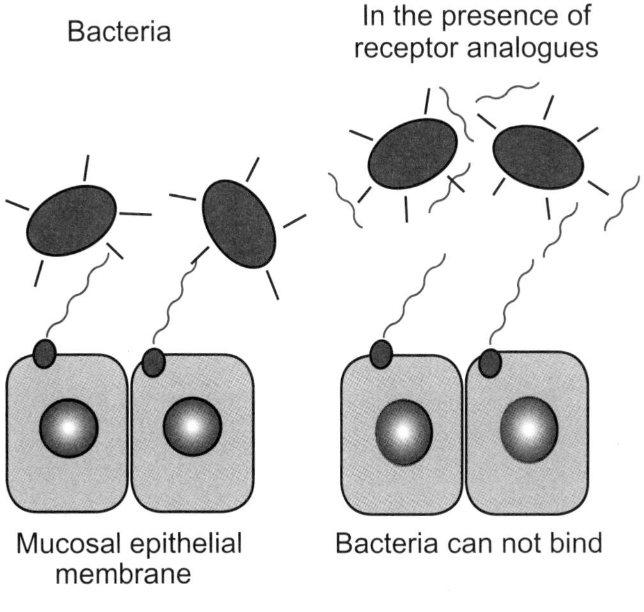

Figure 3. This figure shows how bacteria attach to epithelial cells. The bacteria may carry specific structures called adhesins, or pili, for that purpose. They attach to specific structures on the epithelial cells, usually oligosaccharide side chains of glycoproteins or glycolipids, as indicated in the left part of this figure. To the right can be seen structures in milk similar to the cellular receptor that can block the bacterial attachment.

Hygienic measures often instituted at delivery and thereafter are usually applied to prevent the newborn from being exposed to potentially dangerous bacteria, but may also limit the normal colonization. Lying down, as opposed to squatting, during delivery also limits the normal transfer of bacteria from mother to baby. Thus, the procedures used today usually result in a reduced exposure to the bacteria that normally colonize the gut and other sites and help protect the baby by competing with more dangerous microbes. The normal colonization of the gut helps reduce potentially dangerous bacteria by competing with them for available nutrients and space (Figure 2). In addition, it seems that strict anaerobic bacteria like the common inhabitant in the intestinal flora, *Bacteroides thetaiotamicron*, have an anti-inflammatory effect that may be especially helpful in the young.[4] Such bacteria may be limited in babies born using strict hygienic measures.

Certain bacteria (like *Klebsiella)* also belonging to the *Enterobacteriaceae* family (Table 2) are not common in the gut of adults, but they frequently appear in the gut of infants obviously coming from sources other than the mother.[1] They may, like *E. coli*, cause septicemia and meningitis. Certain streptococci, like enterococci, are common in infants and may originate from the mother, but this has not been investigated (Table 2). Recent studies suggest that the potential pathogen, *Staphylococcus aureus*, is frequently found in the stool flora of Swedish infants suggesting a reduced competition by other bacteria in the gut microflora.[5] These staphylococci often originate from the parent's skin flora, e.g., the mother's breast nipples or nose. Colonization of the baby could possibly be a risk factor for infection, but there is no evidence that they cause disease in breastfed infants. *Staphylococcus epidermidis* (Table 2) and other so called coagulase-negative staphylococci of low virulence are also very common in the stool of Swedish infants during the first few months of life.[3] These bacteria have traditionally been regarded as skin bacteria.

Against this background, it is clearly important to understand how the infant can balance the presence of such potentially pathogenic bacteria as *Klebsiella*, *S. aureus*, and *E. coli*. Human milk is specially made to support the baby against such threats. The baby receives help from the anaerobic bacteria present in the normal flora. The growth of these and certain other bacteria may actually be supported by special factors in the maternal milk helping them to successfully compete with the potential pathogens. Then, the possibility of their causing an infection is much smaller. A carbohydrate structure on the main antibody in milk, the secretory IgA, favors the growth of *E. coli* of low virulence by promoting the production of an adhesin named type1 fimbriae which functions as a colonization factor.[6] The structure shown in Figure 3 is used to help bacteria bind to an epithelial cell via such an adhesin. Non-virulent bacteria adhere in such a way as to support their presence and growth in the gut. Virulent bacteria use this attachment to initiate an infection through the mucosal epithelium.

As aerobic bacteria increase in number in the gut, they consume the oxygen present. This makes it possible for the anaerobic bacteria to multiply and increase in number (Figure 2). They reach high numbers within a week after birth.[1] The strict anaerobes, *Bacteroides* (Table 2), most likely come from the mother's stool since they are slower to appear in the feces of infants delivered by caesarean section. Colonization with bifidobacteria is also slower indicating that these bacteria may be acquired from the mother during a normal vaginal delivery.[1] Some studies suggest that lactobacilli are established early in the microflora of some infants. Most likely, they come from the mother's oral or fecal flora. Again, infants delivered by caesarean section may have a delayed colonization with these microbes. Bifidobacteria and lactobacilli seem to be able to inhibit growth and other functions of many enteric pathogens in vitro.[7-9] The strict anaerobes, clostridia (Table 2), often reach higher counts in the guts of infants than in adults and appear as the first anaerob after caesarean section.[3] This may be because they are acquired from environmental sources as they are spread by spores resistant to most disinfectants.[1]

> The sterile newborn starts to be colonized with bacteria from delivery and thereafter. In the beginning, potentially harmful bacteria which tolerate oxygen may reach high numbers in the gut. Harmless, strictly anaerobic bacteria that do not tolerate oxygen then increase in number competing for food and space and suppressing the aerobic ones. In modern society, the bacterial colonization of the newborn and infant has changed. This may have negative consequences. The immune defense against potentially harmful microbes is limited, but develops rapidly after birth. Human milk contains numerous factors that protect the baby via its mucosal membranes where the microbial exposure takes place.

Bacterial colonization of the newborn in different countries

There are obvious differences in the early intestinal colonization of microbes in neonates and infants born in different countries. In poor areas, the colonization is earlier and a more diverse spectrum of bacteria is established earlier in the gut. The flora changes continuously as the baby is heavily exposed to different bacteria.[1] This, of course, brings a higher risk of infections as noted in our studies in Pakistan. There, the prevalence of neonatal septicemia is as high as 2% whereas it is 0.1-0.4% in Sweden. In Pakistan, most cases of neonatal septicemia are caused by enterobacteria and other related gut bacteria while in Sweden *Staphylococcus aureus, Staphylococcus epidermidis,* and Group B Streptococci (GBS) are the major causes. Especially in poor countries, diarrhea caused by enteropathogenic *E. coli*, *Campylobacter*, and *Salmonella* may be common.[1] There are also differences among well-to-do countries which seem to be due to variations in hygienic measures applied in early life. Some of these measures may increase the risk of exposure to potentially dangerous microbes which can cause infections partly because the normal gut flora, especially the anaerobic bacteria, are reduced. It is obvious that our knowledge, as well as our awareness, is often not adequate in this area.

Neonatal colonization and breastfeeding

Breastfeeding is an important factor in the development of the intestinal microflora of the offspring. Breastfeeding clearly influences microbes in a number of ways. It affects the *E. coli* in the gut of the baby. *E. coli* in breastfed babies less often carry virulence factors that make them more efficient in causing infections.[1] Breastfed babies also have fewer of the potentially pathogenic bacteria, *Klebsiella* and *Enterobacter*, in their gut. Among the members of the *Enterobacteriacae* family, breastfed babies have a predominance of *E. coli* compared with *Klebsiella* and *Enterobacter*. Further, they have much lower counts of clostridia and enterococci than bottle-fed infants. Older studies indicated less *Bacteroides* and more bifidobacteria among breastfed babies, but this is no longer seen in recent studies. Lactobacilli are mostly found in similar numbers in breastfed and non-breastfed infants.[1]

> Breastfeeding modifies the microflora in the gut. Harmless anaerobic bacteria are favored and the potential pathogens are reduced.

Effects of antibiotic treatment on the infant's gut microflora

Antibiotic treatment of infants usually has strong effects on the gut microflora. With antibiotic use, *Klebsiella* and *Enterobacter* reach high numbers in the gut increasing the risk for translocation resulting in septicemia. Antibiotics also decrease the number of *E. coli.*[1]

Antibiotic-resistant strains of enterobacteria increase and may spread in the hospital nursery. If a number of infants in a nursery are given antibiotics, this often affects the intestinal colonization pattern of other infants in the same nursery.[10] After the treatment, it usually takes a few weeks for the intestinal microflora to return to normal. The suppression of the anaerobic flora by antibiotics may result in a limited colonization rate of neonates in neonatal intensive care units. Thus, they may be at a higher risk for colonization with bacteria of a greater capacity to cause disease.

Risk of infections at delivery and in the neonatal period

At delivery, the baby should be protected against staphylococci, which may infect the umbilicus, group B streptococci (GBS) and *Listeria,* which may be present in the mother's vagina. The latter two microbes cause neonatal septicemia and meningitis, as can *E. coli* and *Klebsiella.* Necrotizing enterocolitis (NEC) is a severe condition mainly occurring in the premature infant. It may be related to the gut microflora among other factors. Damage to the intestinal mucosa increases the risk of perforation of the gut mucosa and septicemia.[1] Absence of breastfeeding is a risk factor for NEC as well as for neonatal septicemia and meningitis.

The pregnant woman should be protected against group A streptococci which may infect the delivery canal. She should also be protected against *Listeria* which can cause abortion or severe infections in the newborn.

Intestinal microbes make the immune system of the infant grow

Now, we know an additional reason why it is important for normal bacterial colonization of the infant's gut with an optimal sequence of bacteria: *these microbes are the main stimulus for the growth of the immune system of the newborn.* There are more than ten times as many antibody-producing cells in the intestinal mucosa of animals with a normal intestinal bacterial flora as in germ-free animals.

Some of the normal bacteria in the gut seem to be important for the maturation of the immune system so that it learns to react mainly against microbes rather than its own tissues. The gut learns to become *tolerant* of such structures. It might be that continuous exposure to new bacteria in the gut is important for the development of the tolerance mechanism. It is being proposed that an abnormal intestinal colonization of the neonate adds to an increased risk of allergic diseases. This is possibly because the infant is unable to develop immunological tolerance to food, pollen, mites, and other structures. Instead, its immune system reacts against such structures causing allergic reactions. This proposal is often called the "Hygiene hypothesis".[11]

> The microbial colonization of the intestine induces the rapid expansion and development of the immune system. In this way, the infant becomes more capable of defending itself against infections. The exposure to microbes also helps the infant's immune system develop the critical ability to become immunologically tolerant to material it should not react against like food, pollen, etc. This tolerance prevents the baby from developing allergic diseases.

Probiotic bacteria

Presently, there is quite an interest in so-called probiotic bacteria, e.g., certain *Lactobacillus* strains. Several such microbes have been suggested to have advantageous effects but these effects are still poorly defined. The probiotic bacterial strains may act by competing with other bacteria for space and nutrients in the gut reducing the numbers of potentially pathogenic microbes. There is some evidence that certain *Lactobacillus* strains may help infants with rotavirus infections to recover faster.[12] A *Lactobacillus* strain used to colonize the mother and neonate has been claimed to reduce the risk of allergy in the offspring.[13] While other studies suggested *Lactobacillus* bacteria had no effect against allergy, it is likely that we will learn much more about the possible effects in the future.

In conclusion:

The newborn needs to have contact with and be colonized by a normal microbial flora. It is safest when these bacteria come mainly from the mother because she provides defenses against them.

This normal bacterial flora colonizes the skin and many mucosal membranes of the baby where they help protect against other potentially more dangerous bacteria by competing with them for nutrients and space.

In the gut where the bacteria normally reach high numbers, it is important that the normal flora dominated by anaerobic bacteria becomes established, competes with, and reduces the number of potentially pathogenic bacteria like E. coli or Klebsiella. Antibiotic treatment severely interferes with the normal gut flora of the treated infant and may affect the gut flora of other infants in the same nursery.

Breastfeeding influences many potentially pathogenic microbes in the gut microflora so that they have a lower capacity to cause infections by limiting their ability to bind to and pass into tissues through the gut mucosa.

The microbes colonizing the newborn, especially those in the gut, are the major stimulus for normal growth and development of the baby's immune system. As a result, the immune system becomes capable of defending the baby against infections. It also develops the selective capacity to limit its reactivity against foods, pollen, and other material that, otherwise, may induce allergic reactions.

Reference List

1. Adlerberth I, Hanson LÅ, Wold AE: Ontogeny of the intestinal flora. In: Sanderson IR, Walker WA, editors. Development of the Gastrointestnal Tract. Hamilton, Ontario: BC Dexter Inc. 279-92, 1999

2. Nowrouzian F, Hesselmar B, Saalman R, Strannegard IL, Aberg N, Wold AE, et al: Escherichia coli in infants' intestinal microflora: colonization rate, strain turnover, and virulence gene carriage. Pediatr Res 54:8- 14, 2003

3. Adlerberth I LE, Ahrne S, Aberg N, et al: The intestinal flora of Swedish infants. In manuscript 2004

4. Kelly D, Campbell J.I., King, T.P., Grant G., Jansson E.A., Coutts A.G.P., Pettersson, S., Conway, S: Commensal anarobic gut bacteria attenuate inflammation by regulat ing nuclear-cytoplasmic shuttling of PPAR-g and ReIA. Nature Immunology 5:104-12, 2004

5. Lindberg E, Nowrouzian F, Adlerberth I, Wold AE: Long-time persistence of super antigen-producing Staphylococcus aureus strains in the intestinal microflora of healthy infants. Pediatr Res 48:741-7, 2000

6. Nowrouzian F, Monstein, H-J.. Wold, A., Adlerberth, I: Effect of human milk on type 1 and P fimbrial mRNA expression in intestinal E. coli strains. In manuscript 2004

7. Lievin V, Peiffer I, Hudault S, Rochat F, Brassart D, Neeser JR, et al: Bifidobac terium strains from resident infant human gastrointestinal microflora exert antimi crobial activity. Gut 47:646-52, 2000

8. Coconnier MH, Lievin V, Lorrot M, Servin AL: Antagonistic activity of Lac tobacillus acidophilus LB against intracellular Salmonella enterica serovar. Ty phimurium infecting human enterocyte-like Caco-2/TC-7 cells. Appl Environ Microbiol 66:1152-7, 2000

9. Coconnier MH, Bernet MF, Kerneis S, Chauviere G, Fourniat J, Servin AL: Inhibition of adhesion of enteroinvasive pathogens to human intestinal Caco-2 cells by Lactobacillus acidophilus strain LB decreases bacterial invasion. FEMS Micro biol Lett 110:299-305, 1993

10. Tullus K, Burman LG: Ecological impact of ampicillin and cefuroxime in neonatal units. Lancet 1:1405-7, 1989

11. Prescott SL: Allergy: the price we pay for cleaner living? Ann Allergy Asthma Im munol 90:64-70, 2003

12. Sullivan A, Nord CE: The place of probiotics in human intestinal infections. Int J Antimicrob Agents 20:313-9, 2002

13. Kalliomaki M, Salminen S, Poussa T, Arvilommi H, Isolauri E: Probiotics and prevention of atopic disease: 4-year follow-up of a randomised placebo-controlled trial. Lancet 361:1869-71, 2003.

2 The Components Of Host Defense

Innate immune defense mechanisms

All living material that can be attacked by infectious agents must develop a host defense to survive. This defense has reached enormous complexity in higher level animals. At birth, the pressure on these defense mechanisms to expand and grow is so high that only the nervous system, including the brain, has a similar priority of expansion and growth.

The problem with developing an efficient host defense is that it should succeed in reacting only against infectious agents and not against its own tissues or other harmless or needed materials like pollen or food. This distinction is complicated by the fact that, in rare instances, some infectious agents are able to disguise themselves by integrating host tissues into their own structures. Furthermore, some bacteria must be accepted because they are normal and needed inhabitants on the skin and some mucosal membranes.

Some of the body's basic defense mechanisms are purely mechanical, like undamaged skin, which prevents most microbes from entering tissues (Table 3). Mucosal membranes are thin structures to which infecting microbes try to attach to initiate an infection (Figure 3). To succeed, they usually have to penetrate a protective, tough mucus layer and resist the flow of saliva, if in the oral cavity, or urine, if in the urinary tract. This explains why any obstruction in the urinary tract of a child is often followed by an

Table 3

Innate Immunity

- **Mechanical defense mechanisms**
  - Skin
  - Mucosal membranes and their mucus secretions
  - Flow of saliva, urine
  - Nasal discharge
  - Ciliar functions in respiratory tract
  - Cough
  - Normal peristalsis of the gut as well as diarrhea

- **Chemical and biochemical components**
  - Chemical – low pH in stomach
  - Biochemical – numerous components in blood, tissues, and secretions

- **Phagocytes (neutrophils, monocytes/macrophages)**
  - Stranger signals
    - Gram-negative bacteria (E. coli, Klebsiella, etc)
    - Gram-positive bacteria (Streptococci, Staphylococci, etc)
    - Fungi (Candida, etc.)
    - Viruses
  - Danger signals
    - Recognize components that might cause damage (example uric acid)

- **Outcome:**
  - Activation of phagocytes
  - Production of cytokines
  - Activation of further leucocytes

increased risk of urinary tract infections. It also explains why diarrhea is a defense mechanism. It is a way to reduce the number of infecting microorganisms in the stools. The normal peristalsis of the intestine moving the gut contents downward adds to the protection of the gut mucosa.

Other mechanical defenses are discharge from the nose during a common cold and coughing during a respiratory tract infection. Impaired capacity to cough is a risk factor during such an infection. The cilia in the respiratory tract, with their upward movements, is another defense mechanism. Their impairment in smokers is considered to be one explanation of why smokers have an increased risk of respiratory infections. In the newborn and infant, these defense mechanisms are often not yet fully functional, limiting the baby's defense against all the new bacteria colonizing its various mucosal membranes. This is discussed in some detail in the next chapter.

There are some *chemical factors* that help defend us. The low pH in the stomach kills many of the microbes passing through on their way to the intestine (Table 3). Oleic acid and lactic acid from sweat and sebaceous glands kill bacteria. Various secretions contain a number of *biochemical compounds* like carbohydrates and glycoconjugates, such as glycoproteins, which can stop infections by preventing the attachment of microbes to the carbohydrate structures on epithelial cells in mucosal membranes (Figure 3). There is also a large group of peptide antibiotics present on skin and mucosal membranes, in leucocytes, and in many tissues. More than 700 such peptides are known.[1] They are divided into three groups based on their basic structure. The most well known consists of the defensins, but man also has a cathelicidin. They may be important for controlling the normal flora and stopping infections. Many other biochemical compounds have the capacity to kill or counteract microbes. Human milk contains a large number of such components that will be presented in greater detail in Chapter 5.

These basic defense mechanisms are insufficient to protect us from many infectious agents which often have the capacity to increase rapidly to try to overcome our defenses. Some bacteria may double their numbers every 20 minutes. Many microbes have developed quite elaborate mechanisms to overcome or get around our defenses. Therefore, man has had to produce a number of additional defense mechanisms to compete with microbes.

These mechanisms try to expand as fast as the microbes grow and limit or even stop their attacks both on the mucosal membranes and in the blood and tissues. Phagocytic cells provide this next level of defense.

The phagocytes

For a long time, we thought that defense cells like phagocytes, *neutrophils*, and *macrophage/monocytes* functioned in a non-specific way, engulfing and killing any microbes appearing in blood or tissues (Figure 4). Neutrophils and monocytes are circulating cells, but they can aggregate at infected sites in tissues in response to signals called *chemokines*. Macrophages are present in various tissues.

These cells carry a number of specific receptors for *"stranger signals"*(Table 3).[2] The signals activating these receptors consist of structures specific to microbes and not found in our own tissues. These receptors serve to sound the alarm that a potentially dangerous stranger is around. The defense cells of the innate immune system also recognize structures that have been called *"danger signals"*. Danger signals originate from our own tissues indicating that something untoward is taking place and defense action may be needed.[3] One such danger signal seems to be uric acid originating from dying cells.[4]

With the help of the receptors for stranger signals, the innate immune system recognizes the presence of most bacteria. In this way, all Gram-negative bacteria, like *E. coli* or *Klebsiella*, appearing in the blood or tissues start host defense because these bacteria carry on their surface a quite toxic structure, a lipopolysaccharide (LPS) called endotoxin, that fits into a special receptor on the cells of the innate immune system. This receptor for a stranger signal is one in a series of structures called Toll-like receptors (TLRs) present throughout the animal kingdom down to the fruit fly where it was originally found.[5] The TLR responding to Gram-negative bacteria is called TLR4. In the same way, all Gram-positive bacteria, like staphylococci or streptococci, carry on their surface a lipoteichoic acid which functions similarly to TLR2. There is also a receptor for mannose which occurs in a specific pattern on the surface structures of fungi, like candida. When such fungi appear in host tissues, this results in an immediate host reactivity. In addition, there are receptors recognizing certain virus structures as well as those that recognize certain components of degraded and/or damaged human tissue.

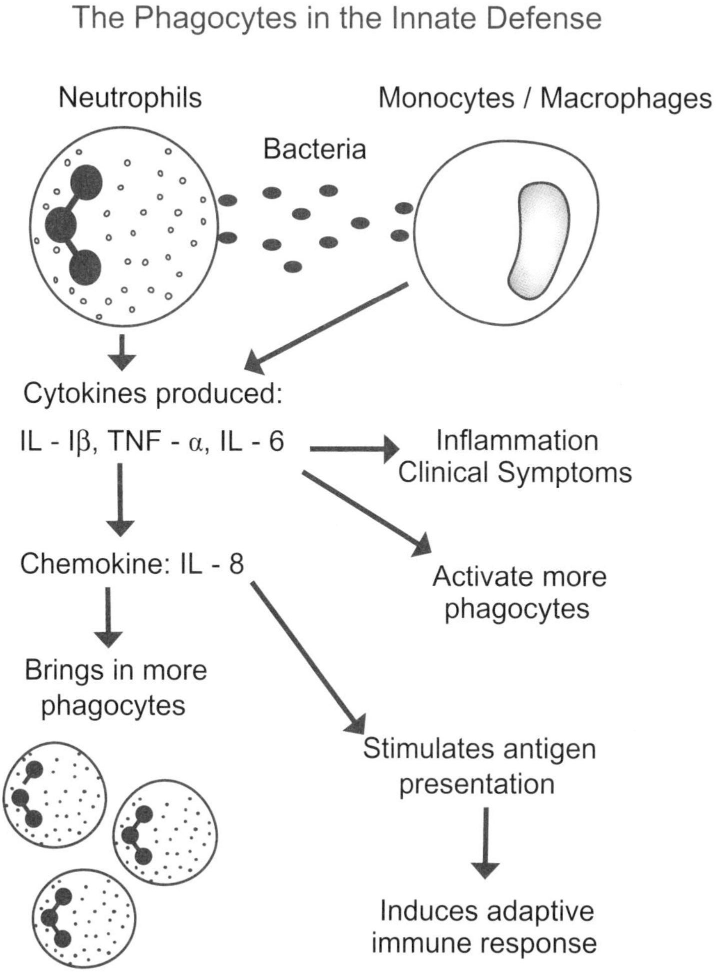

Figure 4. This figure shows the function of phagocytes in the innate immune system. Bacteria in tissues are eaten by phagocytes (neutrophils and monocytes/macrophages). Phagocytes engulf and kill bacteria and produce cytokine signals (IL-1β, TNF-α and IL-6). These pro-inflammatory cytokines cause tissue damage (inflammation) and symptoms of infection. IL-8 acts as a potent chemokine bringing in more phagocytes to insure the death of all bacteria.

> The phagocytes are important for our defense against infections because they engulf and kill microbes. The price we pay for their help is inflammation and tissue damage.

When the phagocytic cells bind to infecting microorganisms via these receptors, they are activated and efficiently engulf and internalize the recognized microbe. The metabolism of the phagocyte is greatly increased which results in the production of a number of components. These components help kill and degrade the engulfed microorganism. There is always leakage of this active material into the surrounding area causing local tissue damage seen as inflammation.

The cytokines

Components called cytokines are most efficient in inducing an inflammatory response. *Cytokines* act as a signal to the immune system.[5] There are at least 150 different cytokines. Of these, about 40 can be called *chemokines* because they serve as signals to bring in more phagocytic cells to an infected or inflamed site. The activated phagocytes then produce cytokines like Interleukin-1β (IL-1β), Tumor Necrosis Factor-α (TNF-α), and IL-6 in an acute situation (Figure 4). These cytokines are called pro-inflammatory because they cause much of the inflammation at an infected site with the typical symptoms of local pain and tenderness, swelling, redness, and increased temperature. Cytokines, like the chemokine IL-8, enhance these symptoms further by bringing in and activating many more phagocytic cells, especially neutrophils. This insures that the infecting agent is efficiently stopped, but there is always a price to pay in the host which includes increased tissue damage and symptoms resulting from the inflammation and ultimately increased energy cost. Other cytokines, like IL-10 and Transforming Growth Factor-β (TGF-β), are produced to balance, control, and down-regulate the defense reaction including inflammation. They are also involved in the repair of the tissues damaged by the inflammatory reaction.

> The cytokines, the signals in the immune system, play a central role in directing most of the functions of the immune system. Some induce inflammation while activating the defense, others down-regulate such effects.

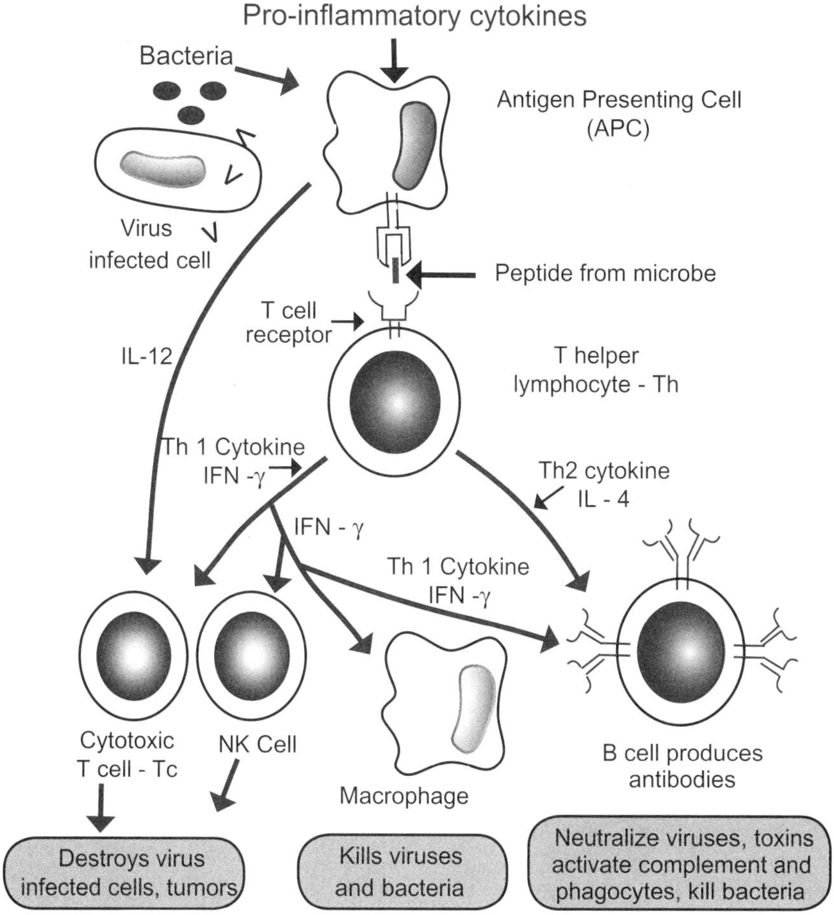

Figure 5. This figure shows the pro-inflammatory cytokines stimulating Antigen Presenting Cells (APCs). APCs, usually dendritic cells, degrade microbes. Peptides from these microbes are present on the surface of the APCs in their HLA (tissue type) receptors. This complex of bacterial peptide and host HLA is recognized by T helper (Th) lymphocytes. Th cells direct the adaptive immune response into a Th1 response where the cytokines, IFN-γ from the Th cells and IL-12 from the APCs, support the development of cytotoxic T lymphocytes or Killer cells. This is cell-mediated immunity in contrast to antibody-mediated immunity. The Killer cells defend against intracellular parasites like viruses via IFN-γ and certain bacteria by destroying infected cells. The released microbes are killed by macrophages stimulated by IFN-γ. INF-γ also activates NK cells to destroy infected cells and tumor cells. Th1 cells stimulate B cells to produce IgG1 antibodies against viruses. IgG1 antibodies protect by neutralizing viruses such as those released from infected tissue cells after attack by Killer cells. Th2 cells provide IL-4 which stimulates B lymphocytes to produce IgG2 antibodies against bacterial peptides. The antibodies also appear as immunoglobulins IgM, IgA, IgE which are specific for the presented peptide since they have the same structure in their binding portion.

Another form of defense cells that are presently less well understood are the natural killer (NK) cells. They are a form of lymphocytes, but they lack the receptors of the adaptive immune system described below. When stimulated, they have the capacity to produce large amounts of Interferon-γ (IFN-γ) and IL-4. NK cells kill virus-infected cells and induce the production of cytokines. They can be stimulated by IFN-γ and act against tumor cells (Figure 5).

During certain forms of inflammation, like infections from large parasites, special chemokines bring in other types of inflammatory cells such as *eosinophils* and *basophils*. These cells use somewhat different killing mechanisms adapted to fighting such infecting agents. The same inflammatory cells are important in allergic inflammation when the immune system makes the mistake of attacking materials like food, inhaled pollen, or similar harmless structures.

Since the defense provided by phagocytes causes tissue destruction in the host and may be insufficient for stopping the infection, another more specific and advanced form of host defense has developed. This is the adaptive immunity which has the capacity to produce defense cells specific for each type of infecting microbe. Adaptive immunity builds on lymphocytes with highly variable receptors. These cells divide and multiply reaching high numbers. Each cell and all its daughter cells recognize the infecting microbe. Even an efficiently invading and multiplying microbe that produces various virulence factors may be efficiently stopped by the combined forces of the innate and adaptive immune defense.

The adaptive immune system

Antigen presentation

An infecting microbe that has been engulfed by phagocytic cells within the innate immune system (Figure 4) will cause these cells to produce cytokines which activate Antigen Presenting Cells (APC) (Figure 5).[5] *Antigen* is the name for any structure that induces a specific response in the adaptive immune system. Thus, all bacteria, viruses, and other microbes contain antigens and elicit immune responses. A vaccine also consists of antigens from a certain microorganism. Various parts of a bacterium can act as an

> The antigen-presenting cells have a central role in initiating a specific immune response to an infecting microbe or a vaccine.

antigen whether from the cell wall, like the lipopolysaccharide (LPS) from Gram-negative bacteria, or a soluble toxin produced by the bacterium, like the tetanus toxin. The most efficient APCs are the *dendritic* cells found in all mucosal membranes and most other tissues. They are readily activated when they receive cytokine signals from phagocytes which have taken up infecting microbes.

The cytokine-activated APCs engulf the microbes and their products. Actually, the cytokine stimulation increases that capacity more than 100-1000 fold. They kill and degrade the microbes they have taken in while migrating to local lymph glands. This migration is directed by a series of chemokines. In the lymph gland, the APCs express small portions of proteins from the microbe as a peptide on the cell surface in a preformed receptor consisting of that individual's tissue type, or *HLA (Human Leucocyte Antigen)* (Figure 5). Thus, the immune response is controlled by the individual's genetic tissue type. These combined structures of self HLA binding a foreign peptide sequence activates T lymphocytes via their T cell receptor (TCR).

T lymphocytes, the thymus, and cell-mediated immunity

From fetal life on, each individual has a family of preformed T cell receptors (TCR) with tremendous diversity on their T lymphocytes. These fit a number of antigens, both microbial and other sources, when presented in the HLA receptor.[5] The genes for these receptors can be reorganized in an efficient manner so that an enormous number of different specific lymphocyte receptors can be produced. These lymphocyte receptors recognize most structures they meet on microbes and other potentially hostile material. Thus, the APC presenting an antigen from a microbe is likely to meet T lymphocytes with a receptor that recognizes that microbial structure.

T lymphocytes are born in the bone marrow and mature in the *thymus* under the influence of a number of factors including cytokines hence the name T lymphocytes. The thymus is a central lymphoid organ located under the breastbone.[5] In the thymus, T lymphocytes start to mature in fetal life. They appear with receptors of many specificities against their own tissues.

Table 4

Adaptive Immunity – The Effector Mechanisms

- ❖ Cytokines
  - ➢ From phagocytes stimulated in innate immune system
  - ➢ Activate Antigen Presenting Cells (APCs)
    - ▪ Present components of degraded microbes and antigens to lymphocytes
- ❖ T lymphocytes
  - ➢ Develop T cell receptors (TCR) specific for antigen
  - ➢ Become cytotoxic T lymphocytes (Killer T cells)
    - ▪ Kill tissue cells infected with intracellular parasites (Listeria, Mycobacteria, or viruses)
    - ▪ Produce Interferon-γ (IFN-γ)
      - • Makes them able to kill
      - • Stimulates NK cells to destroy infected cells, tumor cells
- ❖ B lymphocytes
  - ➢ Produce specific antibodies against microbial antigens
    - ▪ IgM
      - • Low specificity
      - • Produced first
      - • Activate complement system
        - ♦ Kill bacteria
        - ♦ Stimulates phagocytosis
        - ♦ Enhances inflammation
      - • Found in blood and tissues
    - ▪ IgG
      - • Higher specificity
      - • Neutralizes viruses and toxins
      - • Less efficiently activates complement system
    - ▪ IgE
      - • Defends against parasites
      - • Can mediate allergy
      - • Found in blood and tissues
    - ▪ SIgA
      - • Protect mucosal membranes – primary route of most infections
- ❖ Regulatory T lymphocytes (Treg)
  - ➢ Control T and B lymphocytes
  - ➢ Prevent autoimmune/allergic reactivity

Most of the auto-reactive T cells are eliminated by "programmed cell death" or apoptosis in the thymus. Only about 1% of the pre-T cells that enter the thymus leave this immunological organ reaching the periphery.

T lymphocytes with a receptor which recognizes the antigen presented by the APC (Figure 5) can become a T helper cell of type 1 (Th1) if the APC predominantly produces IL-12. This cytokine together with IFN-γ supports the development of *cytotoxic T lymphocytes*, or *Killer cells*, with receptors specifically fitting to the presented antigen. Such cells provide cell-mediated immunity and fight infections from intracellular pathogens, like viruses, which are not efficiently reached by antibodies (Table 4).[5] The tissue cell infected with a certain virus will display proteins originating from the infecting agent in the HLA molecules on the surface of the cell. This is recognized by the cytotoxic T cells with TCRs specific for that virus. Such Killer cells can also destroy a cell infected with other intracellular pathogens like mycobacteria, the bacteria that cause tuberculosis. The cytotoxic T cells act by producing IFN-γ. This activates phagocytic cells, like macrophages, so they become capable of killing intracellular parasites, like *Listeria* which is a dangerous pathogen in pregnant women and infants (Figure 5).

> T helper lymphocytes with a T cell receptor (TCR) that fits a presented antigen, for instance from a virus, respond when exposed to the virus by increasing in number. They support the production of large numbers of Killer T cells with TCRs specific for the presented virus.

The IFN-γ produced by the Th1 cells activate NK cells to kill virus-infected cells and tumor cells. This cytokine also stimulates macrophages to kill viruses.

There are *regulatory T lymphocytes (Treg)* which help control the immune system to prevent autoimmune and allergic diseases and, presumably, protect the fetus from the potential threat of attacks by the mother's immune system as discussed in the next chapter. The Treg may use cytokines, like IL-10, to protect the fetus.[6]

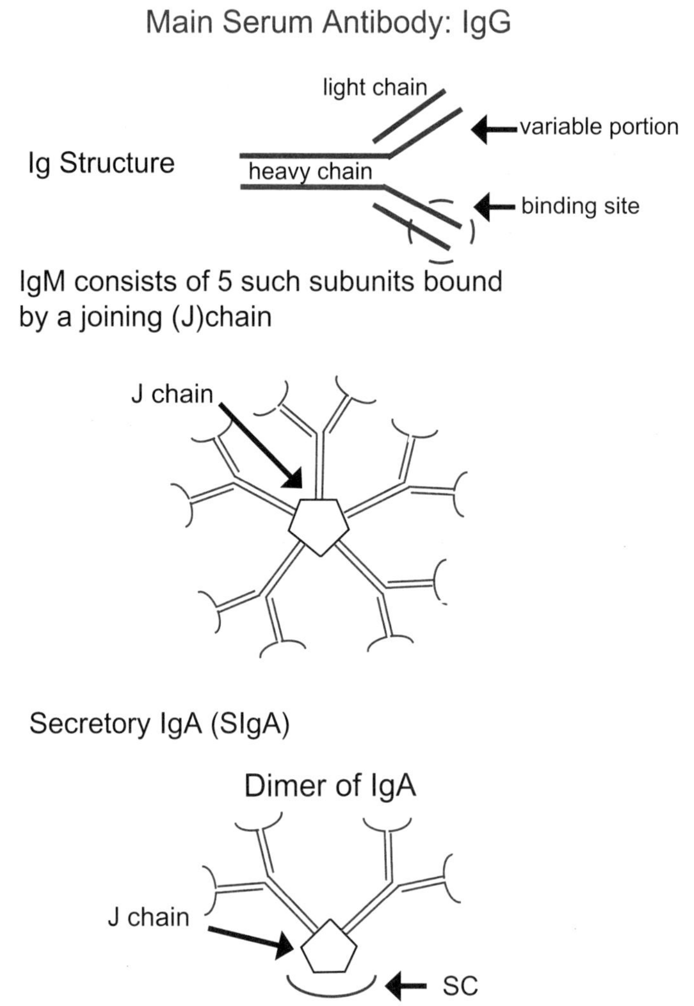

Figure 6. Immunoglobulins all have a basic structure of 4 polypeptide chains: two light and two heavy chains. In one end, they have a unique variable structure. This structure forms the specific binding site for the antigen, e.g. a bacterial peptide. IgG, serum IgA, and IgE are recognized as different entities because they show special structural characteristics in their heavy chains even though their binding sites may be the same. The end opposite the antibody binding site, called Fc, activates complement and makes IgG able to bind to the Fc receptors in the placenta which transports it across to the fetus. IgM consists of 5 identical subunits each with 2 heavy and 2 light chains with an additional joining (J) chain. Secretory IgA (SIgA) is composed of a dimer of IgA with a J chain. When transported into secretions, it takes up a part of the polyIg receptor (polyIgR), called Secretory Component (SC), see Figure 8.

Antibody production

T lymphocytes, named T helper cells of type 2 (Th2), that produce the cytokine IL-4 effectively support another kind of lymphocytes, called *B lymphocytes*, to begin producing *antibodies* specific for the presented antigen (Figure 6) (Table 4). These proteins called *immunoglobulins* make up a family of antibodies made up of basically two types of peptide chains both of which have a variable portion in one end (Figure 6). The structure of this variable portion is determined by the genes of the B lymphocytes producing the antibodies. The diversity is acquired in a very similar manner as the T cell receptor. The antibodies produced by an initially responding B lymphocyte and all its daughter cells have the same structure and will be specific for the same antigen (Figure 5).

In serum, most of the antibodies are made up of a structure called immunoglobulin G (IgG). It appears in the form of four subclasses IgG1 – 4. Most are in the form of IgG1. Very few are in the form of IgG4. They have somewhat different roles in the defense against infections. The Th2 helper cells promote production of anti-microbial IgG antibodies of various subclasses by producing IL-4. Th1 cells via IFN-γ may also support production of certain IgG antibodies, like IgG1.

In serum, there is more IgG than IgA and IgM (Figure 6). IgM is the first antibody produced in an immune response (Figure 7). It has a lower specificity than the other immunoglobulins and can react against more structures which are similar but not identical. Later, with the help provided by T cells, the B cell switches to IgG production increasing the specificity and binding capacity (affinity) by further mutating its genes. Thus, the antibodies bind more strongly to the antigen. In the first or *primary response* to an antigen, the IgG antibodies reach high levels and inhibit further production of the IgM antibodies (Figure 7). They remain in the circulation for a long time at lower levels. On renewed encounter with the antigen, a *secondary response* quickly results in IgG antibodies. In this way, there is a good chance that on a second encounter with a microbe the antibody response may be protective. The faster secondary response is due to long-lived *memory lymphocytes* remaining from the first encounter with the antigen.

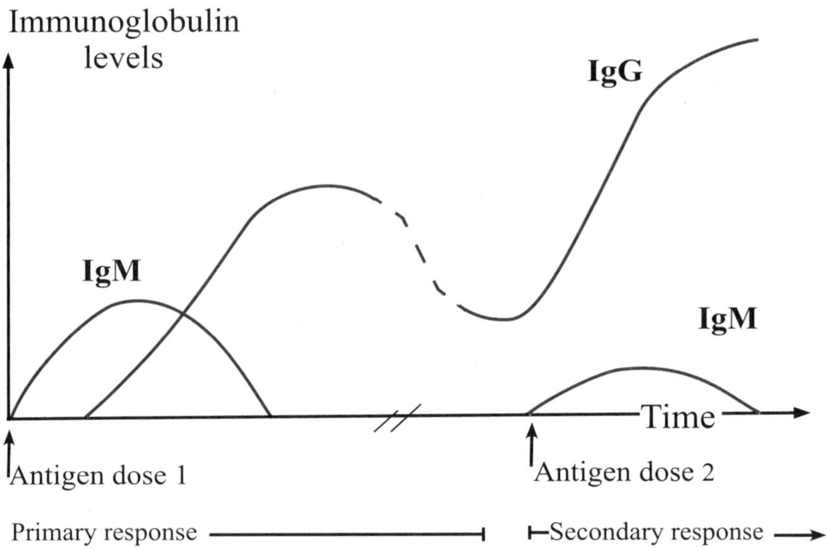

Figure 7. After a first encounter with an antigen, a primary immune response is induced. First, IgM antibodies are formed, then IgG production starts. IgG inhibits the production of IgM. Each renewed exposure to the antigen yields a secondary immune response with rapid production of high levels of IgG . The response is similar whether the antigen is a bacterium, virus, or vaccine. Long-lived memory lymphocytes remain after the primary immune response and provide the quicker, higher production of IgG antibodies upon repeated exposure. Usually, less IgM is produced after a second exposure to the antigen.

T helper cells support B lymphocytes to produce antibodies specific for the antigen. IgM is produced first, then IgG. On the next encounter with the same antigen from an infecting microbe or a vaccine, long-lived memory cells recognize the antigen and large numbers of antibodies specific for the antigen are quickly produced. The Killer T cells also show immunological memory on a renewed encounter with the antigen.

IgM antibodies activate a complex series of serum proteins called the *complement system.* The complement system kills the infecting microbe. Complement activation induces inflammation by bringing in many stimulated phagocytic neutrophils with increased capacity to ingest and kill the infecting microbe. These cells produce cytokines which add to the inflammation. This is yet another mechanism efficiently enhancing host defense directed against an infecting agent. The IgG antibodies also activate complement, but less well than the IgM antibodies.

IgG antibodies bind and neutralize bacterial toxins and viruses as well. In that situation, a good fit and strong binding of the antibodies is an advantage because the toxin or the virus is safely neutralized and rendered harmless. In contrast, the lower specificity and broader fit of the IgM antibodies can be an advantage in the early stage of an infection. The IgM, IgA and IgG antibodies occur and act primarily in blood and tissues.

> IgM and IgG antibodies neutralize toxins and viruses and activate the complement system to kill bacteria. Phagocytes are then stimulated to further increase the killing. But, complement and phagocytes cause inflammation and tissue damage.

IgE antibodies are mainly directed against parasites and activate a specialized host defense with potent inflammatory cells such as eosinophils, basophils, and mast cells. In developed societies where parasitic diseases are rare, IgE mediated inflammation is mainly seen in allergic individuals who erroneously produce IgE antibodies against antigens from pollen, food, dogs, cats, etc.

Secretory IgA (SIgA) - the main antibodies on mucosal membranes and in human milk

As discussed above, most infections reach man via the mucosal membranes. Man (and large apes) have a fully developed additional antibody system to protect the mucosal level.[7] Man's mucosal immune system consists almost exclusively of specially structured antibodies adapted to stop infections on the mucosa. These antibodies prevent the entry of microbes into tissues. Were microbes to reach into tissues, they would activate host defense and cause inflammation, tissue damage, clinical symptoms, and high energy cost.[8;9]

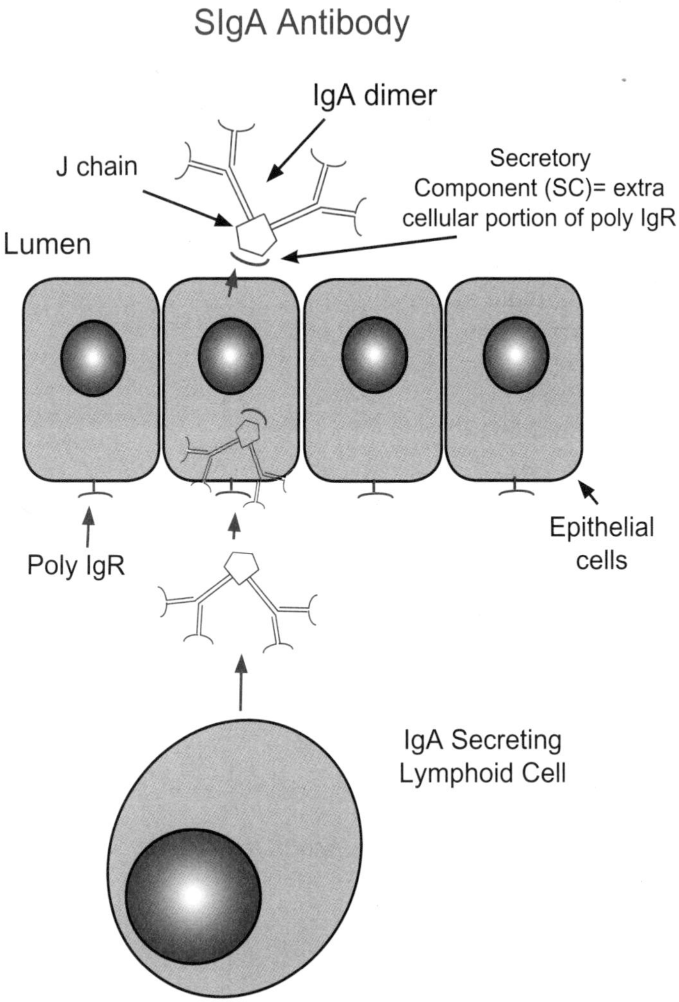

Figure 8. SIgA is produced by lymphocytes under the epithelial cells of exocrine glands, like the mammary glands, or in mucosal membranes, like the gut mucosa. The lymphocytes produce the IgA dimers with J chain which together bind to the special receptor, the polyIgR, on the basal portion of the epithelial cells. The complex migrates through the epithelial cell and appears with the extramural portion of the polyIgR, the Secretory Component (SC), as the complete SIgA molecule in the external secretion on the surface of the epithelium.

The SIgA antibodies consist of a dimer of IgA with a joining (J) chain produced by lymphocytes located under epithelial cells in mucosal membranes as in the gut, or exocrine glands like the mammary glands (Figure 8). The IgA dimer together with the J chain binds to a receptor called polyIgR on the basal portion of the epithelial cells. Together with a portion of this receptor, named secretory component (SC), the complete SIgA molecule migrates through the epithelial cell onto the cell surface. These special antibodies, the secretory IgA (SIgA), make up 80% of all antibodies in man. They were first discovered in human milk where they are the dominant antibody fraction.[10] SIgA and its protective functions will be discussed further in Chapter 3 and Chapter 5.

Most antibodies in man are secretory IgA (SIgA) antibodies appearing on mucosal membranes in the respiratory and gastrointestinal tract where most infections start. SIgA binds microbes and blocks them from entering tissues. Thus, immune defense in tissues is not activated. IgM and IgG antibodies, the complement system, and phagocytes are not engaged. Inflammation, tissue damage, clinical symptoms, and energy consumption are prevented.

Vaccination

Vaccination works by exposing the specific immune system to a microorganism to induce a protective immune response against the disease-causing microbe.[11] The vaccine can be composed of a live but attenuated microorganism like the live oral poliovirus vaccine. It can also consist of a killed microorganism or a crucial part of a microbe like the tetanus or diphtheria toxoid (detoxified toxin). The goal is to induce an immune response as protective and long lasting as possible with as harmless a microbial material as can be produced. Some vaccines protect by inducing antibody-mediated immunity. These antibodies are usually IgG found in serum. A vaccinated mother will transfer these antibodies via the placenta to her fetus. If they are SIgA, they may be transferred via the milk. If the vaccine-induced immunity is based on protective T cells, like the BCG vaccine against mycobacteria, there is no transfer of immunity from mother to fetus.

Some vaccines induce protection with a single dose giving a primary response. Other vaccines require several doses inducing secondary responses to reach a protective level of immunity (Figure 7). The resulting immunological memory is due to lymphoid cells surviving for decades.[5] Revaccination induces secondary immune responses with the same specificity as the primary response in T as well as B cells.

Mistakes by the immune system: autoimmune and allergic diseases

Developing an immune system which protects us selectively against threatening microbes without causing damage to our tissues has only been partly successful. This is the reason why our host defense mechanisms can cause autoimmune diseases in just about every organ by reacting with various parts of our own tissues or various forms of allergic diseases by reacting with food, pollen, or mites.

There is much interest in the subset of regulatory T lymphocytes (Treg) which, by producing down-regulating cytokines, like IL-10 and Transforming Growth Factor-β (TGF-β), seem to control and down regulate normal as well as abnormal responses. If the Treg do not suppress and control the immune system adequately, this may result in tissue damage and disease caused by the immune system.[12]

In conclusion:

The defense against infection is based on several levels of mechanisms within the innate and adaptive immune systems. The first level of the innate defense system provides protection via non-specific mechanisms like mechanical factors such as skin, cough, and diarrhea, as well as chemical factors like the low pH in the stomach. There are many biochemical compounds in blood, secretions, and tissues that support the defense. Some act non-specifically, others are specific for certain microbial structures. Human milk has many such components.

The next level of the innate immune system consists of cells like neu-

trophils and monocytes/macrophages which function as phagocytes capable of engulfing and killing infecting microbes. They act by recognizing groups of microbes and certain tissue components via special receptors including Toll-like receptors. Upon recognizing microbes or damaged tissue, these cells are activated and produce a number of active components, especially cytokines. These components function by bringing in many more stimulated phagocytes to further support the defense. While acting in defense, the activated phagocytes and cytokines that are released cause clinical symptoms of infection, and a tissue damaging and energy-consuming inflammation.

Since the innate level of defense may be insufficient, an additional adaptive immunity develops against invading microbes. Lymphocytes have the capacity to produce receptors which are specific for certain parts of an infecting microbe, named antigens. B lymphocytes produce antibodies which have the structure of the specific receptor fitting to an antigen in one end. The serum IgG and IgM antibodies bind to microbes and activate the complement system which can kill bacteria and activate more phagocytes. The SIgA antibodies present in secretions stop infecting agents at the mucosal level by preventing them from entering tissues. Thus inflammation, clinical symptoms, tissue damage, and energy loss is prevented.

Receptors specific for microbial antigens are also found on T lymphocytes. Cytotoxic Killer T cells with such receptors can destroy virus-infected cells as well as tumor cells. T helper cells also support B cells to produce more, better, and more specific antibodies. In addition, by producing IFN-γ (Interferon-γ) the Killer T cells can activate macrophages to be highly efficient in ingesting and killing microbes, including viruses.

Reference List

1. Boman HG: Innate immunity and the normal microflora. Immunol Rev 173:5-16, 2000

2. Bendelac A, Medzhitov R: Adjuvants of immunity: harnessing innate immunity to promote adaptive immunity. J Exp Med 195:F19-F23, 2002

3. Gallucci S, Matzinger P: Danger signals: SOS to the immune system. Curr Opin Immunol 13:114-119, 2001

4. Shi Y, Evans JE, Rock KL: Molecular identification of a danger signal that alerts the immune system to dying cells. Nature 425:516-521, 2003

5. Janeway CA, Travers P, Walport M, et al: Immunobiology (5th Edition). New York, Garland Publishing, 2001

6. Takahashi T, Sakaguchi S: The role of regulatory T cells in controlling immunologic self-tolerance. Int Rev Cytol 225:1-32, 2003

7. Goldman AS: Evolution of the mammary gland defense system and the ontogeny of the immune system. J Mammary Gland Biol Neoplasia 7:277-289, 2002

8. Brandtzaeg P: Role of secretory antibodies in the defence against infections. Int J Med Microbiol 293:3-15, 2003

9. Hanson LA, Korotkova M, Telemo E: Human milk, its components and their immunobiological function, in J Mestecky JB, Lamm ME, Mayer L, et al (eds): Mucosal Immunology. 3rd Edition. San Diego, Academic Press, 2004

10. Hanson LA: Comparative immunological studies of the immune globulins of human milk and of blood serum. Int Arch Allergy Appl Immunol 18:241-267, 1961

11. Zinkernagel RM: On natural and artificial vaccinations. Annu Rev Immunol 21:515-546, 2003

12. Zhang X, Koldzic DN, Izikson L, et al: IL-10 is involved in the suppression of experimental autoimmune encephalomyelitis by CD25 + CD4+ regulatory T cells. Int Immunol 16:249-256, 2004

3 The Development Of Host Defense In The Fetus And Baby

The immunology of pregnancy

During pregnancy, the mother's immune system is capable of damaging the fetus and the placenta. Such damage may occur because the mother reacts with the "foreign" structures in the fetus and the placenta based on genes from the father. Both the maternal cytotoxic T cells and her NK cells and macrophages present in the placenta during pregnancy are, in principle, capable of destroying the fetus. However, the NK cells and macrophages may need to be activated by IFN-γ to do so (see Figure 5). The Th1-directed part of the maternal immune system which can induce IFN-γ production is normally down-regulated during pregnancy to prevent such anti-fetal reactivity. In the meantime, the antibody-mediated immunity is up-regulated. This is, presumably, not harmful to the fetus and may, possibly, be protective because antibodies against the fetal structures of paternal origin may cover such structures so they are not recognized by the maternal Th1 immune response.

The Th1/Th2 concept is an oversimplification when explaining why the fetus and the placenta are not rejected by the mother as a foreign transplant.[1;2] There are potentially harmful NK cells in the placenta. They make up about 70% of the mononuclear cells in the decidua, the maternal part of the placenta.[3] But, they also produce down-regulatory and, presumably, protective IL-10.[4] The trophoblasts, the fetal cells forming the placenta, do not carry the classical tissue type antigens, HLA class I and II. If they did, they would be rejected. Instead, they carry other HLA antigens, like

HLA-G, which are recognized by the placental NK cells. Recognition of this unusual HLA blocks the NK cells so they cannot destroy the placental trophoblasts.[3]

At the time of implantation, there are as many as 20-30% macrophages among the decidual cells.[5] The macrophages may be important for eliminating apoptotic cells killed by programmed cell death which, otherwise, could cause inflammation.

There are also a few T lymphocytes in the epithelium of the uterus which may act by producing IL-10 as well as TGF-β. Both of these cytokines are down-regulatory.[6] It seems that regulatory T cells (Treg) known to protect against autoimmune diseases also play a role in protecting the fetus.[7] In experiments with pregnant mice lacking Treg, they lost the fetuses by immunological rejection.[8]

The down-regulation of the maternal Th1 cell-mediated immunity during pregnancy is suggested to result in less efficient defense against certain infections in the mother. In some cases, there is improvement of Th1-mediated autoimmune diseases like rheumatoid arthritis.[9] In agreement with this, the mainly Th2 dominated autoantibody-mediated autoimmune disease, Systemic Lupus Erythematosus (SLE), may worsen during pregnancy.[10]

The normal maternal immune response against the fetus is not just a risk factor. It also seems to be an important driving force and regulator of pregnancy. The implantation of the fertilized egg in the decidua or epithelium in the uterus requires a number of growth factors and cytokines, especially the Leukemia Inhibiting Factor (LIF). Recently, it has been suggested that sterility may, in some instances, be due to a deficiency of LIF.[4;11]

The outgrowth of trophoblasts from the egg into the decidua forming the placenta is stimulated by several cytokines.[12] There is evidence that the larger the genetic difference between the parents, the larger the placenta and the fetus. This is important because low birth weight is a major risk factor for newborns. Cousin marriages may result in lower birth weight and higher mortality of the offspring.[13]

The hormones necessary for a successful pregnancy are influenced by maternal cytokines. Delivery is induced by prostaglandins released by maternal cytokines, including IL-1β. This may explain why infections during the latter part of pregnancy may induce early delivery since infections are followed by an increase in pro-inflammatory cytokines.

The mother's immune system reacts against the fetus because of the paternal contribution to its genetic makeup. This immune response is a threat to the fetus and we do not fully understand how rejection is avoided. It is clear that maternal cytokines and growth factors play an important role in the implantation of the fertilized egg in the uterus, growth of the placenta, hormone balance during pregnancy, and initiation of delivery.

The innate defense mechanisms

Defense in the fetus

Most of the components of the host defense system are developed during fetal life. Fetuses exposed to infectious agents like mumps, CMV and rubella virus, or Toxoplasma respond with both antibody responses and cytotoxic T cells. Still, infections occur, but they may be mild like toxoplasmosis.[14;15] These observations agree with the fact that functional T lymphocytes are present in the fetus by the gestational age of 16 weeks and B lymphocytes are present by 12-13 weeks. They mount cell-mediated immunity and produce antibodies.

Some innate immune mechanisms are already in place in the fetus. Receptors for microbes, like the TLRs, were found on gut mucosal epithelium in the fetus and an excessive IL-8 response was obtained on exposure to LPS from Gram-negative bacteria.[16] IL-8 is such a strong chemokine for neutrophils that TLR receptors might add to the damage of the intestinal mucosa as seen in premature infants with necrotizing enterocolitis (NEC).

Mechanical and chemical defense factors

At birth, most natural immune defense mechanisms like secretions on mucosal membranes are in place. The newborn can cough, but it may be inefficient. The low pH that normally kills many of the microbes passing through the stomach is not as acidic in the newborn (Table 5). This reduced protection against infections may be very obvious in the premature infant. The more premature a newborn, the less efficient are such functions. Therefore, the risk of getting infections as well as the problem of getting rid of them is greater in premature infants.

Biochemical defense factors

Bactericidal fatty acids in sweat may be reduced in early life. Recently, it has been suggested that a group of peptide antibiotics, the defensins, and a cathelicidin, are present in the amniotic fluid and in the newborn. They are found on the skin and may help control the early microbial colonization by potential pathogens. They actually kill group B streptococci.[17] *Vernix caseosa*, the creamy white substance that covers the skin of term babies, contains these peptide antibiotics.[18] There are higher levels of defensins in certain intestinal epithelial cells in infants with necrotizing enterocolitis.[19] Defensins that have anti-microbial capacity can act as chemokines and induce pro-inflammatory cytokines such as TNF-α and IL-1β while diminishing the suppressive IL-10. At the same time, they favor maturation of Antigen-Presenting dendritic Cells (APCs).[20]

The complement system efficiently enhances the effects of IgM and IgG antibodies against microbes by activating phagocytosis and increasing the inflammatory response. Full term newborns have decreased levels of many of the complement components with a complement activity about half that of an adult (Table 5).[21] Preterm infants have even lower complement activity. By 3 months of age, the complement levels reach normal adult range.

> Some protective functions, like the acid pH in the stomach, cough, and gut peristalsis, have reduced capacity in early life. The complement system is subnormal in the first 3 months limiting the efficiency of bacterial killing. Defensins are present in the newborn and may act in a pro-inflammatory way, but little is known about their role.

Table 5

Examples of Host Defense Mechanisms That May Not Be Fully Developed in Early Infancy

- Innate Immunity
  - Mechanical, chemical, biochemical
    - Cough, gut peristalsis
    - Low pH in stomach, fatty acids in sweat
    - Complement system
  - Phagocytes – produce fewer up and down regulating cytokines
    - Neutrophils
      - Fewer in bone marrow
      - Poor response to activating signals⇨fewer neutrophils at infected sites
      - Good capacity to kill bacteria, but due to low complement levels, fewer neutrophils are activated
      - Reduced production of new neutrophils
      - Severe prematurity and on-going sepsis, pneumonia, or respiratory distress⇨impaired capacity of neutrophils to kill bacteria
    - Monocytes/macrophages
      - Poorer response to signals⇨less efficient killing of Candida
      - Less production of activating signals⇨poorer response to Gram negative bacteria
- Adaptive Immunity
  - Antigen Presenting Cells (APCs)
    - Immature cytokine production⇨reduced specific immune responses
  - Thymus
    - Small size⇨low birthweight, malnutrition, intrauterine infections, increased mortality
    - Size can be doubled by breastfeeding
  - Cell-mediated immunity
    - T lymphocytes – low capacity to produce cytokines⇨ reduced cell-mediated immune response

Table 5 cont.

- Adaptive Immunity cont.
  - Antibody-mediated immunity
    - IgG
      - Maternal IgG via placenta – high at birth, decreases during first month of life
        - Protects infant
        - Inhibits infant's own antibody responses
      - Infant's IgG production takes over during first year
    - IgM antibody production – more prominent in neonate
    - SIgA
      - Increases in first few weeks in heavily exposed infants
      - Takes many months to increase in less exposed infants

The phagocytes

The innate immune response provided by phagocytes is reduced in the full-term newborn (Table 5). The bone marrow reserve of neutrophils is small. Once they appear in the circulation, they respond poorly to chemotaxis. Therefore, these defense cells do not migrate and do not aggregate efficiently at infected sites.[22] This is probably the most consistent defect of the neonatal neutrophils and a major reason why the inflammatory response is reduced in the neonate, especially in the premature neonate. The limited activation of neutrophils in the neonate is due to its decreased capacity to activate the complement system. More of a neonate's neutrophils are immature and their capacity to handle Gram-negative bacteria is reduced because they produce less of a bactericidal/permeability-increasing protein, BP1. This protein normally helps neutralize the LPS of these bacteria and prepares them for phagocytosis.[23] After the uptake of the bacteria, killing is as efficient as with adult neutrophils. The production of superoxide is increased in neonatal compared to adult neutrophils.[24] On the other hand, the bactericidal capacity of the neonatal neutrophils is decreased by severe prematurity, ongoing sepsis, pneumonia, or respiratory distress.

Normally, cells no longer needed in the defense against an infection are eliminated by "programmed cell death" or apoptosis. This is a carefully balanced process. The cytokines, Granulocyte Colony-Stimulating Factor (G-CSF) and Granulocyte-Macrophage Colony-Stimulating Factor (GM-

CSF), cannot prevent apoptosis of neutrophils in newborns as efficiently as in adults. This may result in the elimination of too many cells allowing neutropenia to develop which impairs the defense of the neonate.[25]

Neutrophils in the neonate respond poorly to chemotaxis. They migrate and aggregate poorly and are inefficiently activated. As a result, they are less efficient in killing bacteria. The bone marrow reserve of neutrophils is small with an increased risk of neutropenia.

Macrophages and monocytes

Macrophages and monocytes are very important for defense in early life before the adaptive immune system has expanded. Neonatal mononuclear phagocytes have several characteristics that are different from adult cells. Neonatal macrophages do not respond to IFN-γ as efficiently as adult cells. They also show deficient killing of Candida and depressed release of superoxide.[26] Preterm cord blood monocytes produce lower levels of pro-inflammatory cytokines like IFN-γ, G-CSF, IL-6, IL-8, and TNF-α. However, lung macrophages from term and preterm infants with respiratory failure had almost identical production of TNF-α, but lower synthesis of the anti-inflammatory IL-10.[27] Exposing neonatal mononuclear cells to Gram positive bacteria induce higher levels of IL-12 and TNF-α in both cord and adult cells than when they are exposed to Gram negative bacteria. The pro-inflammatory IL-6 was higher in neonatal than adult cells whereas IL-10 was similar in both. Gram negative bacteria induced similar levels of IL-6 and IL-10 in both neonatal and adult cells. This suggests that the receptors for bacteria function well on neonatal cells; although, there is evidence that the TLR receptors, e.g., the TLR4 for Gram negative bacteria may have impaired responses.[28;29]

The inflammatory reactivity of lymphocytes and monocytes in term and preterm neonates indicate that they produce somewhat less of the up-regulating cytokines IL-1β, IL-6, IL-8, and TNF-α, but considerably less of the down-regulating IL-10 and TGF-β. Since IL-10 and TGF-β are so important for the control of the inflammatory process during an infection, infected neonates may have more inflammation-induced tissue damage.[30]

The monocytes/macrophages of newborns are different from mature cells in their responsiveness and cytokine production. This may result in unbalanced reactivity, less efficient defense, and potentially more damaged tissue during infection-induced inflammation.

NK cells

NK cells in the neonate seem to be somewhat immature because they mainly produce IL-4 on stimulation whereas adult NK cells make IFN-γ as well as IL-4.[31] NK cells are present in low numbers in the blood of newborns and adults. They may have important functions in the defense against tumors and viral infections and possibly in the control of the immune system preventing autoimmune reactivity.

Antigen-presenting cells

Antigen-presenting cells (APCs) (mostly dendritic cells) are not fully developed at birth. They have a delayed capacity to produce IL-12.[32] IL-12 is important during infections because it induces production of IFN-γ from NK cells and naive T cells. It also enhances production of T Killer cells in cell-mediated immunity. IL-12 production which to a lesser extent originates from monocytes and macrophages is low in early childhood, but can increase with proper stimulation. Presumably, the responsiveness rests mainly on the number and function of dendritic cells.[33] The newborn's APCs produce TNF-α and IL-10 at adult levels, but they have fewer stimulatory molecules on their surface. The main limitation of immune responsiveness in early life may be due to deficiencies in antigen presentation (Table 5).[34]

Antigen-presenting cells in the neonate are immature, especially in the production of cytokines. These cells are important for an efficient and balanced immune responsiveness. Their immaturity is a major reason for the decreased immune responsiveness in early infancy.

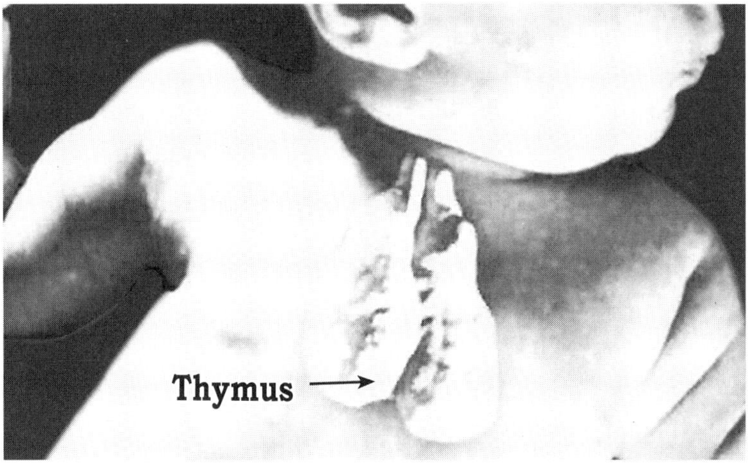

Figure 9. Photo of the location of the thymus.

The adaptive immune system

The thymus

Bone marrow is the birth place of the lymphocytes and it is active at birth. Production and distribution of lymphocytes has already taken place.[35] The helper T lymphocytes which recognize the presented antigen have matured in the central lymphoid organ, the thymus (Figure 9). The size of the thymus at birth is related to the weight, height, and arm circumference of the newborn. It is a little larger in boys than in girls and smaller in premature infants. The larger the size of the thymus, the lower the infant mortality rate according to a study which compensated for low birth weight and malnutrition, both known to reduce the size of the thymus (Table 5).[36] The incidence of chorioamnionitis, the most common cause of fetal death, was related to a smaller thymus in infants of different gestational ages having this condition.[37] A fully breastfed baby has a thymus twice the size of a non-breastfed baby, possibly due to the content in the mother's milk of important signals to the infant's immune system like the cytokine IL-7 (Chapter 5).[38]

> A small thymus at birth relates to low birth weight, malnutrition, intrauterine infection, and higher infant mortality. Breastfeeding can double the size of the thymus.

T lymphocytes

Neonatal cytotoxic T cells produce lower levels of IL-4, IL-10, and IFN-γ, but higher levels of IL-13 than adult cells produce.[39] During the first year of life, the number and proportion of T cells producing IFN-γ and IL-4 increase, but do not reach adult levels.[40] This low capacity of neonatal and infantile T cells may be due to immaturity and decreased production of IFN-γ (Table 5). It seems that IL-7 is important for neonatal T cell maturation.[41] The Th1 mediated protection providing cell-mediated immunity in the form of cytotoxic Killer T cells (Figure 5) is down-regulated at delivery. Instead, the Th2 antibody-mediated immunity is up-regulated similar to the maternal immune system during pregnancy. After microbial exposure in neonatal life, the Th1/Th2 balance is the same as in adults.

> The cytokine production by cytotoxic Killer T cells is immature and poorly balanced in early life so that cell-mediated immunity is somewhat reduced.

While there is a small number of regulatory T cells (Treg) in the circulation, they seem to have an important role in balancing the immune response.[7] They are present in cord blood, but their functional role has not been well studied in infants.[42]

B lymphocytes

B lymphocytes form B cell aggregates called germinal centers in lymphoid tissues, like lymph nodes and spleen, where antibody production takes place. This is slow to develop during the first few weeks of life. The serum antibody response of the neonate to a microbe is based on responding B cells and is characterized by more IgM antibodies than is seen later in life when IgG antibodies take over and suppress the continued production of the IgM antibodies against the microbe (Figure 7). The IgM antibodies have a lower specificity and can, therefore, react with a broader range of antigens of somewhat similar structure. This can be an advantage in the early phase of an infection. IgM antibodies are more efficient than IgG in activating the complement system and stimulating phagocytosis and, thereby, defense and inflammation. On the other hand, the complement system is quite deficient in early life.

As described in more detail in the next chapter, maternal IgG is transferred via the placenta during pregnancy (Figure 11). As a result, the newborn has about the same concentration of IgG in the blood as the mother. The more premature the baby, the less IgG has been transferred and the lower the serum IgG levels. While these antibodies are metabolized and vanish from the infant's circulation, the infant's own immune system starts to produce IgM and IgG antibodies in response to the microbial and food antigens it meets from birth on. As a result, the IgG levels in the serum diminish at first (figure 12). Around 2-4 months of life, the IgG levels start to increase. In parallel, the serum levels of IgM and IgA also increase.

> The newborn has obtained IgG antibodies from the mother in fetal life. These survive through the first months of life while the baby starts its own antibody production when it begins to meet many antigens after delivery, like bacteria, viruses, and food. At first, IgM antibodies predominate in the infant's response. As the maternal IgG vanishes, the infant's IgG antibodies take over and the levels in the blood increase.

Immunological memory, in the form of memory lymphocytes specific for the antigen, remains after each primary immune response. They provide a quick secondary response mainly from IgG antibodies already in the infant's circulation (Figure 7).

Antibody responses to protein antigens become quite functional early in life. Antibody responses to polysaccharides are usually subnormal during the first two years of life. The risk of infections from bacteria covering themselves with a polysaccharide capsule, like meningococci, *H. influenzae* type b, pneumococci, and certain *E. coli*, is, therefore, increased in early childhood. Antibody responses against vaccines consisting only of polysaccharides are also inefficient at that age, especially in the form of IgG2 antibodies (see section on Vaccinations below).

The mucosal defense system

As already mentioned, most infections reach us via mucosal membranes. The surface area of such membranes, for instance in the respiratory and gastrointestinal tracts, is vast. The area of mucosal surfaces may be more than 100 times larger than that of the skin.[43] After birth, the intestine grows 20-25 centimeters during the first days of life. In parallel to the bacterial colonization of the intestines, the adaptive immune system is stimulated to expand, especially in the intestinal mucosa. Prior to 10 days of age, there are few IgA-producing cells in the mucosal membranes of infants. After 2-4 weeks, there is a rapid increase. After 1-2 months, these are the predominant Ig-producing cells in mucosal membranes, like the gut.[44] Colonizing germfree animals with only one bacterial species increases the number of mucosal lymphocytes 10-fold.

Exposure to foods includes several antigens. A crude estimate suggests that by 6-12 months of age an infant may have been exposed to some 500-1000 antigens.[45] From studies of experimental animals, it is clear that exposure to food proteins in early life contributes to the expansion of the immune system. When fully developed, 70-80% of the whole immune system is located in the intestinal mucosa with about 10^{10} IgA-producing cells for each meter of gut.[43]

In the intestinal mucosa, there are numerous aggregates of T and B lymphocytes together with antigen-presenting dendritic cells. These aggregates are called Peyer's patches (Figure 10). The number of patches in the gut increases from 80-120 at gestation to about 250 in the mid-teens and then starts to decline.[45] Special epithelial cells, named M cells, cover the Peyer's patches and smaller similar lymphoid aggregates. The M cells have the capacity to sample material from the gut content containing food and microbes. This antigenic material is brought into contact with the dendritic cells, the APCs, which present it to the T and B lymphocytes in the patches. Macrophages are also present. They may be important in taking care of potentially harmful live pathogens brought into the patches.

By means of local cytokine signals, the antibody response in the Peyer's patches consists mainly of B lymphocytes with the capacity to produce dimers of IgA with an additional polypeptide chain, the joining (J) chain, as described in the previous chapter (Figure 8).[46] These lymphocytes leave the patches and migrate via the lymph nodes and blood to various mucosal membranes, like other parts of the gut and the respiratory tract. They also reach exocrine glands, like salivary glands and active lactating mammary glands (Figure 10). Arriving at these various sites, the specialized B cells mature into plasma cells and produce the IgA dimers with J chain (Figure 8). The complete SIgA molecules formed during transport through the epithelial cells appear on the mucosal epithelium and in exocrine secretions. In this way, lymphocytes in the lactating mammary glands produce SIgA antibodies against the microbes which are or have been present in the mother's gut.[43;47]

The memory cells appearing in T and B cell responses also produce a SIgA response in the lactating mammary glands. Since the milk of any mother tested contains a very broad spectrum of SIgA antibodies to many different microbes, it seems unlikely that it only reflects recent encounters.[47] A primary SIgA antibody response usually lasts for 3 months unless there is a renewed exposure to the same microbe.

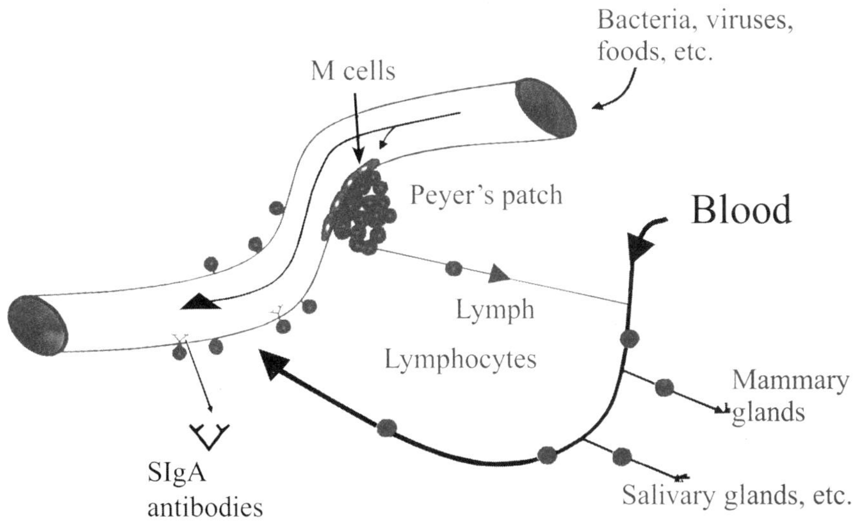

Figure 10. The M cells covering the Peyer's patches in the gut take up bacteria, viruses, food, and other antigenic material from the gut. This material is presented to lymphocytes in the Peyer's patches which are directed to produce IgA dimers and J chain (Figure 8). These cells migrate via the lymph and blood to other mucosal sites and to exocrine glands. There, the SIgA antibodies are produced. As a result, protection against the microbes present or passing through the gut is spread to other sites. Human milk contains large amounts of SIgA antibodies against the microbes in the mother's gut which the baby is normally colonized with at delivery and thereafter and may need defense against.

The SIgA antibodies function in secretions and on mucosal membranes by binding microbes, preventing them from attaching to and entering mucosal membranes and deeper tissues. They also neutralize viruses and toxins. During their passage through epithelial cells bound to the secretory component (SC), they neutralize viruses infecting the cells (Figure 8). The SC also has an anti-microbial effect on its own.[43;48]

The mucosal immune system is continuously expanding in the infant and young child. In Pakistani children with a heavy and early microbial exposure, we noted that the salivary SIgA antibodies to *E. coli* increased to adult levels within the first several weeks of life. For the less exposed Swedish children, it took almost a year before adult levels were attained.[49] Obviously, the mucosal immune system can expand very quickly when needed at least as measured above.

If the infectious dose of microbes is sufficiently large, the mucosal defense will still be too limited to stop the attack. Too much energy is required to have an immune system that can handle any infectious dose. We can only have the immune system we can afford as far as energy cost and space. Such limitations become obvious in poor, malnourished children heavily exposed to infectious agents. But, protein/calorie malnutrition must be severe before the capacity of the immune system becomes inadequate.[50] Unfortunately, malnourished children often live in poor, unhygienic, and crowded conditions so the infectious dose is larger. Out of 100 children dying from infections in poor countries, malnutrition contributes to the death in about 56% of the cases.[51] Deficiencies of specific micronutrients like vitamin A and zinc are important and contribute to child mortality.[50]

SIgA antibodies prevent microorganisms from entering tissues via mucosal membranes. SIgA is produced in the gut in early life. If the child is heavily exposed, this defense system develops more quickly. Once the mucosal immune system is initiated in the gut, it sends out cells to other mucosal membranes and exocrine glands so that SIgA antibodies appear in saliva, milk, and other secretions. While the young infant is developing this defense system, it receives huge amounts of SIgA antibodies against microbes from the mother's surroundings via the maternal milk (Figure 10).

Small for gestational age (SGA) and intrauterine growth retardation (IUGR)

There are many risk factors known for IUGR, but we know little about the mechanisms behind this condition. There seems to be decreased levels of IL-10 produced by decidual cells in placentas from IUGR deliveries. This may possibly be linked to an insufficient suppression of the maternal immune response against the fetus.[52] We have confirmed that observation in a study from Pakistan where IUGR is as common as 15-25% of newborns.[53]

Little is known about the immune capacity of small for gestational age (SGA) babies and intrauterine growth retarded (IUGR) neonates. Those with IUGR have low numbers of B cells, low IgG levels, and low numbers of T cells. They also have depressed levels of serum thymic hormone and poor T cell responsiveness to antigens. The capacity to produce IFN-γ was markedly reduced.[54;55] This results in poor responses to infections and vaccines.

The effects of vaccinations on infants, young children, and pregnant mothers

Vaccination is such an efficient way to prevent many infections that it is important to administer these procedures in early life when there is an increased risk of infections.

In spite of the limited maturity of many aspects of the immune system in the newborn, it is still possible to induce protection against mycobacteria by vaccinating the neonate with the BCG vaccine. Neonatal BCG vaccinations are part of many national vaccination programs. In poor countries, premature infants are vaccinated as well.[56] Unfortunately, infants with intra-uterine growth retardation may have an inadequate response.[57]

The BCG vaccine is based on an attenuated bovine strain of mycobacteria. This strain gives a cross-reactive immune response which protects against *Mycobacterium tuberculosis,* the main cause of tuberculosis in man. There are, however, problems with the BCG vaccine in that the protection induced varies between 0-80% in different populations. In some regions, various other mycobacterial strains have induced cross-reactive immunity which seems to diminish the response to the BCG vaccine. The only available test for possible mycobacterial infection or remaining immune reactivity is the tuberculin test which brings out a T cell-mediated immune reactivity to mycobacteria present in the infant. The tuberculin extract contains some 200 different mycobacterial antigens. Therefore, a positive skin test may also have been induced by cross-reactive mycobacteria.[58]

Infections with bacteria carrying a polysaccharide capsule as a virulence factor are particularly dangerous in infancy. This is partly due to the fact that the most efficiently protective antibodies are IgG of the subclass IgG2. Before two years of age, children are inefficient in producing these antibodies and respond poorly to vaccines consisting of polysaccharides from meningococci, pneumococci, and *Haemophilus influenzae* with the polysaccharide capsule b (Hib). Because these are important pathogens in childhood, it was a very important discovery that if these polysaccharides are linked to a protein carrier like diphtheria or tetanus toxoid they induce a reliable response in infants.[59] Such conjugate vaccines are now widely used and some function well in both rich and poor countries. A pneumococcal capsular polysaccharide conjugate vaccine consisting of 11 different capsules initiates the immune response adequately in infants.[60] The use of the polysaccharide–conjugate vaccines have proven to function well in low birth weight infants; although, some reports contradict this finding.[61;62]

Vaccines composed of proteins, such as tetanus and diphtheria toxoids, pertussis vaccines, and viral vaccines against poliovirus and hepatitis B normally induce adequate responses in infancy.

Vaccination of the pregnant mother results in good responses against pneumococcal polysaccharides.[63] The IgG antibodies induced by the vaccine pass the placenta and reach the fetus. The transplacental antibodies protect the fetus by passive immunity. However, those passively transferred IgG antibodies are metabolized and vanish during the first several months of life (see next chapter for further details). Therefore, it is necessary to induce an active immune response by vaccinating the offspring so that lasting immunity results. If passively transferred antibodies remain at vaccination, then the vaccine response may be hampered.

In conclusion:

The fetus is exposed to an immune response from the mother against structures inherited from the father. Normally, this immune response is sufficiently controlled so as not to destroy the fetus. In contrast, many cytokines and other factors from the mother are important monitoring signals for the implantation of the egg, the growth of the placenta, the course of the pregnancy, and finally the delivery.

The host defense of neonates is not fully functional at birth. Mechanical and chemical defenses, like cough and the low pH of the stomach, are not adequate until the infant is older. Components of the innate immunity, like defensins, are present at birth, but the complement system important for the activation of phagocytes that kill bacteria remains reduced for some months.

Among the phagocytes, the neutrophils have reduced migration and aggregation at infected sites. They are immature and less able to kill microbes. The neutrophils of newborns cannot resist apoptosis (programmed cell death) as efficiently as adult cells and this can result in low numbers of neutrophils. The neonate's monocytes/macrophages have some deficiencies compared to adult cells. They do not respond as well to activation with IFN-γ. Their production of superoxide is low and killing of Candida is reduced. Their cytokine production after exposure to microbes seems adequate in full term, but not in preterm infants.

In the inflammatory response, the term and pre-term neonates produce less of several pro-inflammatory cytokines and considerably less of the down-regulating IL-10. There seems to be more limited control of the tissue damage that can be caused by inflammation at an early age.

As to the adaptive immune mechanisms, the antigen-presenting cells have reduced capacity. This may be a major reason for the limited immune responsiveness of the newborn. The T lymphocytes have different cytokine responses in the newborn. Also, the antibody producing B lymphocytes function somewhat differently in early life responding

with more IgM antibodies. There is a decreased capacity during the first two years or so to efficiently produce protective IgG antibodies to the polysaccharide capsules on pathogens like pneumococci, meningococci, H. influenzae type b, and certain E. coli. This is why it is important to protect the infants against these pathogens with breastfeeding and effective vaccinations.

The mucosal defense in the form of SIgA antibodies in various secretions is inadequate in the young infant. This form of immunity protects against many of the common viral and bacterial infections in childhood without causing inflammation and tissue engagement. The early deficiency in mucosal protection is counterbalanced by breastfeeding. Breastfeeding provides protection while the infant builds up its own SIgA system. Human milk provides large amounts of SIgA antibodies against the pathogens in the infant's surroundings (Chapters 5 and 6).

Today numerous well controlled, defined vaccines with very limited side effects are available for the infant.

Reference List

1. Clark DA, Arck PC, Chaouat G: Why did your mother reject you? Immunogenetic determinants of the response to environmental selective pressure expressed at the uterine level. Am J Reprod Immunol 41:5-22, 1999

2. Zenclussen AC, Fest S, Busse P, et al: Questioning the Th1/Th2 paradigm in re production: peripheral levels of IL-12 are down-regulated in miscarriage patients. Am J Reprod Immunol 48:245-251, 2002

3. Moffett-King A: Natural killer cells and pregnancy. Nat Rev Immunol 2:656-663, 2002

4. Chaouat G, Zourbas S, Ostojic S, et al: A brief review of recent data on some cytokine expressions at the materno-foetal interface which might challenge the classical Th1/Th2 dichotomy. J Reprod Immunol 53:241-256, 2002

5. Mor G, Abrahams VM: Potential role of macrophages as immunoregulators of pregnancy. Reprod Biol Endocrinol 1:119, 2003

6. Nagaeva O, Jonsson L, Mincheva-Nilsson L: Dominant IL-10 and TGF-beta mRNA expression in gammadeltaT cells of human early pregnancy decidua sugg ests immunoregulatory potential. Am J Reprod Immunol 48:9-17, 2002

7. Takahashi T, Sakaguchi S: The role of regulatory T cells in controlling immunologic self-tolerance. Int Rev Cytol 225:1-32, 2003

8. Aluvihare VR, Kallikourdis M, Betz AG: Regulatory T cells mediate maternal tolerance to the fetus. Nat Immunol 5:266-271, 2004

9. Ostensen M, Villiger PM: Immunology of pregnancy--pregnancy as a remission inducing agent in rheumatoid arthritis. Transpl Immunol 9:155-160, 2002

10. Cervera R, Font J, Carmona F, et al: Pregnancy outcome in systemic lupus erythe matosus: good news for the new millennium. Autoimmun Rev 1:354-359, 2002

11. Ledee-Bataille N, Lapree-Delage G, Taupin JL, et al: Concentration of leukaemia inhibitory factor (LIF) in uterine flushing fluid is highly predictive of embryo implantation. Hum Reprod 17:213-218, 2002

12. Bowen JM, Chamley L, Mitchell MD, et al: Cytokines of the placenta and extra-placental membranes: biosynthesis, secretion and roles in establishment of pregnancy in women. Placenta 23:239-256, 2002

13. Yaqoob M, Cnattingius S, Jalil F, et al: Risk factors for mortality in young children living under various socio-economic conditions in Lahore, Pakistan: with particular reference to inbreeding. Clin Genet 54:426-434, 1998

14. Malhotra I, Ouma J, Wamachi A, et al: In utero exposure to helminth and mycobacterial antigens generates cytokine responses similar to that observed in adults. J Clin Invest 99:1759-1766, 1997

15. Nahmias AJ, Kourtis AP: The great balancing acts. The pregnant woman, placenta, fetus, and infectious agents. Clin Perinatol 24:497-521, 1997

16. Nanthakumar NN, Fusunyan RD, Sanderson I, et al: Inflammation in the developing human intestine: A possible pathophysiologic contribution to necrotizing enterocolitis. Proc Natl Acad Sci USA 97:6043-6048, 2000

17. Dorschner RA, Lin KH, Murakami M, et al: Neonatal skin in mice and humans expresses increased levels of antimicrobial peptides: innate immunity during devel opment of the adaptive response. Pediatr Res 53:566-572, 2003

18. Yoshio H, Tollin M, Gudmundsson GH, et al: Antimicrobial polypeptides of human vernix caseosa and amniotic fluid: implications for newborn innate defense. Pediatr Res 53:211-216, 2003

19. Salzman NH, Polin RA, Harris MC, et al: Enteric defensin expression in necrotiz ing enterocolitis. Pediatr Res 44:20-26, 1998

20. Ganz T: Defensins: antimicrobial peptides of innate immunity. Nat Rev Immunol 3:710-720, 2003

21. Berger M, Frank MM: The serum complement system, in Stiehm ER (ed): Immunologic Disorders in Infants & Children. 4th Edition. Philadelphia, W.B. Saunders, 1996

22. Schelonka RL, Infante AJ: Neonatal immunology. Semin Perinatol 22:2-14, 1998

23. Levy O, Martin S, Eichenwald E, et al: Impaired innate immunity in the newborn: newborn neutrophils are deficient in bactericidal/permeability-increasing protein. Pediatrics 104:1327-1333, 1999

24. Komatsu H, Tsukimori K, Hata K, et al: The characterization of superoxide production of human neonatal neutrophil. Early Hum Dev 65:11-19, 2001

25. Uguz A, Coskun M, Yuzbey S, et al: Apoptosis of cord blood neutrophils and their response to colony-stimulating factors. Am J Perinatol 19:427-434, 2002

26. Marodi L: Deficient interferon-gamma receptor-mediated signaling in neonatal macrophages. Acta Paediatr Suppl 91:117-119, 2002

27. Blahnik MJ, Ramanathan R, Riley CR, et al: Lipopolysaccharide-induced tumor necrosis factor-alpha and IL-10 production by lung macrophages from preterm and term neonates. Pediatr Res 50:726-731, 2001

28. Karlsson H, Hessle C, Rudin A: Innate immune responses of human neonatal cells to bacteria from the normal gastrointestinal flora Infect Immun 70:6688-6696, 2002

29. De Wit D, Tonon S, Olislagers V, et al: Impaired responses to toll-like receptor 4 and toll-like receptor 3 ligands in human cord blood. J Autoimmun 21:277-281, 2003

30. Schultz C, Temming P, Bucsky P, et al: Immature anti-inflammatory response in neonates. Clin Exp Immunol 135:130-136, 2004

31. Kadowaki N, Antonenko S, Ho S, et al: Distinct cytokine profiles of neonatal natural killer T cells after expansion with subsets of dendritic cells. J Exp Med 193:1221-1226, 2001

32. Liu E, Tu W, Law HK, et al: Decreased yield, phenotypic expression and function of immature monocyte-derived dendritic cells in cord blood. Br J Haematol 113:240-246, 2001

33. Upham JW, Lee PT, Holt BJ, et al: Development of interleukin-12-producing capacity throughout childhood. Infect Immun 70:6583-6588, 2002

34. Langrish CL, Buddle JC, Thrasher AJ, et al: Neonatal dendritic cells are intrinsically biased against Th-1 immune responses. Clin Exp Immunol 128:118-123, 2002

35. Kelly D, Coutts AG: Early nutrition and the development of immune function in the neonate. Proc Nutr Soc 59:177-185, 2000

36. Aaby P, Marx C, Trautner S, et al: Thymus size at birth is associated with infant mortality: a community study from Guinea-Bissau. Acta Paediatr 91:698-703, 2002

37. De Felice C, Vacca P, Presta G, et al: Small thymus at birth and neonatal outcome in very-low-birth-weight infants. Eur J Pediatr 162:204-206, 2003

38. Ngom PT, Collinson A, Pido-Lopez J, et al: Improved thymic function in exclusively breast-fed babies is associated with higher breast milk IL-7. Am J Clin Nutr 2004 (in press)

39. Ribeiro-do-Couto LM, Boeije LC, Kroon JS, et al: High IL-13 production by human neonatal T cells: neonate immune system regulator? Eur J Immunol 31:3394-3402, 2001

40. Buck RH, Cordle CT, Thomas DJ, et al: Longitudinal study of intracellular T cell cytokine production in infants compared to adults. Clin Exp Immunol 128:490-497, 2002

41. Marshall-Clarke S, Reen D, Tasker L, et al: Neonatal immunity: how well has it grown up? Immunol Today 21:35-41, 2000

42. Wing K, Ekmark A, Karlsson H, et al: Characterization of human CD25+ CD4+ T cells in thymus, cord and adult blood. Immunology 106:190-199, 2002

43. Brandtzaeg P: Role of local immunity and breast-feeding in mucosal homeostasis and defence against infections, in Calder PC, Field CJ, Gill HS (eds): Nutrition and Immune Function Oxon: CABI Publ 273-319, 2002

44. Brandtzaeg P: The secretory immunoglobulin system: regulation and biological significance. Focusing on human mammary glands, in David MK, Isaacs CE, Hanson LA, et al (eds): Integrating population outcomes, biological mechanisms and research methods in the study of human milk and lactation. New York, Kluwer Academic/Plenum Publishers 1-16, 2002

45. Cummins AG, Thompson FM: Postnatal changes in mucosal immune response: a physiological perspective of breast feeding and weaning. Immunol.Cell Biol 75:419-429, 1997

46. Janeway CA, Travers P, Walport M, et al: Immunobiology (5th Edition). New York, Garland Publishing, 2001

47. Goldblum R, Hanson L, Brandtzaeg P: The Mucosal Defense System, in Stiehm E (ed): Immunologic Disorders in Infants & Children. 3rd Edition. Philadelphia, 159-199, 1996

48. Phalipon A, Corthesy B: Novel functions of the polymeric Ig receptor: well beyond transport of immunoglobulins. Trends Immunol 24:55-58, 2003

49. Mellander L, Carlsson B, Jalil F, et al: Secretory IgA antibody response against Escherichia coli antigens in infants in relation to exposure. J Pediatr 107:430-433, 1985

50. Hanson LA, Robertson AK, Bjersing J, et al: Undernutrition, immunodeficency and mucosal infections, in J. Mestecky JB, Lamm ME, Mayer L, et al (eds): Mucosal Immunology. 3rd Edition (in press). San Diego, Academic Press, 2004

51. Pelletier DL: The potentiating effects of malnutrition on child mortality: epidemiologic evidence and policy implications. Nutr Rev 52:409-415, 1994

52. Hahn-Zoric M, Hagberg H, Kjellmer I, et al: Aberrations in placental cytokine mRNA related to intrauterine growth retardation. Pediatr Res 51:201-206, 2002

53. Amu S, Malik A, Hahn-Zoric M, et al: Studies of cytokines in placentas from Pakistani newborns with intrauterine growth retardation compared to prematures and those of normal birth weight. In manuscript 2004

54. Chandra RK: Serum thymic hormone activity and cell-mediated immunity in healthy neonates, preterm infants, and small-for-gestational age infants. Pediatrics 407-411, 1989

55. Saito S, Kato Y, Maruyama M, et al: A study of interferon-gamma and interleu kin-2 production in premature neonates and neonates with intrauterine growth retardation. Am J Reprod Immunol 27:63-68, 1992

56. Kaur S, Faridi MM, Agarwal KN: BCG vaccination reaction in low birth weight infants. Indian J Med Res 116:64-69, 2002

57. Manerikar SS, Malaviya AN, Singh MB, et al: Immune status and BCG vaccination in newborns with intra-uterine growth retardation. Clin Exp Immunol 26:173-175, 1976

58. Vekemans J, Ota MO, Sillah J, et al: Immune responses to mycobacterial antigens in the Gambian population: implications for vaccines and immunodiagnostic test design. Infect Immun 72:381-388, 2004

59. Robbins JB, Schneerson R, Anderson P, et al: The 1996 Albert Lasker Medical Research Awards. Prevention of systemic infections, especially meningitis, caused by Haemophilus influenzae type b. Impact on public health and implications for other polysaccharide-based vaccines. JAMA 276:1181-1185, 1996

60. Wuorimaa T, Dagan R, Vakevainen M, et al: Avidity and subclasses of IgG after immunization of infants with an 11-valent pneumococcal conjugate vaccine with or without aluminum adjuvant. J Infect Dis 184:1211-1215, 2001

61. Khalak R, Pichichero ME, D'Angio CT: Three-year follow-up of vaccine response in extremely preterm infants. Pediatrics 101:597-603, 1998

62. Munoz A, Salvador A, Brodsky NL, et al: Antibody response of low birth weight infants to Haemophilus influenzae type b polyribosylribitol phosphate-outer membrane protein conjugate vaccine. Pediatrics 96:216-219, 1995

63. Lehmann D, Pomat WS, Riley ID, et al: Studies of maternal immunisation with pneumococcal polysaccharide vaccine in Papua New Guinea. Vaccine 21: 3446-3450, 2003

4 Maternal Defense Of The Fetus Via The Placenta

The newborn needs help from its mother after delivery when its own immune system is still incomplete. At this time, the neonate is exposed to numerous microbes many of which are potentially dangerous if they reach high numbers (see Chapter 1). One way for the mother to help her offspring is by selective transfer of her own plasma IgG antibodies via the placenta. The surface area in the placenta where fetal blood meets maternal blood is enormous. The transfer of the maternal IgG to the fetal circulation occurs via an active, selective binding to receptors specific for the end of the antibodies, called Fc. The Fc end is opposite the antibody binding sites (Figure 6).[1] The placental Fc receptors are named Fcn, or Brambell receptors, after their discoverer. These receptors efficiently transfer the maternal IgG to the fetal circulation so that the full term newborn has approximately 90% of the maternal blood concentration of IgG antibodies. In some studies, the newborn had 150% (Figure 11).[1-3] For unknown reasons, the transfer of antibodies of certain specificities and high binding capacity are favored.[4]

The transfer of IgG during fetal life gives the fetus a continuous increase in blood IgG concentrations. The more premature the delivery, the lower the blood IgG levels in the neonate (Figure 11). Figure 12 illustrates the rapid decline in the level of maternal IgG in the infant after delivery. At that time, the half-life of IgG is approximately 25-30 days. Later, it is reduced to 21-25 days as the infant's own IgG production takes over and increases the total IgG towards the levels normal for a child (Figure 12). The figure shows that the IgG from the maternal cir-

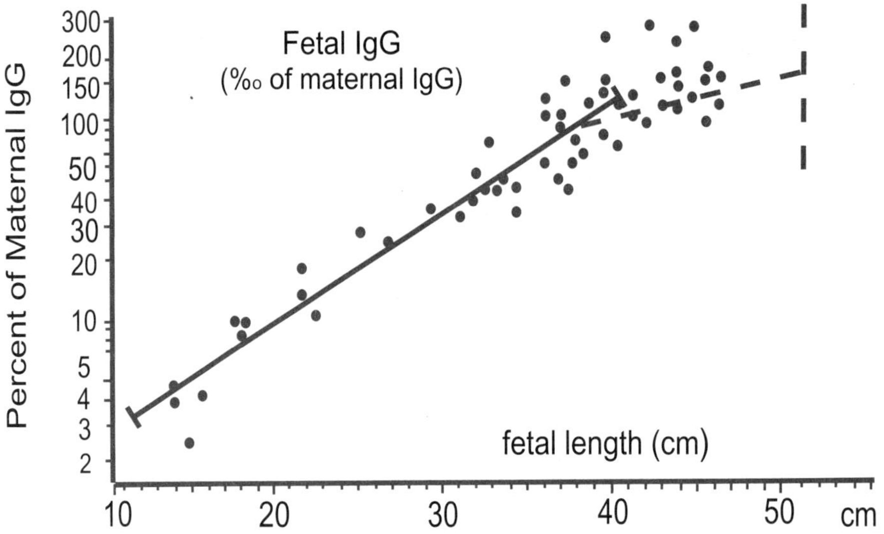

Figure 11. This figure illustrates the continuous active transfer of maternal IgG through the placenta by means of the Brambell receptor binding to the Fc portion of the IgG. The level of IgG in the serum during pregnancy is expressed in percent of maternal serum IgG in relation to fetal length. In this study, the continuous line shows fetal length up to 45 centimeters, the broken line shows fetal lengths from 42 centimeters up. Note, the transfer slopes off towards the end of pregnancy. (Reference 3, Chapter 4)

culation starts to decrease after birth and the serum IgG levels decrease. The levels start to increase at about 3-4 months of life as the infant begins to produce IgG.[5]

As long as they are present, maternal IgG antibodies in the newborn's circulation provide good defense against infections from many different microbes in blood and tissues. But, they do so at a price. When reacting with the infecting microbes they meet in blood and tissues, they activate the complement system which stimulates phagocytes. Phagocytes then attack the invading microbes, but also produce pro-inflammatory cytokines like IL-1β, TNF-α and IL-6. They enhance defense, but cause tissue damage including inflammation. Pro-inflammatory cytokines are the main mechanism behind the symptoms the infant develops - fever, listlessness, tiredness, pain, and loss of appetite. Cytokine IL-8 is also produced during infections. Cytokine IL-8 is a strong chemokine for neutrophils. These cells are brought in to reinforce the defense, but they further increase the inflammatory and symptom-causing process.

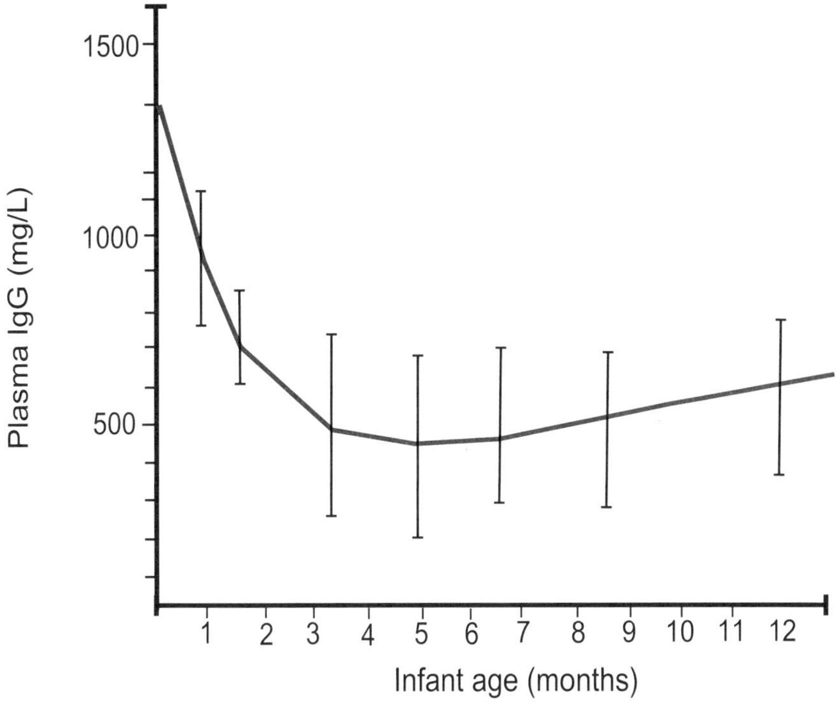

Figure 12. After birth, the maternal antibodies transferred to the infant are metabolized with a half-life of about 25-30 days. The IgG level in the serum of the infant reaches a minimum around 2-4 months of life when the IgG antibodies produced by the infant begin taking over. Figure 12 is based on reference 5 in Chapter 4.

Pro-inflammatory cytokines increase the level of the appetite-regulating hormone, leptin, which reduces the appetite (Chapter 5). The inflammation and subsequent tissue repair costs energy. This energy comes from the energy that should be used for growth of the infant. This is one reason why severe and/or repeated infections can impair growth.

As mentioned in the previous chapter, vaccination of the mother with vaccines which induce a protective vaccine response in the form of IgG antibodies results in protection of the infant via the transplacental IgG.[6] It should be noted that while remaining in the infant's circulation such antibodies may inhibit vaccine responses of the infant. This effect can last through the first year of life for the measles vaccine.[7]

In conclusion:

During fetal life, there is a continuous transfer of IgG antibodies from the maternal circulation to the fetus by means of a special receptor in the placenta. A full term newborn will have a concentration of maternal IgG antibodies similar to its mother for its defense against infections. This maternal IgG has a half-life of about 25-30 days. Most will vanish during the first several months of life in parallel with an increase in IgG antibodies produced by the infant.

The maternal IgG antibodies in the infant's circulation defend efficiently against microbial infections in blood and tissues. But, they do so by inducing a cytokine driven pro-inflammatory defense which causes symptoms of infection and tissue damage, and is energy-costly. The maternal IgG antibodies can interfere with certain vaccinations given to the infant during the first year of life.

Reference List

1 Hanson LA, Korotkova M, Lundin S, et al: The transfer of immunity from mother to child. Ann NY Acad Sci 987:199-206, 2003

2. Landor M: Maternal-fetal transfer of immunoglobulins. Ann Allergy Asthma Immunol 74:279-283, 1995

3. Berg T, Nilsson BA: The foetal development of serum levels of IgG and IgM. Acta Paediatr Scand 58:577-583, 1969

4. Avanzini MA, Pignatti P, Chirico G, et al: Placental transfer favours high avidity IgG antibodies. Acta Paediatr 87:180-185, 1998

5 Berg T: The immunoglobulin development during the first year of life. A longitudinal study. Acta Paediatr Scand 58:229-236, 1969

6. Shahid NS, Steinhoff MC, Roy E, et al: Placental and breast transfer of antibodies after maternal immunization with polysaccharide meningococcal vaccine: a ran domized, controlled evaluation. Vaccine 20:2404-2409, 2002

7. Siegrist CA: Mechanisms by which maternal antibodies influence infant vaccine responses: review of hypotheses and definition of main determinants. Vaccine 21:3406-3412, 2003

5 Mother's Defense Of The Offspring Via Milk

Components Of Human Milk With Immunobiological Activities

Antibodies

The predominant antibody in human colostrum and mature milk is SIgA.[1;2] As described in earlier chapters, it consists of two IgA molecules bound to a J chain and the polyIgR (Figure 8). SIgA makes up 80-90% of the immunoglobulins in colostrum and milk. The concentration can be as high as 12 grams/liter in colostrum, decreasing to about 1 gram/liter in mature milk. A fully breastfed infant will consume about 125 mg/kg/day at the age of one month and around 75 mg/kg/day by 4 months.[3] In comparison, a nonlactating adult produces about 40 mg/kg/day. The adult makes 25% more SIgA than the major serum immunoglubulin, IgG.[4] The high concentration of SIgA in colostrum rapidly decreases during the first few days. Mature milk has lower concentrations that parallel the increase in milk volume (Figure 13).[5] The level of SIgA is higher in milk from mothers of premature infants than mothers of full term babies.[6]

Although SIgA antibodies do not activate inflammatory reactivity via complement and cytokines, they can induce eosinophils to release their pro-inflammatory granular content.[7] Experimental studies in mice suggest that SIgA antibodies can prevent lung eosinophilia, airway hyper-responsiveness, and production of IgE antibodies.[8]

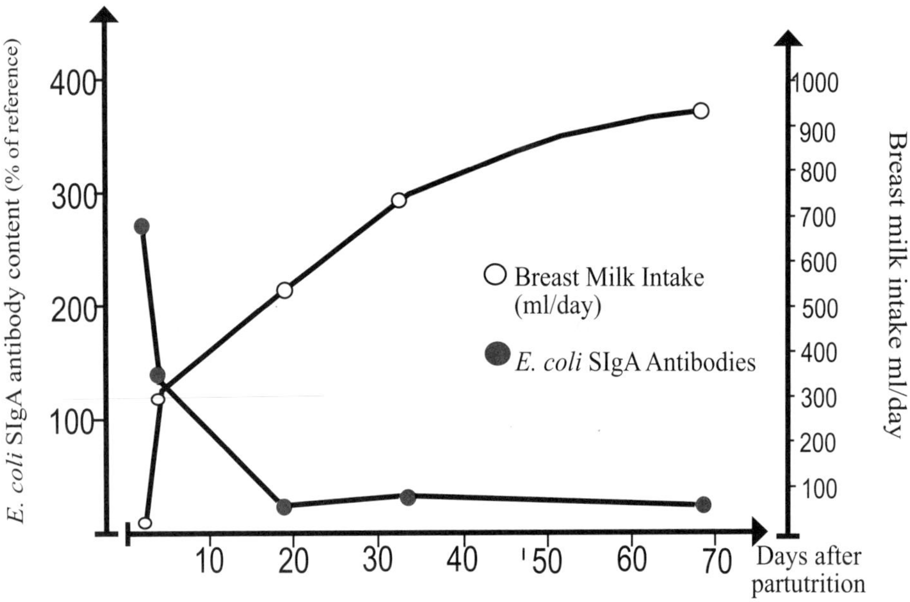

Figure 13. This figure shows the titers of SIgA antibodies against *E.coli* bacteria in human milk during lactation. The high titers in colostrum are followed by lower titers in mature milk. This decrease is offset by the increase in milk volume. The antibody levels measured reflect the SIgA content of the milk. (Reference 5, Chapter 5)

Due to its special structure, SIgA is much more resistant to proteolytic enzymes than other forms of antibodies like IgG which primarily occur in blood and tissues. IgG normally does not to any large extent come in contact with the proteolytic enzymes present in various secretions, such as in the gut, whereas SIgA functions in those sites. SIgA is more resistant than serum IgA to proteases produced by bacteria like *H. influenzae* or pneumococci which often occur in the upper respiratory tract. Furthermore, milk contains SIgA antibodies that neutralize those bacterial enzymes.[9;10]

It was noted that human milk contains SIgA antibodies against a wide range of bacteria, especially of intestinal origin.[11] The reason for this became apparent when it was shown that lactogenic hormones affecting the mammary glands toward the end of pregnancy directed migration of lymphocytes originating from the Peyer's patches in the gut to the mammary glands.[12;13] In the mammary glands, these cells produce SIgA antibodies against the microbes they encounter in the gut. This is called the *entero-mammaric link* (Figure 10). This link explains why milk provides such good protection against a very wide range of microbes which tend to infect the infant via its mucosal membranes. Thus, milk SIgA antibodies cover not only pathogens in the gastrointestinal tract, but also the respiratory tract. This is advantageous for the infant because the mother may swallow aero-pathogens which may activate the SIgA response in the gut via the Peyer's patches.

At any given time, human milk has SIgA antibodies against a wide range of microbial antigens. It also has memory lymphocytes directed toward the lactating mammary glands. The primary SIgA response via mucosal membranes is reported to last about three months. Supported by the hormone-directed migration of lymphoid cells to the mammary glands, the milk may contain SIgA antibodies not only against the microbes the mother presently carries, but also against those she has been exposed to earlier in life.

The presence of a stable microflora with many bacterial species in the gut (Chapter 1) also supports the presence of SIgA antibodies with a broad range of specificities. One report suggested that ongoing intestinal infections in lactating mothers caused by pathogens like *Shigella* and *Giardia lamblia* induced a temporary decrease of SIgA antibodies in the milk in 91% of the cases.[14] It is likely that the mothers could still protect their babies against these pathogens as illustrated by the original observation of Mata et al.[15] They showed that a few mothers with diarrhea caused by *Shigella* protected their babies from symptomatic dysentery by breastfeeding; although, the same bacteria grew from the stool of the infants.

The major function of SIgA antibodies is to bind microbes already on the surface of mucosal membranes. This prevents bacteria and viruses from attaching to the epithelial cells in the mucosa and blocks them from entering tissues - a prerequisite for establishing infections (Figures 3 and 10).

SIgA antibodies bind and neutralize viruses and bacterial toxins. The breastfed baby has many milk SIgA antibodies to protect it against bacteria and viruses from its mother and surroundings in early life.

A small study suggested that vaccination against pneumococcal polysaccharides during lactation increased the level of SIgA antibodies against pneumococci in the milk.[16]

The predominant antibody in human milk is SIgA. It is a stable antibody, more resistant to proteolytic enzymes than blood antibodies. It binds microbes on mucosal membranes during its passage down to and through the gastrointestinal tract. Thus, milk antibodies prevent microbes from attaching to the epithelial cells which is their first step when starting an infection. Lymphocytes from the mother's gut migrate to the mammary glands where they produce milk antibodies. This explains why the milk contains SIgA antibodies against the microbes in the mother's gut flora, reflecting the microbes in the mother's surrounding.

Clinical studies have shown that the level of SIgA antibodies in human milk specific for *Vibrio cholerae*, enterotoxigenic *E. coli, Campylobacter, Shigella,* and *Giardia lamblia* provides protection against gastroenteritis caused by each of these agents.[17-22]

The importance for the baby is not only the efficiency of this ready-made defense, but also the low energy cost of this form of defense.[11] The defense conveyed by milk SIgA prevents activation of the tissue-damaging, energy-consuming, pro-inflammatory defense of IgG antibodies, complement activation, phagocytes, etc. as described in Chapter 2. With this form of milk-mediated mucosal defense, the newborn can be colonized with a microbial flora primarily from its mother after delivery with little risk of infection as discussed in more detail in Chapter 6.

Milk SIgA antibodies protect without inducing energy-consuming, symptom-causing inflammatory defense. This is important for the child needing the energy for growth and development.

Recently, it has been shown that the carbohydrate side chains of SIgA promote the growth of *E. coli* with type1 pili.[23;24] Such *E. coli* are generally of low virulence. It is presumably helpful that their growth is promoted in the gut of the breastfed infant by the milk SIgA. Human SIgA is also reported to favor the formation of a biofilm of microbes on an epithelial surface. This function may possibly promote the normal microbial colonization of the gut.[25]

Milk SIgA antibodies promote growth of certain *E. coli* bacteria of low virulence in the gut of the breastfed baby.

Milk also contains free secretory component (SC) which is the extra-membranous part of the polyIgR, the receptor bringing the IgA dimers with J chain through the epithelial cell (Figure 8). In colostrum, there may be as much as 2 grams/liter of free SC. It has been suggested that the free SC may limit infections from enterotoxin-producing *E. coli* by binding to the bacteria among other effects.[26;27]

Human milk contains smaller amounts of IgM and IgG antibodies. IgM reaches the milk via the same transport mechanism as SIgA and carries the same extra-membranous portion of the polyIgR as SIgA, the SC. In colostrum, there is up to 0.6 grams/liter of SIgM.[28] The possible biological relevance of milk IgG and SIgM has not been determined. There are some recent studies indicating that milk IgG has enzyme activity that hydrolyzes nucleotides and DNA.[28-30] It is not clear why this happens. We have recently found that germ-free animals absorb such nucleotides and this enhances their growth. The nucleotides seem to come from gut bacteria.[31]

In conclusion:

Colostrum and mature milk transfer considerable amounts of SIgA antibodies to the breastfed infant. These antibodies have a more stable structure than serum antibodies and can resist proteolytic enzymes on mucosal membranes. This is especially important in the gut where such enzymes are prevalent. The SIgA antibodies in milk are part of a special defense system for mucosal membranes. They make up 80% of all the antibodies in the body. The large size of this immune system presumably suggests that most infections reach humans via the extensive mucosal membranes in the respiratory and gastrointestinal tracts.

SIgA antibodies are important because they bind to the microbes they meet on mucosal membranes. SIgA antibodies prevent the microbes from attaching to mucosal membranes and entering tissues. If the microbes do enter the tissues, they cause infections that will be met by activation of defense forces in the tissues. This defense always results in an inflammatory response with engagement of phagocytes, like neutrophils and monocytes/macrophages, and production of pro-inflammatory cytokines giving the clinical symptoms of infection, tissue damage, and increased energy consumption. Thus, the SIgA antibodies in milk protect by preventing tissue engagement caused by infecting microorganisms. This is a form of defense which is especially helpful for the newborn and growing young infant. They are rather slow to produce these antibodies on their own.

The SIgA antibodies in milk are efficient for the baby because they are produced by lymphoid cells which migrate to the mammary glands from the mother's gut. In the mother's gut, the lymphoid cells have responded to the gut microbes. When they arrive in the mammary glands, they produce SIgA antibodies directed against the gut bacteria (Figure 10). Having been delivered next to the mother's anus, the normal exposure of the newborn to the mother's gut bacteria is not dangerous. The colostrum and milk contain large amounts of SIgA antibodies against her gut bacteria thanks to the entero-mammaric link in her immune system. Obviously, it is helpful for the newborn to receive the colostral SIgA antibodies soon after delivery to handle the bacteria it meets from delivery and thereafter. Even if the volumes of the early colostrum are small, the concentration of SIgA is very high. At the same time, these milk antibodies permit the normal colonization of the gut of the newborn which is so important for its health and normal development as described in Chapter 1. The milk SIgA antibodies promote the growth of *E. coli* of low virulence in the infant's gut because such *E. coli* carry adhesins, or pili, which bind to a carbohydrate side chain present only on the SIgA molecules.

Clinical studies have shown that milk SIgA antibodies protect the baby against intestinal pathogens like *Campylobacter*, *Shigella*, enterotoxin-producing *E. coli*, *Vibrio cholerae*, and *Giardia lamblia*. The milk SIgA antibodies neutralize viruses and toxins.

The newborn's natural instinct is to reach the mammary glands right after delivery and begin breastfeeding. This helps the baby obtain ready made immune protection. The baby also receives a number of other milk components important for its own active development as described below.

Lactoferrin

Human milk is low in protein compared to many other species milk. Yet two of the major protein components in human milk are not primarily for nutrition but for defense: SIgA and lactoferrin. Colostrum contains 5-7 grams/liter of lactoferrin. The lactoferrin in mature milk decreases to1-3 grams/liter.[32;33] This decrease is partly compensated by the increase in milk production. By 1 month of age, a breastfed infant consumes about 260 mg/kg/day of lactoferrin. By 4 months of age, the breastfed infant consumes about 125 mg/kg/day.[3]

Lactoferrin consists of a single polypeptide chain glycoprotein forming two lobes. Each lobe binds iron. Lactoferrin is one of the iron-binding proteins in the transferrin family. It is present in all exocrine secretions including milk, but is also present in granulocytes. It has a molecular weight of 78 kD.[11]

Lactoferrin is quite resistant to degradation in the gut by trypsin and chymotrypsin. This presumably explains why the stools of breastfed babies contain significant amounts of lactoferrin and large fragments thereof.[34] In the gut, there is a special receptor for the uptake of lactoferrin and large lactoferrin fragments.[35] In vitro studies suggest that lactoferrin promotes the growth of the intestinal epithelium.[36]

Lactoferrin and certain of its fragments are bactericidal for many Gram-negative and Gram-positive bacteria. It was previously thought that a major cause of the bactericidal capacity of lactoferrin was due to its capacity to bind iron which is needed by most bacteria. This has not been confirmed. More important for the bactericidal effect against Gram-negative and -positive bacteria seems to be the capacity of lactoferrin to react with and destabilize their outer cell membrane. Then, the bacteria become more sensitive to killing by lysozyme, another milk protein, described below.[37;38] Lactoferrin has anti-viral effects and acts against fungi like *Candida albicans*.[39]

Lactoferrin has multiple enzyme activities, one of which is serine protease which cleaves two colonization factors on *H. influenzae* possibly decreasing the pathogenic potential of these bacteria.[40] In addition, lactoferrin was found to hinder the adherence of enteropathogenic *E. coli* (EPEC) to intestinal epithelial cells presumably via a similar mechanism.[41] These effects may help prevent intestinal infections. Lactoferrin is a ribonuclease. It interacts with nucleic acids, proteins, and polysaccharides.[42] At the same time, it seems to promote the growth of Bifidobacteria.[43]

> Lactoferrin is another major enzyme-resistant milk protein which, like SIgA antibodies, may relatively help protect the breastfed baby. It can kill bacteria, viruses, and fungi like *Candida*.

Lactoferrin provides yet another example of a defense factor in milk which kills microbes without inducing tissue engagement and inflammation. In addition, it is efficiently anti-inflammatory. Thus, it prevents the production of several pro-inflammatory cytokines.[44] Lactoferrin has the capacity to enter leucocytes and their nuclei. There, lactoferrin binds to the Nuclear Factor κB (NFκB) which is the transcription factor directing the production of several pro-inflammatory cytokines including IL-1β, TNF-α and IL-6. Inhibiting NFκB blocks the pro-inflammatory effects of an infection. In contrast, the anti-inflammatory cytokines IL-4 and IL-10 are upregulated by lactoferrin.[45]

> Lactoferrin, like SIgA, defends against infections without causing inflammation. Entering the nuclei of leucocytes, lactoferrin blocks the mechanisms which induce the production of the pro-inflammatory and symptom-inducing cytokines IL-1β, TNF-α and IL-6.

To prove that one single factor in human milk, like lactoferrin, protects against a certain infection on its own is very difficult. It has only been done for SIgA antibodies in milk. It is possible to determine the protection against a certain infection in relation to the amount of SIgA antibodies in the milk to that infectious agent. There are still no human studies proving the clinical relevance of the anti-infectious and anti-inflammatory capacities of lactoferrin.

However, there are some experimental studies. Letting mice drink human lactoferrin or certain active fragments thereof significantly inhibited urinary tract infections caused by *E. coli*.[46] It is interesting to note that breastfed babies have lactoferrin and lactoferrin fragments from the milk in the urine and breastfeeding seems to protect against urinary tract infection.[34] Other experimental studies suggest that lactoferrin may act against *E. coli* and *Shigella Flexneri*.[47;48] In a mouse model, it was shown that orally administered human lactoferrin and certain of its fragments significantly diminished the inflammatory reaction of dextran sulphate-induced colitis.[49] The level of IL-1β in the blood and the number of TNF-α-producing cells were decreased among other effects.

> Although there are no clinical studies, one study in mice showed that human lactoferrin and certain lactoferrin fragments could protect against urinary tract infection. Another study showed the anti-inflammatory activity of lactoferrin and lactoferrin fragments in mice with experimental colitis.

In conclusion:

Lactoferrin, like SIgA, is a major milk protein that is likely to play an important role in the defense of the breastfed baby. Lactoferrin has the capacity to kill bacteria, both Gram-negative and Gram-positive, as well as viruses and fungi. At the same time, it blocks production of the pro-inflammatory cytokines which are, otherwise, always induced in tissue defense when antibodies in blood and tissues become engaged in host defense along with activated complement and phagocytes. The blocking effect results from lactoferrin entering the nuclei of leucocytes, preventing the transcription factor NFκB from inducing production of the symptom- and inflammation-inducing cytokines IL-1β, TNF-α and IL-6.

Lactoferrin is quite resistant to the proteolytic enzymes in the intestine. Many lactoferrin fragments also have similar effects on microbes. Lactoferrin and its fragments are taken up by special receptors in the gut. As a result, the breastfed baby has lactoferrin and fragments thereof in the urine. This may be one reason why breastfed infants have fewer urinary tract infections than non-breastfed infants.

Lactoferrin has several other suggested effects which may be beneficial for the baby like promotion of the growth of Bifidobacteria in the infant's gut.

Human lactoferrin and certain fragments thereof given perorally to experimental animals prevent urinary tract infections caused by E. coli and down-regulate the inflammation in chemically induced colitis.

α–*Lactalbumin*

Another of the main milk proteins, α-lactalbumin, has been shown to appear as an aggregate of several α-lactalbumin molcules and is then able to induce apoptosis in all transformed embryonic and lymphoid cells. In contrast, there is no effect on mature epithelial cells.[50] It has been shown that a lower number of such aggregated molecules of α-lactalbumin that have been unfolded, binding as a cofactor oleic acid, can kill malignant cells.[51;52] The resulting structure is called HAMLET, **h**uman α-lactalbumin **m**ade **le**thal to **t**umor cells. In this form, the molecule elevates Ca^{2+} and induces apoptosis. It seems that the change into HAMLET may be supported by the low pH in the infant's stomach which releases Ca^{2+} and activates lipases cleaving off free fatty acids from the milk triglycerides adding to the oleic acid already present in the milk. The change in the conformation of the α-lactalbumin makes it release its strongly bound Ca^{2+} and expose a binding site for oleic acid.

The resulting HAMLET molecule kills cancer cells only, not normal differentiated cells. This anti-tumor activity has been demonstrated against more than 40 different carcinoma and lymphoma cell lines. Ongoing studies suggest effects in vivo against human papilloma and also human glioblastoma cells in an animal model.[53] HAMLET may be the reason breastfeeding is suggested to result in a reduction in childhood leukemia. The intestine contains some 70-80% of the whole lymphoid system. HAMLET may reach sites of proliferation in the gut mucosa purging pre-malignant perversions of rapidly growing enterocytes and lymphocytes. It is not known if HAMLET has any preventive effects against breast cancer but this could explain why breastfeeding prevents this form of cancer (also discussed in Chapter 6).

In conclusion:

Another major milk component with a specialized function, α-lactalbumin, has recently been found as a large complex in human milk binding oleic acid. In this form, called HAMLET, it induces apoptosis of all malignant cells tested, but not normal cells. This change in the milk protein is favored by the low pH in the stomach. It may be that α-lactalbumin plays a role in preventing malignancies in the mammary glands as well as in the gut of the infant.

Lysozyme

Lysozyme increases during lactation in contrast to SIgA and lactoferrin. Colostrum contains about 70 ng/ml. By 1 month, there is 20 ng/ml. By 6 months of lactation, 250 ng/ml is present.[6;32] An exclusively breastfed baby receives 3-4 mg/kg/day at 1 month and 6 mg/kg/day at 4 months.[3]

The cell walls of certain bacteria is split by this glycoprotein enzyme in cooperation with lactoferrin and SIgA antibodies when attacking *E. coli.*[54] The possible protective value of lysozyme in milk has not been determined.

In conclusion:

Lysozyme is another milk protein with anti-microbial capacities particularly when combined with other milk proteins like SIgA antibodies and lactoferrin. There are no studies testing the biological value of lysozyme in the protection of breastfed infants.

Carbohydrate components

Human milk contains oligosaccharides and glycoconjugates, many of which may be involved in host defense against various mucosal infections like otitis media, respiratory tract infections, and diarrhea.[55] Their major function is to act as blocking analogues to receptors on the mucosal epithelium. Microbes and microbial toxins attach to such receptors as the first step in a mucosal attack (Figure 3).

The *oligosaccharides* consist of various combinations of the five different monosaccharides - glucose, fucose, galactose, N-acetylamine, and sialic acid in chains of 3-10 of the mono-components. They are produced in the mammary gland epithelium and make up the third largest solid component of human milk.[56;57] Over 90 different oligosaccharides have been isolated from milk. There are more than 900 different fucosyloligosaccharides.[58;59]

Most of the milk oligosaccharides pass through the gut unchanged and about 1% of the daily intake appears in the urine.[60;61] Formula-fed infants have less oligosaccharides in the stool and urine and they are of a different composition than those of breastfed infants.

The milk oligosaccharides seem to affect the composition of the gut microflora and its capacity to cause infections. The oligosaccharides may partly explain why breastfed infants have fewer different serogroups of *E. coli* in their gut microflora than formula-fed infants and why breastfed infants less often carry pathogenic *E. coli, Klebsiella,* and other *Enterobacteriacae* strains.[62]

Microbial adhesion to various mucosal epithelium has been shown to be inhibited by milk oligosaccharides for diarrhea-causing *E. coli* and *Campylobacter jejuni*, for otitis-causing *Streptococcus pneumoniae* and *H. influenzae*, for HIV-1, and for several other microorganisms (Figure 3).[58;63-65]

> Human milk is rich in sugar chains – oligosaccharides. They seem to affect the composition of the bacterial flora in the baby's gut and may be one reason why breastfed babies have a different gut microflora than non-breastfed babies. Oligosaccharides block adherence of microbes to epithelial cells helping to prevent infections.

Several *glycoconjugates* in milk also block mucosal attachment by various microbes and toxins. The ganglioside, GM1, prevents adherence of *V. cholerae* and binds the enterotoxins of *E. coli, V. cholerae* and *C. jejuni*.[66-68] The milk glycolipid, Gb3, blocks binding of *S. dysenteriae* and a Shiga-like toxin from entero-hemorrhagic *E. coli*.[55] One high molecular weight glycoprotein in human milk binds and neutralizes respiratory syncytial virus and another hepatitis A virus.[69;70] A Mac-2 binding protein richly present in milk helps bind macrophages to microbes. It has been suggested that higher levels of this protein may lead to a reduced risk of respiratory tract infections in breastfed infants.[71;72]

Mucin, which is found mainly on milk fat globules, contains sialic acid. Mucin and milk fat globules prevent binding of *E. coli* via their attachment structure S-fimbriae to epithelial cells.[73] Mucin inhibits replication of rotavirus, most likely via its carbohydrate component.[74] The mucin-associated glycoprotein, lactadherin, also binds to and inhibits rotavirus and blocks its replication. The lactadherin in milk may protect against rotavirus infection.[75] Components of casein seem to prevent cellular adhesion of *Actinomyces* and streptococci, and κ-casein blocks *Helicobacter pylori*.[76-78]

> Human milk contains several glycoproteins and glycolipids which can block the adherence of bacteria and viruses to epithelial cells, presumably preventing infections. This form of defense does not cause inflammation.

E. coli with type 1 pili or fimbriae, which are of low virulence, bind to a carbohydrate portion of SIgA.[79] Therefore, the presence of SIgA in the gut, which is especially high in breastfed infants, seems to favor the growth of type 1 piliated, low virulence *E. coli*.[24] This is supported by the fact that individuals lacking IgA have less *E. coli* with type 1 pili in their gut microflora.[80]

In conclusion:

Human milk contains a number of different oligosaccharides, glycoproteins, and glycolipids. These sugar molecules may play an important role in the defense of breastfed infants because they carry structures which function as analogues to receptors on the infants' mucosal epithelium that are subsequently used by microbes for the initial step of attaching to host cells (Figure 3). This is yet another anti-microbial function of a group of human milk components which function without inducing inflammation.

Certain glycoproteins, like SIgA, enhance the growth of gut bacteria of low virulence. This may be one reason why breastfed babies have less virulent microbes among their intestinal microflora than non-breastfed babies.

Some studies suggest that receptor analogues may prevent infections. This is further discussed in the next chapter.

Lipids and milk fat globules

Human milk contains lipids which are hydrolyzed by lipoprotein lipase, bile salt-stimulated lipase, and gastric lipase. The resulting fatty acids and monoglycerides are often anti-microbial and can attack certain bacteria and enveloped viruses, e.g. *G. lamblia* and *Entamoeba histolytica.*[81-85] The bile salt-stimulated lipase liberates free fatty acids which kill *G. lamblia.*[86] Human milk fat also binds and neutralizes Shiga-like toxin.[87] Several *E. coli* strains produce a toxin, also called Shiga-like toxin, similar to the toxin produced by one type of *Shigella dysenteriae*. Such toxins can cause severe diseases like hemorrhagic colitis and hemolytic-uremic syndrome.[88]

The milk fat globules not only carry mucin, but also SIgA and HLA tissue type structures.[89-91] It is possible that the SIgA antibodies in this form may provide anti-microbial activity through the intestinal passage.

The content in human milk of unsaturated fatty acids and specifically a low ratio of n-6/n-3 fatty acids seems to influence the immune system of the offspring so that the risk of developing allergic disease may be reduced. This is discussed in more detail in Chapter 6.

In conclusion:

Lipid components of human milk have anti-microbial activity. There are no studies available to evaluate their possible clinical relevance.

The fat composition of human milk may reduce the risk of the baby developing allergic diseases. This is still under investigation.

Nucleotides

Human milk contains more nucleotides than ruminant milk, some 2-5% of the total non-protein nitrogen.[92] In colostrum, there is 53-58 mg/liter and in mature milk about 33 mg/liter.[93] Nucleotides are important because they are the building blocks of nucleic acids, DNA, and RNA. The young infant's fast growing organ systems, such as the immune system and the central nervous system, require many nucleotides.

Nucleotides enhance the maturation and rapid growth of the intestinal mucosa and the mucosal immune system from the neonatal period and thereafter. This enhancement is initiated by exposure to the gut microflora (Chapter 1). Our recent observation from studies in germ-free rats suggests that nucleotides are a growth factor and may, in addition, originate from gut bacteria.[31] The enzyme activities of milk IgG and lactoferrin may help degrade bacterial nucleotides. Human milk as well as the intestinal mucosa contain additional enzymes which can partly degrade the milk nucleotides.[94]

The effect of adding nucleotides to formula has been tested. One study showed that higher serum levels of IgA and IgM resulted.[95] Another study showed higher numbers of NK cells and NK cell activity.[96] Less risk of diarrheal disease and increased responses to vaccination against *H. influenzae* type b and diphtheria toxoid were also reported.[97-99]

In conclusion:

The growing infant with its quickly expanding immune and central nervous systems presumably needs more nucleotides to make DNA than it can produce on its own. It is likely that the nucleotides in mother's milk are a helpful source. It may even be that milk components kill bacteria in the gut and degrade their nucleotides for the use of the infant. The addition of nucleotides to formula seems to support antibody production, NK cells, and protective capacity in the baby.

Defensins

Of the many known defensins, the β-defensin LBD-1 has been found in milk.[100] It has anti-microbial activity against *E. coli* and is present at levels of 1-10 ng/liter.[101] Defensins are cytotoxic without any specificity and act against mycobacteria, fungi, some enveloped viruses, and Gram-positive as well as Gram-negative bacteria. They lyse the membranes of the bacteria. In addition, defensins influence T cells and dendritic cells possibly enhancing and regulating adaptive immune mechanisms directed against microorganisms.[102]

In conclusion:

The defensins comprise an interesting group of antimicrobial compounds with very broad reactivity. They also have effects on the immune system. There are no studies of the potential biological value of the defensins found in milk.

Cytokines

Many cytokines are present in human milk.[103] Among them is TGF-β which has an anti-inflammatory effect by suppressing T cells. In an experimental model in mice, TGF-β was absorbed from milk and depressed the inflammatory conditions that occurred in mice lacking the gene for TGF-β.[104] It was recently suggested that the TGF-β provided by long-term breastfeeding might contribute to a decreased risk of developing allergies.[105] This may be linked to the possibility that TGF-β makes B lymphocytes produce SIgA antibodies. Another recent study suggested that the TGF-β provided by breastfeeding related to a decreased risk of wheezing, possibly signifying that the milk TGF-β affects lung development.[106]

IL-10 is another down-regulating cytokine present in milk.[103] It may moderate inflammatory activity in the gut of the breastfeeding baby, but this has not yet been studied. The IL-1β present in milk inhibits the production of IL-2 that normally stimulates expansion of T cells.[107]

The pro-inflammatory cytokine, TNF-α, is present in milk in substantial amounts.[108] It acts as a chemokine for the milk phagocytes and stimulates the production of polyIgR which transports the IgA dimers into milk (Figure 8).[109;110] Milk contains soluble TNF-α receptors which may modify the effects of the TNF-α present in milk.[111]

IL-6 in milk, like TGF–β, promotes the differentiation of B cells and also seems to promote the production of α1-antitrypsin by phagocytes.[112] This may explain why breastfed infants have this protein in their stools.[113]

It is interesting that IL-7 is found in human milk because it is known to promote the development of small aggregates of lymphocytes, the cryptopatches, that support the production of a special T cell population called Tγδ in the gut mucosa and in the thymus.[114] These cells appear as intraepithelial lymphocytes in the intestinal mucosa and in milk.[115] The function of these cells is not quite clear at this time.

Breastfeeding increases the size of the thymus, the central organ of the immune system (Figure 9).[116] Its size even relates to the number of breastfeeds per day. Exclusively breastfed babies had a thymus that was twice the size of non-breastfed babies' thymus. This is an interesting observation because of the central role of the thymus in the maturation of T lymphocytes, including both the Killer cells, very important for defense, and regulatory T cells (Treg), important for prevention of autoimmune diseases.[117]

It was recently found that the size of the thymus in exclusively breastfed infants was correlated to the milk content of IL-7.[118] The larger the thymus, the higher the output of T lymphocytes. Severe malnutrition results in a small thymus that expands on re-feeding. A smaller thymus at birth predicted a higher infant mortality from infections in a study from Africa independent of other factors known to reduce the size of the thymus such as birth weight and malnutrition.[119] The effect of thymus size on mortality was not seen after 1 year of age.

> There are numerous cytokines, chemokines, and colony-stimulating factors in human milk. We do not know their functions in most instances. They may act as signals from the mother to her baby. The thymus is the central immunological organ important for the development and function of the immune system The IL-7 in milk may be one factor that explains why the thymus is signifcantly larger in breastfed than in non-breastfed babies.

Whereas many of the cytokines in milk originate from the milk cells, some like IL-18 are produced by the mammary gland epithelium.[120] Numerous other cytokines like IL-12, G-CSF, M-CSF, IFN-γ, IFN-α, and macrophage migration inhibitory factor (MIF) are found in milk. So are several chemokines like IL-8, eotaxin, IL-16, Monocyte Chemotactic Factor, and RANTES (Regulated on Activation, Normal T cell Expressed and Secreted).[11] It will be interesting to learn about their effects on the breastfed infant. At this time, it has been shown that blood lymphocytes in breastfed 6 month old infants had significantly less of the receptors for cellular signaling (the integrins) compared to non-breastfed infants.[121] At that age, breastfed infants also had significantly less of one T cell population and more NK cells.[122]

In conclusion:

Human milk contains numerous cytokines with multiple activities on many different cells including those of the immune system. Some of these signals act as chemokines bringing in inflammatory cells. While these components may be used if infections occur in the mammary glands, their output in the milk is most likely for the use of the breastfed infant. The milk cytokines presumably act as signals for the immune system of the baby, supporting its growth and development. Our information is still limited, except for the effects of breastfeeding on the thymus.

The fact that fully breastfed babies have been reported to have a thymus twice the size of the thymus in a non-breastfed infant seems to relate to the content of the cytokine IL-7 in the milk. The thymus is the central organ in the lymphoid system and the site where T lymphocytes

mature. There was an inverse relationship between the size of the thymus and infant mortality from infections in an African study. This observation was unrelated to the fact that malnutrition and birth weight also influence the size of the thymus. Presumably, the link to infant mortality illustrates the importance of the thymus for host defense.

Hormones and growth factors

There are numerous hormones and growth factors in human milk. Most likely, they act as signals from the mother to the offspring, like the cytokines and several other components in the milk. A description of hormones and growth factors in milk is included because the immune system and the neuro-endocrine system have a functional closeness and cooperate.[123] Some hormones have the structure of cytokines. The brain produces and has receptors for many cytokines. The pro-inflammatory cytokines, IL-1β, TNF-α and IL-6, activate the hypothalamus-pituitary-adrenal (HPA) stress axis and induce production of glucocorticoids.[124]

Table 6

Hormones And Growth Factors In Human Milk

- Epidermal growth factor (EGF)
- Fibroblast growth factor (FGF)
- Insulin like growth factor-1 (IGF-1)
- Vascular endothelial growth factor (VEGF)
- Growth hormone releasing factor (GH-releasing factor)
- Hepatocyte growth factor (HGF)
- Erythropoietin
- Prolactin
- Thyroid hormone
- Leptin
- Transforming growth factor (TGF)

The young infant has low enzymatic activity and enhanced uptake in the gut helping the transfer of biological information in the form of hormones, etc..[125] This is even more evident in the premature neonate.[126] In man, steroid hormones and non-protein hormones, like the thyroid hormone, are well absorbed by the gut.[127]

There are several animal studies indicating that milk components like epidermal growth factor (EGF) and insulin-like growth factor 1 (IGF-1) are transferred (Table 6).[128;129] Growth hormone (GH) which has cytokine structure is increased in rats due to the GH-releasing factor in milk.[130] There are similar observations of effects from the transfer via milk of luteinizing hormone-releasing hormone (LHRH) and erythropoietin (EPO).[131;132]

IGF-1, epidermal growth factor (EGF), and prolactin in milk may act as immunomodulatory components in the infant's gut.[133] Prolactin can bind to a receptor belonging to the IL-2 receptor superfamily.[134] In this way, prolactin enhances T cell activation which results in stimulation of macrophages and NK cells.[135] Growth factors in human milk like IGF-1, EGF, and fibroblast growth factor (FGF) stimulate development of intestinal epithelium.[136] Milk-borne EGF was shown to modulate the levels of TGF-α in the gut of newborn rats.[136] The vascular endothelial growth factor present in human milk may have immunomodulatory effects via its receptors on intestinal epithelium.[137] The hepatocyte growth factor (HGF) present in milk may stimulate the development of the gastrointestinal tract.[138]

The appetite regulating hormone, leptin, which has a cytokine-like structure, is present in mammary epithelial cells, milk fat globules, and milk as well as in a number of other tissues in man.[139] The receptor for leptin, which also binds IL-6 and LIF (leukemia inhibiting factor), is present in numerous organs, including the hypothalamus, and on T cells.[140] Leptin regulates appetite.[141] Increased levels lower appetite, decreased levels increase appetite. These activities are part of a system that controls feeding behavior. Leptin counteracts the characteristics of starvation such as decreased body temperature, activation of the stress axis, and reduced immune and reproductive functions.[142]

Increased levels of the pro-inflammatory cytokines IL-1β, TNF-α and IL-6, for instance during an infection, increase the level of leptin.[139] This results in a lower appetite and explains the commonly noted loss of appetite during infections which has drastic consequences for children in poor countries living under unhygienic, crowded conditions who attract frequent infections. The infections and the subsequent loss of appetite contribute to undernutrition. Breastfeeding not only prevents many such infections, but also seems to depress the anorectic response to immunization from the quadruple vaccine (DPTH) against diphtheria, pertussis, tetanus and *Hemophilus influenzae* type b noted in formula-fed infants according to one study.[143] This is an interesting possible effect of breastfeeding not previously noted.

Leptin stimulates differentiation and proliferation of hematopoietic cells and up regulates monocyte/macrophage functions. It also modifies T cell responses by increasing the production of IL-2 and IFN-γ from Th1 cells and IL-4 and IL-10 from Th 2 cells.[139] Leptin has direct, as well as indirect, effects on the thymus by enhancing proliferation and survival of T cells which mature in that site before reaching the periphery where they act in our defense.

Breastfeeding is linked to increased numbers of NK cells in the blood and more cytotoxic T lymphocytes than helper T lymphocytes in breastfed infants compared to non breastfed infants.[122] This may relate to the presence of factors like leptin and/or certain cytokines and growth factors in human milk.

> Human milk contains numerous hormones and growth factors. Among the hormones is leptin which is involved in regulation of appetite. Leptin has several effects on the immune system. Little is known about the potential roles of this and other hormones and growth factors for the breastfed baby.

Leptin seems to be absorbed by the baby from the mother's milk.[144] It may be involved in the preventive effects of breastfeeding on obesity as suggested by some studies discussed in Chapter 6.

In conclusion:

There are numerous hormones and growth factors in human milk. They may direct several functions in the breastfed infant including effects on the immune system. The neuro-endocrine and the immune systems show several modes of cooperation. Some hormones, like growth hormone and leptin, have cytokine structures and bind to cytokine receptors. The brain also produces many cytokines and has specific receptors for them.

Human milk contains several factors like insulin-like growth factor-1 (IGF-1), epidermal growth factor (EGF), prolactin etc, which may have immunomodulatory effects in the gut. The recently discovered hormone, leptin, has immunomodulatory effects on T cells and monocytes/macrophages. Increased levels of leptin reduce appetite, whereas low levels have the opposite effect. It is being discussed whether the presence of leptin in milk relates to the possibility that breastfeeding may prevent obesity in the infant (Chapter 6).

Anti-secretory factor

The anti-secretory factor (AF) was discovered through its effect to prevent the intestinal fluid secretion caused by the cholera toxin.[145] AF is produced in many localities including the pituitary gland, the placenta, by lymphocytes and epithelium in the intestine, and in the mammary gland.[146] Its mode of function is not known in detail. Its anti-secretory effect prevents or blocks inflammatory processes like diarrhea in piglets and in man.[147] It can be induced by giving a specially treated cereal. Early data suggest that inflammatory bowel disease can be successfully treated with AF.[148;149]

AF has been found in some samples of human milk from mothers in poor countries possibly induced by exposure to enterotoxin-producing bacteria.[150] In a preliminary study, a significant reduction in the prevalence of mastitis in Swedish lactating women resulted when AF was induced in their milk with a specially treated cereal.[151] It needs to be determined whether inducing AF can prevent sub-clinical mastitis linked to an increased risk of transfer of HIV-1 from mother to infant via breastfeeding.

In conclusion:

The anti-secretory factor (AF) seems to have an anti-inflammatory effect by reducing fluid secretion. AF can be induced by eating a specially treated cereal. Early data suggest that this can be used to treat inflammatory bowel disease and other inflammatory conditions.

In a preliminary study, we have seen a preventive effect against clinically apparent mastitis in lactating women after inducing AF in milk with specially treated cereal. We hope to determine if AF can also be used for treatment of ongoing mastitis.

Anti-inflammatory components

Human milk contains numerous components with anti-inflammatory capacities.[103] This agrees with the function of milk in the baby: to defend without inducing inflammation and if inflammation occurs, to counteract it.

There are pro-inflammatory systems in the milk, like the complement system, the coagulation system, and the kallikrein-kininogen system, but the levels are low. There are few pro-inflammatory antibodies like IgM, IgG, and IgE and relatively few phagocytes and lymphocytes in the milk.[103] The milk SIgA antibodies bind microbes and prevent them from getting into tissues where they would induce inflammatory reactivity.

There are several different forms of anti-inflammatory factors in milk (Table 7). Some have been mentioned above, like the immunomodulatory cytokines IL-10 and TGF-β. Soluble cytokine receptors for IL-1β (IL-1βRa) and for TNF-α (TNF-α RI and II) function similarly by blocking the pro-inflammatory cytokines.[103] As mentioned above, one of the major milk proteins, lactoferrin, has a strong anti-inflammatory capacity. It blocks the transcription factor, NFκB, which brings about production of the pro-inflammatory cytokines IL-1β, TNF-α, and IL-6.[44]

> Human milk contains numerous components with anti-inflammatory activities. There are no studies to permit us to evaluate the possible role of all these factors. Presumably, they support the type of defense provided by the milk SIgA antibodies and lactoferrin without inducing inflammation.

Table 7

Anti-inflammatory Factors In Milk

- **Protective antibodies that do not induce inflammation**
  - SIgA
- **Immunomodulatory cytokines**
  - IL-10 (Interleukin-10)
  - TGF-β (Transforming Growth Factor-β)
- **Factors blocking cytokine receptors**
  - IL-1β Ra (Interleukin-1β Receptor antagonist)
  - TNF-α RI, RII (Tumor Necrosis Factor-α soluble Receptors I, II)
- **Factor blocking cytokine production via NFκB**
  - Lactoferrin
- **Complement inhibiting factors**
  - Lysozyme
  - Lactoferrin
  - α-Lactalbumin
  - Soluble complement inhibitors
  - Complement regulatory factors
- **Growth factors that promote maturation of epithelial cells**
  - EGF (Epidermal Growth Factor)
  - TGF-β1 and 2
- **Prostaglandins that inhibit neutrophil enzymes and are cytoprotective**
  - PGE1 and 2 (Prostaglandins 1 and 2)
- **Anti-proteases that block potentially tissue-damaging enzymes**
  - Against α1-antitrypsin
  - α1-antichymotrypsin
  - Elastase inhibitor

Complement activity is inhibited by numerous milk components like lysozyme, lactoferrin, α-lactalbumin, complement regulatory factors, and soluble inhibitors of complement.[152] Growth factors like EGF and TGF-α promote expansion and maturation of gut epithelial cells. The prostaglandins, PGE1 and 2, inhibit neutrophil enzymes and are cytoprotective in the gut. The anti-proteases against α1-antitrypsin and α1-antichymotrypsin as well as the elastase inhibitor block potentially tissuc-damaging proteolytic enzymes (Table 7).[103]

There are several antioxidants like catalase, lactoferrin, glutathione peroxidase, α-tocopherol, ascorbic acid, β-carotene, and L-histidine which degrade superoxide, prevent hydroxyl radical formation and lipid peroxidation, and scavenge oxygen radicals (Table 7).[103]

In conclusion:

Again, it appears that human milk has multiple capacities to prevent and/or down-regulate various mechanisms and forms of inflammation. These effects are provided by a large number of components with a wide range of functions. This suggests that it is important to prevent any form of energy-consuming, symptom-inducing inflammation in the growing infant and child.

Again, however, it is very difficult to separately evaluate the biological role of these factors by critical clinical studies.

Soluble CD14 and soluble Toll-Like Receptor

Colostrum and milk contain high concentrations of soluble CD14, more than 20 times the serum concentration.[153] This molecule helps the surface structure lipopolysaccharide (LPS) on Gram-negative bacteria (Table 2) bind to the Toll-Like Receptor 4 (TLR4) which activates phagocytes (Chapter 2). Intestinal epithelium carries TLRs, but not CD14. By means of the milk CD14, phagocytes in the intestine are activated by Gram-negative as well as Gram-positive bacteria since they both require both CD14 and the latter TLR2.[154]

Recently, it was found that human milk contains soluble TLR2 which can bind Gram-positive bacteria, mycobacteria, a measles virus protein, and several other microbial components.[155] It is possible that this soluble TLR in milk modifies the response to Gram-positive bacteria, suggesting yet another anti-inflammatory component in milk.

Soluble CD14 promotes differentiation and expansion of B lymphocytes and synergizes with the anti-inflammatory capacity of lactoferrin.[156;157]

In conclusion:

Milk contains significant quantities of soluble CD14 which may help the breastfed infant respond to exposure to many bacteria in the gut including Gram-positive and Gram-negative bacteria. On the other hand, milk contains soluble Toll-Like Receptor (TLR) 2 which may down-modulate the reactivity induced by Gram-positive bacteria and other microbes.

This is yet another illustration of the complexity of the many components in milk that can modify the breastfed baby's response to microbial exposure. And, again, we have no data to evaluate the likely biological role of these mechanisms.

Leucocytes in milk

During the first days of lactation, human milk contains live activated macrophages, neutrophils, and lymphocytes at levels of 1-3x10^6 cells/ml.[6] By 2-3 months of lactation, the number of these leucocytes have decreased and are less than 1x10^6/ml.[6;158] By 4-6 months, epithelial cells have increased to about 80% of the milk cells.[6;158] Obviously, the breastfed infant obtains many millions of leucocytes via the milk daily. About 4% of them are lymphocytes.[159]

The milk cells spontaneously produce less IL-1β, TNF-α, and IL-6 than mononuclear cells from the blood. After exposure to endotoxin (LPS) from Gram-negative bacteria, they also respond with less of these cytokines than the blood cells.[160]

Neutrophils

Milk neutrophils show characteristics of activation by expression of certain surface structures, decreased adherence, and motility. Blood neutrophils exposed to milk react similarly.[161]

Macrophages

Milk macrophages also show signs of activation.[162] They spontaneously produce the pro-inflammatory cytokines IL-1β, TNF-α and IL-6, but they produce less than blood mononuclear cells. They produce less of these cytokines after exposure to LPS. The milk macrophages produce prostaglandin E2, complement factor 3, lysozyme, and plasminogen activator, and may be the source of these components in milk.[162;163]

The milk macrophages act as antigen-presenting cells (APCs) and carry the receptor typical of dendritic cells (DCs), the most effective APC (see Chapter 2). They also carry the receptor DC-Sign typical for DCs.[164;165] This structure functions as a receptor for human immunodeficiency virus (HIV). As a consequence, milk macrophages may add to the risk of HIV-1 transfer via the milk from the mother to the infant (Chapter 7).

Milk macrophages can be activated to phagocytose (engulf bacteria). They have a receptor for SIgA; binding to that receptor activates the cells.[166;167] Enteropathogenic *E. coli* to which SIgA antibodies are bound are killed by milk macrophages.[168]

It is likely that the major role of neutrophils and macrophages in milk are to defend the mammary glands. The protein, fibronectin, the IgG antibodies, and the complement factor 3 present in milk may support phagocytic activity.[169]

Lymphocytes

The milk lymphocytes are mainly T cells (83%) with some B cells (6%) and some NK cells.[159;170] There are T helper cells as well as cytotoxic T cells and Tγδ cells.[117] They show characteristics of being activated and having immunological memory - the capacity to give a secondary, memory immune response when meeting the antigen specific to their T cell receptor (TCR) (Chapter 2).

There is evidence that T lymphocytes in milk may be a selected population due to directed migration to the mammary glands.[171;172] The milk T cells mainly produce IFN-γ, but also produce Macrophage Inhibiting Factor (MIF) and Monocyte Chemotactic Factor.[173;174]

The maternal lymphocytes carry the mother's HLA tissue type which is somewhat different from that of her offspring, who also carries genes from the father. We would not expect milk lymphocytes to be absorbed by the breastfed baby. However, there is considerable evidence from experimental animals of various species that this happens.[175-182] One study done in sheep transfered technetium-labeled milk lymphocytes from the dams to the lambs' intestine via a catheter. The maternal lymphocytes then appeared in the gut mucosa, mesenteric lymph ducts, and cortical zone of mesenteric lymph nodes of the lambs.[182] Using cells from dams vaccinated against tetanus, the lambs after transfer showed an enhanced response to tetanus vaccination suggesting that the milk lymphocytes were not only absorbed by the lamb but that immunological information was transferred via these cells.[183] Another study in B lymphocyte deficient mice showed that newborn mice could avoid severe infections by foster-feeding using normal mothers providing B cells via the milk.[177] In one animal model, transfer of maternal cells to the offspring occurred not only via the milk, but also via the placenta during pregnancy.[184]

> Human milk contains lymphocytes, both T and B cells. Several experimental studies indicate that these maternal cells can be absorbed by the breastfed offspring. Some studies suggest that these cells may transfer immunological information and protective capacity. There is evidence in humans that a breastfed baby may become tolerant to its mother's tissue type (HLA). This may permit the maternal cells to be absorbed by the baby and possibly transfer immune functions.

The exposure to milk cells obviously leads to the development of immunological tolerance to the maternal tissue type in the offspring. Such tolerance to maternal HLA after breastfeeding has been shown to result in better survival of a transplanted kidney if it comes from the mother, but not from the father. If the mother had not breastfed, the outcome would be the same as if the kidney came from the father.[185-186] Foster feeding experiments in rats confirm these findings.[188] Breastfed individuals show fewer precursors of T cells reactive with maternal HLA than non-breastfed individuals.[187]

It has been shown that tuberculin positivity can be transferred to the infant via the milk, possibly due to T cell transfer.[189;190] Another study did not confirm this observation.[191]

In conclusion:

It is likely that the primary task of neutrophils and macrophages present in milk may be the defense of the mammary glands.

Lymphocytes seem to be absorbed by the breastfed offspring. This is quite surprising since milk lymphocytes come from a different individual, the mother, who has a somewhat different HLA tissue type than her baby. Therefore, these milk cells should be rejected. There are several studies in experimental animals to suggest that maternal lymphocytes are absorbed and even confer immunological information to the offspring, such as the enhanced responsiveness to a vaccine. Breastfed children seem to become tolerant to the mother's HLA. Thus, it may be possible for the baby to absorb and accept these maternal milk lymphocytes.

This tolerance to the maternal tissue type induced by breastfeeding has an interesting side effect. A kidney donated by a mother to her child will survive and function better even in adulthood if the mother breastfed that offspring as a baby. This tolerance to the maternal HLA seems to have long lasting effects.

Reference List

1. Hanson LA: Comparative immunological studies of the immune globulins of human milk and of blood serum. Int Arch Allergy Appl Immunol 18:241-267, 1961

2. Hanson LA, Johansson BG: Immunological characterization of chromatographically separated protein fractions from human colostrum. Int Arch Allergy Appl Immunol 20:65-79, 1962

3. Butte NF, Goldblum RM, Fehl LM, et al: Daily ingestion of immunologic components in human milk during the first four months of life. Acta Paediatr Scand 73:296-301, 1984

4. Brandtzaeg P: The secretory immunoglobulin system: regulation and biological significance. Focusing on human mammary glands, in David MK, Isaacs CE, Hanson LA, et al (eds): Integrating Population Outcomes, Biological Mechanisms and Research Methods in the Study of Human Milk and Lactation. New York, Kluwer Academic/Plenum Publishers 1-16, 2002

5. Carlsson B, Gothefors L, Ahlstedt S, et al: Studies of Escherichia coli O antigen specific antibodies in human milk, maternal serum and cord blood. Acta Paediatr Scand 65:216-224, 1976

6. Goldblum RM, Goldman AS, Garza C, et al: Human milk banking. II. Relative stability of immunologic factors in stored colostrum. Acta Paediatr Scand 71:143-144, 1982

7. Abu-Ghazaleh RI, Fujisawa T, Mestecky J, et al: IgA-induced eosinophil degranulation. J Immunol 142:2393-2400, 1989

8. Schwarze J, Cieslewicz G, Joetham A, et al: Antigen-specific immunoglobulin-A prevents increased airway responsiveness and lung eosinophilia after airway challenge in sensitized mice. Am J Respir Crit Care Med 158:519-525, 1998

9. Plaut AG: Microbial IgA proteases. N Engl J Med 298:1459-1463, 1978

10. Gilbert JV, Plaut AG, Longmaid B, et al: Inhibition of bacterial IgA proteases by human secretory IgA and serum. Ann NY Acad Sci 409:625-636, 1983

11. Hanson LA, Korotkova M, Telemo E: Human milk, its components and their immunobiological function, in J Mestecky JB, Lamm ME, Mayer L, et al (eds): Mucosal Immunology. 3rd Edition. San Diego, Academic Press, 2004 (in press)

12. Roux ME, McWilliams M, Phillips-Quagliata JM, et al: Origin of IgA-secreting plasma cells in the mammary gland. J Exp Med 146:1311-1322, 1977

13. Weisz-Carrington P, Roux ME, McWilliams M, et al: Hormonal induction of the secretory immune system in the mammary gland. Proc Natl Acad Sci USA 75:2928-2932, 1978

14. Cruz JR, Cano F, Caceres P: Association of human milk SIgA antibodies with maternal intestinal exposure to microbial antigens. Adv Exp Med Biol 310:193-199, 1991

15. Mata LJ, Urrutia JJ, Garcia B, et al: Shigella infection in breast-fed Guatemalan indian neonates. Am J Dis Child 117:142-146, 1969

16. Finn A, Zhang Q, Seymour L, et al: Induction of functional secretory IgA responses in breast milk, by pneumococcal capsular polysaccharides. J Infect Dis 186:1422-1429, 2002

17. Glass RI, Svennerholm AM, Stoll BJ, et al: Protection against cholera in breast-fed children by antibodies in breast milk. N Engl J Med 308:1389-1392, 1983

18. Cruz JR, Gil L, Cano F, et al: Breast milk anti-Escherichia coli heat-labile toxin IgA antibodies protect against toxin-induced infantile diarrhea. Acta Paediatr Scand 77:658-662, 1988

19. Ruiz-Palacios GM, Calva JJ, Pickering LK, et al: Protection of breast-fed infants against Campylobacter diarrhea by antibodies in human milk. J Pediatr 116:707-713, 1990

20. Hayani KC, Guerrero ML, Morrow AL, et al: Concentration of milk secretory immunoglobulin A against Shigella virulence plasmid-associated antigens as a predictor of symptom status in Shigella-infected breast-fed infants. J Pediatr 121:852-856, 1992

21. Walterspiel JN, Morrow AL, Guerrero ML, et al: Secretory anti-Giardia lamblia antibodies in human milk: protective effect against diarrhea. Pediatrics 93:28-31, 1994

22. Long K, Vasquez-Garibay E, Mathewson J, et al: The impact of infant feeding patterns on infection and diarrheal disease due to enterotoxigenic Escherichia coli. Salud Publica Mex 41:263-270, 1999

23. Nowrouzian F, Adlerberth I, Wold AE, et al: The Escherichia coli mannose-specific adhesin, which binds to IgA carbohydrate, is a colonization factor in the human large intestine. In manuscript 2004

24. Nowrouzian F, Monstein HJ, Wold A, et al: Effect of human milk on type 1 and P fimbrial mRNA expression in intestinal E. coli strains. In manuscript 2004

25. Bollinger RR, Everett ML, Palestrant D, et al: Human secretory immunoglobulin A may contribute to biofilm formation in the gut. Immunology 109:580-587, 2003

26. Brandtzaeg P: Role of local immunity and breast-feeding in mucosal homeostasis and defence against infections, in Calder PC, Field CJ, Gill HS (eds): Nutrition and Immune Function. Oxon: CABI Publ 273-319, 2002

27. Phalipon A, Corthesy B: Novel functions of the polymeric Ig receptor: well beyond transport of immunoglobulins. Trends Immunol 24:55-58, 2003

28. Kanyshkova TG, Semenov DV, Khlimankov DY, et al: DNA-hydrolyzing activity of the light chain of IgG antibodies from milk of healthy human mothers. FEBS Lett. 416:23-26, 1997

29. Semenov DV, Kanyshkova TG, Kit YY, et al: Human breast milk immunoglobulins G hydrolyze nucleotides. Biochemistry (Mosc.) 63:935-943, 1998

30. Semenov DV, Kanyshkova TG, Karotaeva NA, et al: Catalytic nucleotide-hydrolyzing antibodies in milk and serum of clinically healthy human mothers. Med Sci.Monit. 10:BR23-BR33, 2004

31. Banasaz M, Hanson LA, Midtvedt T, et al: Dietary nucleotides increase weight gain and enhance intestinal rate of mitosis in germfree rats. In manuscript 2004 (in press)

32. Goldman AS, Garza C, Nichols BL, et al: Immunologic factors in human milk during the first year of lactation. J Pediatr 100:563-567, 1982

33. Hennart PF, Brasseur DJ, Delogne-Desnoeck JB, et al: Lysozyme, lactoferrin, and secretory immunoglobulin A content in breast milk: influence of duration of lactation, nutrition status, prolactin status, and parity of mother. Am J Clin Nutr. 53:32-39, 1991

34. Goldblum RM, Schanler RJ, Garza C, et al: Human milk feeding enhances the urinary excretion of immunologic factors in low birth weight infants. Pediatr Res 25:184-188, 1989

35. Kawakami H, Lonnerdal B: Isolation and function of a receptor for human lactoferrin in human fetal intestinal brush-border membranes. Am J Physiol 261: G841-G846, 1991

36. Nichols BL, McKee KS, Henry JF, et al: Human lactoferrin stimulates thymidine incorporation into DNA of rat crypt cells. Pediatr Res 21:563-567, 1987

37. Ellison RT, III: The effects of lactoferrin on gram-negative bacteria. Adv Exp Med Biol 357:71-90, 1994

38. Leitch EC, Willcox MD: Synergic antistaphylococcal properties of lactoferrin and lysozyme. J Med Microbiol 47:837-842, 1998

39. Nikawa H, Samaranayake LP, Tenovuo J, et al: The effect of antifungal agents on the in vitro susceptibility of Candida albicans to apo-lactoferrin. Arch Oral Biol 39:921-923, 1994

40. Hendrixson DR, Qiu J, Shewry SC, et al: Human milk lactoferrin is a serine protease that cleaves Haemophilus surface proteins at arginine-rich sites. Mol Microbiol 47:607-617, 2003

41. Ochoa TJ, Noguera-Obenza M, Ebel F, et al: Lactoferrin impairs type III secretory system function in enteropathogenic Escherichia coli. Infect Immun 71:5149-5155, 2003

42. Kanyshkova TG, Buneva VN, Nevinsky GA: Lactoferrin and its biological functions. Biochemistry (Mosc.) 66:1-7, 2001

43. Duffy LC, Byers TE, Riepenhoff-Talty M, et al: The effects of infant feeding on rotavirus-induced gastroenteritis: a prospective study. Am J Public Health 76:259-263, 1986

44. Haversen L, Ohlsson BG, Hahn-Zoric M, et al: Lactoferrin down-regulates the LPS-induced cytokine production in monocytic cells via NF-kappa B. Cell Immunol 220:83-95, 2002

45. Togawa J, Nagase H, Tanaka K, et al: Lactoferrin reduces colitis in rats via modulation of the immune system and correction of cytokine imbalance. Am J Physiol Gastrointest Liver Physiol 283:G187-G195, 2002

46. Haversen LA, Engberg I, Baltzer L, et al: Human lactoferrin and peptides derived from a surface-exposed helical region reduce experimental Escherichia coli urinary tract infection in mice. Infect Immun 68:5816-5823, 2000

47. Edde L, Hipolito RB, Hwang FF, et al: Lactoferrin protects neonatal rats from gut-related systemic infection. Am J Physiol Gastrointest Liver Physiol 281:G1140-G1150, 2001

48. Gomez HF, Herrera-Insua I, Siddiqui MM, et al: Protective role of human lactoferrin against invasion of Shigella flexneri M90T. Adv Exp Med Biol. 501:457-467, 2001

49. Haversen LA, Baltzer L, Dolphin G, et al: Anti-inflammatory activities of human lactoferrin in acute dextran sulphate-induced colitis in mice. Scand J Immunol 57:2-10, 2003

50. Hakansson A, Zhivotovsky B, Orrenius S, et al: Apoptosis induced by a human milk protein. Proc Natl Acad Sci USA 92:8064-8068, 1995

51. Svensson M, Sabharwal H, Hakansson A, et al: Molecular characterization of alpha-lactalbumin folding variants that induce apoptosis in tumor cells. J Biol Chem 274:6388-6396, 1999

52. Svensson M, Hakansson A, Mossberg AK, et al: Conversion of alpha-lactalbumin to a protein inducing apoptosis. Proc.Natl.Acad.Sci.U.S.A 97:4221-4226, 2000

53. Svanborg C, Agerstam H, Aronson A, et al: HAMLET kills tumor cells by an apoptosis-like mechanism--cellular, molecular, and therapeutic aspects. Adv Cancer Res 88:1-29, 2003

54. Adinolfi M, Glynn AA, Lindsay M, et al: Serological properties of gamma-A antibodies to Escherichia coli present in human colostrum. Immunology 10:517-526, 1966

55. Newburg DS: Human milk glycoconjugates that inhibit pathogens. Curr Med Chem 6:117-127, 1999

56. Kunz C, Rudloff S: Biological functions of oligosaccharides in human milk. Acta Paediatr. 82:903-912, 1993

57. McVeagh P, Miller JB: Human milk oligosaccharides: only the breast. J Paediatr. Child Health 33:281-286, 1997

58. Newburg DS: Do the binding properties of oligosaccharides in milk protect human infants from gastrointestinal bacteria? J Nutr 127:980S-984S, 1997

59. Stahl B, Thurl S, Zeng J, et al: Oligosaccharides from human milk as revealed by matrix-assisted laser desorption/ionization mass spectrometry. Anal Biochem 223:218-226, 1994

60. Rudloff S, Pohlentz G, Diekmann L, et al: Urinary excretion of lactose and oligosaccharides in preterm infants fed human milk or infant formula. Acta Paediatr 85:598-603, 1996

61. Chaturvedi P, Warren CD, Buescher CR, et al: Survival of human milk oligosaccharides in the intestine of infants. Adv Exp Med Biol 501:315-323, 2001

62. Gothefors L, Olling S, Winberg J: Breast feeding and biological properties of faecal E. coli strains. Acta Paediatr Scand 64:807-812, 1975

63. Korhonen TK, Valtonen MV, Parkkinen J, et al: Serotypes, hemolysin production, and receptor recognition of Escherichia coli strains associated with neonatal sepsis and meningitis. Infect Immun 48:486-491, 1985

64. Andersson B, Porras O, Hanson LA, et al: Inhibition of attachment of Streptococcus pneumoniae and Haemophilus influenzae by human milk and receptor oligosaccharides. J Infect Dis 153:232-237, 1986

65. Ruiz-Palacios GM, Cervantes LE, Ramos P, et al: Campylobacter jejuni binds intestinal H(O) antigen (Fuc alpha 1, 2Gal beta 1, 4GlcNAc), and fucosyloligosaccharides of human milk inhibit its binding and infection. J Biol Chem 278:14112-14120, 2003

66. Holmgren J, Svennerholm AM, Lindblad M: Receptor-like glycocompounds in human milk that inhibit classical and El Tor Vibrio cholerae cell adherence (hemagglutination). Infect Immun 39:147-154, 1983

67. Ruiz-Palacios GM, Torres J, Torres NI, et al: Cholera-like enterotoxin produced by Campylobacter jejuni. Characterisation and clinical significance. Lancet 2:250-253, 1983

68. Otnaess AB, Laegreid A, Ertresvag K: Inhibition of enterotoxin from Escherichia coli and Vibrio cholerae by gangliosides from human milk. Infect Immun 40:563-569, 1983

69. Laegreid A, Otnaess AB, Fuglesang J: Human and bovine milk: comparison of ganglioside composition and enterotoxin-inhibitory activity. Pediatr Res 20:416-421, 1986

70. Zajac AJ, Amphlett EM, Rowlands DJ, et al: Parameters influencing the attachment of hepatitis A virus to a variety of continuous cell lines. J Gen Virol 72 (Pt 7):1667-1675, 1991

71. D'Ostilio N, Sabatino G, Natoli C, et al: 90K (Mac-2 BP) in human milk. Clin Exp Immunol 104:543-546, 1996

72. Fornarini B, Iacobelli S, Tinari N, et al: Human milk 90K (Mac-2 BP): possible protective effects against acute respiratory infections. Clin Exp Immunol 115:91-94, 1999

73. Schroten H, Hanisch FG, Plogmann R, et al: Inhibition of adhesion of S-fimbriated Escherichia coli to buccal epithelial cells by human milk fat globule membrane components: a novel aspect of the protective function of mucins in the nonimmunoglobulin fraction. Infect Immun 60:2893-2899, 1992

74. Yolken RH, Peterson JA, Vonderfecht SL, et al: Human milk mucin inhibits rotavirus replication and prevents experimental gastroenteritis. J Clin Invest 90:1984-1991, 1992

75. Newburg DS, Peterson JA, Ruiz-Palacios GM, et al: Role of human-milk lactadherin in protection against symptomatic rotavirus infection. Lancet 351:1160-1164, 1998

76. Parker F, Migliore-Samour D, Floch F, et al: Immunostimulating hexapeptide from human casein: amino acid sequence, synthesis and biological properties. Eur J Biochem 145:677-682, 1984

77. Neeser JR, Chambaz A, Del Vedovo S, et al: Specific and nonspecific inhibition of adhesion of oral actinomyces and streptococci to erythrocytes and polystyrene by caseinoglycopeptide derivatives. Infect Immun 56:3201-3208, 1988

78. Stromqvist M, Falk P, Bergstrom S, et al: Human milk kappa-casein and inhibition of Helicobacter pylori adhesion to human gastric mucosa. J Pediatr Gastroenterol Nutr 21:288-296, 1995

79. Wold AE, Mestecky J, Tomana M, et al: Secretory immunoglobulin A carries oligosaccharide receptors for Escherichia coli type 1 fimbrial lectin. Infect Immun 58:3073-3077, 1990

80. Friman V, Adlerberth I, Connell H, et al: Decreased expression of mannose-specific adhesins by Escherichia coli in the colonic microflora of immunoglobulin A-deficient individuals. Infect Immun 64:2794-2798, 1996

81. Gillin FD, Reiner DS, Wang CS: Human milk kills parasitic intestinal protozoa. Science 221:1290-1292, 1983

82. Gillin FD, Reiner DS, Gault MJ: Cholate-dependent killing of Giardia lamblia by human milk. Infect Immun 47:619-622, 1985

83. Resta S, Luby JP, Rosenfeld CR, et al: Isolation and propagation of a human enteric coronavirus. Science 229:978-981, 1985

84. Isaacs CE, Thormar H, Pessolano T: Membrane-disruptive effect of human milk: inactivation of enveloped viruses. J Infect Dis 154:966-971, 1986

85. May JT: Microbial contaminants and antimicrobial properties of human milk. Microbiol Sci 5:42-46, 1988

86. Hernell O, Ward H, Blackberg L, et al: Killing of Giardia lamblia by human milk lipases: an effect mediated by lipolysis of milk lipids. J Infect Dis 153:715-720, 1986

87. Herrera-Insua I, Gomez HF, Diaz-Gonzalez VA, et al: Human milk lipids bind Shiga toxin. Adv Exp Med Biol 501:333-339, 2001

88. Fraser ME, Fujinaga M, Cherney MM, et al: Structure of shiga toxin type 2 (Stx2) from Escherichia coli 0157:H7. J Biol Chem Apr. 9, 2004

89. Schroten H, Bosch M, Nobis-Bosch R, et al: Secretory immunoglobulin A is a component of the human milk fat globule membrane. Pediatr Res 45:82-86, 1999

90. Wiman K, Curman B, Tragardh L, et al: Demonstration of HLA-DR-like antigens on milk fat globule membranes. Eur J Immunol 9:190-195, 1979

91. Newman RA, Ormerod MG, Greaves MF: The presence of HLA-DR antigens on lactating human breast epithelium and milk fat globule membranes. Clin Exp Immunol 41:478-486, 1980

92. Cosgrove M: Perinatal and infant nutrition. Nucleotides. Nutrition 14:748-751, 1998

93. Kuchan M, Winship T, Masor M: Nucleotides in Infant Nutrition: Effects on Immune Function, in Reifen R, Lerner A, Branski D, et al (eds): Pediatric Nutrition. Basel: Pediatr Adolesc Med, Karger 80-94, 1998

94. Thorell L, Sjoberg LB, Hernell O: Nucleotides in human milk: sources and metabolism by the newborn infant. Pediatr Res 40:845-852, 1996

95. Navarro J, Maldonado J, Narbona E, et al: Influence of dietary nucleotides on plasma immunoglobulin levels and lymphocyte subsets of preterm infants. Biofactors 10:67-76, 1999

96. Carver JD, Pimentel B, Cox WI, et al: Dietary nucleotide effects upon immune function in infants. Pediatrics 88:359-363, 1991

97. Brunser O, Espinoza J, Araya M, et al: Effect of dietary nucleotide supplementation on diarrhoeal disease in infants. Acta Paediatr 83:188-191, 1994

98. Pickering LK, Granoff DM, Erickson JR, et al: Modulation of the immune system by human milk and infant formula containing nucleotides. Pediatrics 101:242-249, 1998

99. Ostrom KM, Cordle CT, Schaller JP, et al: Immune status of infants fed soy-based formulas with or without added nucleotides for 1 year: part 1: vaccine responses, and morbidity. J Pediatr Gastroenterol Nutr 34:137-144, 2002

100. Tunzi CR, Harper PA, Bar-Oz B, et al: Beta-defensin expression in human mammary gland epithelia. Pediatr Res 48:30-35, 2000

101. Jia HP, Starner T, Ackermann M, et al: Abundant human beta-defensin-1 expression in milk and mammary gland epithelium. J Pediatr 138:109-112, 2001

102. Yang D, Biragyn A, Kwak LW, et al: Mammalian defensins in immunity: more than just microbicidal. Trends Immunol 23:291-296, 2002

103. Garofalo RP, Goldman AS: Expression of functional immunomodulatory and anti-inflammatory factors in human milk. Clin Perinatol 26:361-377, 1999

104. Letterio JJ, Geiser AG, Kulkarni AB, et al: Maternal rescue of transforming growth factor-beta 1 null mice. Science 264:1936-1938, 1994

105. Saarinen KM, Vaarala O, Klemetti P, et al: Transforming growth factor-beta1 in mothers' colostrum and immune responses to cows' milk proteins in infants with cows' milk allergy. J Allergy Clin Immunol 104:1093-1098, 1999

106. Oddy WH, Halonen M, Martinez FD, et al: TGF-beta in human milk is associated with wheeze in infancy. J Allergy Clin Immunol 112:723-728, 2003

107. Hooton JW, Pabst HF, Spady DW, et al: Human colostrum contains an activity that inhibits the production of IL-2 Clin Exp Immunol 86:520-524, 1991

108. Rudloff HE, Schmalstieg FC, Jr., Mushtaha AA, et al: Tumor necrosis factor-alpha in human milk. Pediatr Res 31:29-33, 1992

109. Mushtaha AA, Schmalstieg FC, Hughes TK, Jr., et al: Chemokinetic agents for monocytes in human milk: possible role of tumor necrosis factor-alpha. Pediatr Res 25:629-633, 1989

110. Nilsen EM, Johansen FE, Kvale D, et al: Different regulatory pathways employed in cytokine-enhanced expression of secretory component and epithelial HLA class I genes. Eur J Immunol 29:168-179, 1999

111. Buescher ES, McWilliams-Koeppen P: Soluble tumor necrosis factor-alpha (TNF-alpha) receptors in human colostrum and milk bind to TNF-alpha and neutralize TNF-alpha bioactivity. Pediatr Res 44:37-42, 1998

112. Kono Y, Beagley KW, Fujihashi K, et al: Cytokine regulation of localized inflammation. Induction of activated B cells and IL-6-mediated polyclonal IgG and IgA synthesis in inflamed human gingiva. J Immunol 146:1812-1821, 1991

113. Davidson LA, Lonnerdal B: Fecal alpha 1-antitrypsin in breast-fed infants is derived from human milk and is not indicative of enteric protein loss. Acta Paediatr Scand 79:137-141, 1990

114. Laky K, Lefrancois L, Freeden-Jeffry U, et al: The role of IL-7 in thymic and extrathymic development of TCR gamma delta cells. J Immunol 161:707-713, 1998

115. Bertotto A, Castellucci G, Scalise F, et al: Gamma-delta T cells in human breast milk. Arch Dis Child 66:12621991

116. Hasselbalch H, Jeppesen DL, Engelmann MD, et al: Decreased thymus size in formula-fed infants compared with breastfed infants. Acta Paediatr 85:1029-1032, 1996

117. Wing K, Ekmark A, Karlsson H, et al: Characterization of human CD25+ CD4+ T cells in thymus, cord and adult blood. Immunology 106:190-199, 2002

118. Ngom PT, Collinson A, Pido-Lopez J, et al: Improved thymic function in exclusively breast-fed babies is associated with higher breast milk IL-7. Am J Clin Nutr 2004 (in press)

119. Aaby P, Marx C, Trautner S, et al: Thymus size at birth is associated with infant mortality: a community study from Guinea-Bissau. Acta Paediatr 91:698-703, 2002

120. Takahata Y, Takada H, Nomura A, et al: Interleukin-18 in human milk. Pediatr Res 50:268-272, 2001

121. Bottcher MF, Jenmalm MC, Bjorksten B, et al: Chemoattractant factors in breast milk from allergic and nonallergic mothers. Pediatr Res 47:592-597, 2000

122. Hawkes JS, Neumann MA, Gibson RA: The effect of breast feeding on lymphocyte subpopulations in healthy term infants at 6 months of age. Pediatr Res 45:648-651, 1999

123. Haddad JJ, Saade NE, Safieh-Garabedian B: Cytokines and neuro-immune-endocrine interactions: a role for the hypothalamic-pituitary-adrenal revolving axis. J Neuroimmunol 133:1-19, 2002

124. Koldovsky O: Hormonally active peptides in human milk. Acta Paediatr Suppl 402:89-93, 1994

125. Britton JR, Koldovsky O: Development of luminal protein digestion: implications for biologically active dietary polypeptides. J Pediatr Gastroenterol.Nutr 9:144-162, 1989

126. Bohles H, Aschenbrenner M, Roth M, et al: Development of thyroid gland volume during the first 3 months of life in breast-fed versus iodine-supplemented and iodine-free formula-fed infants. Clin Investig 71:13-20, 1993

127. Berseth CL, Michener SR, Nordyke CK, et al: Postpartum changes in pattern of gastrointestinal regulatory peptides in human milk. Am J Clin Nutr. 51:985-990, 1990

128. Philipps AF, Anderson GG, Dvorak B, et al: Growth of artificially fed infant rats: effect of supplementation with insulin-like growth factor I. Am J Physiol 272: R1532-R1539, 1997

129. Kuhn CM, Pauk J, Schanberg SM: Endocrine responses to mother-infant separation in developing rats. Dev Psychobiol 23:395-410, 1990

130. Baram T, Koch Y, Hazum E, et al: Gonadotropin-releasing hormone in milk. Science 198:300-302, 1977

131. Semba RD, Juul SE: Erythropoietin in human milk: physiology and role in infant health. J Hum Lact 18:252-261, 2002

132. Grosvenor CE, Picciano MF, Baumrucker CR: Hormones and growth factors in milk. Endocr Rev 14:710-728, 1993

133. Viselli SM, Stanek EM, Mukherjee P, et al: Prolactin-induced mitogenesis of lymphocytes from ovariectomized rats. Endocrinology 129:983-990, 1991

134. Bernton EW, Meltzer MS, Holaday JW: Suppression of macrophage activation and T-lymphocyte function in hypoprolactinemic mice. Science 239:401-404, 1988

135. Hirai C, Ichiba H, Saito M, et al: Trophic effect of multiple growth factors in amniotic fluid or human milk on cultured human fetal small intestinal cells. J Pediatr Gastroenterol Nutr 34:524-528, 2002

136. Dvorak B, Williams CS, McWilliam DL, et al: Milk-borne epidermal growth factor modulates intestinal transforming growth factor-alpha levels in neonatal rats. Pediatr Res 47:194-200, 2000

137. Siafakas CG, Anatolitou F, Fusunyan RD, et al: Vascular endothelial growth factor (VEGF) is present in human breast milk and its receptor is present on intestinal epithelial cells. Pediatr Res 45:652-657, 1999

138. Itoh H, Itakura A, Kurauchi O, et al: Hepatocyte growth factor in human breast milk acts as a trophic factor. Horm Metab Res 34:16-20, 2002

139. Lord G: Role of leptin in immunology. Nutr.Rev 60:S35-S38, 2002

140. Tartaglia LA, Dembski M, Weng X, et al: Identification and expression cloning of a leptin receptor, OB-R. Cell 83:1263-1271, 1995

141. Friedman JM, Halaas JL: Leptin and the regulation of body weight in mammals. Nature 395:763-770, 1998

142. Ahima RS, Prabakaran D, Mantzoros C, et al: Role of leptin in the neuroendocrine response to fasting. Nature 382:250-252, 1996

143. Lopez-Alarcon M, Garza C, Habicht JP, et al: Breastfeeding attenuates reductions in energy intake induced by a mild immunologic stimulus represented by DPTH immunization: possible roles of interleukin-1beta, tumor necrosis factor-alpha and leptin. J Nutr 132:1293-1298, 2002

144. Savino F, Costamagna M, Prino A, et al: Leptin levels in breast-fed and formula-fed infants. Acta Paediatr 91:897-902, 2002

145. Lonnroth I, Lange S: Purification and characterization of a hormone-like factor which inhibits cholera secretion. FEBS Lett 177:104-108, 1984

146. Lange S, Lonnroth I: The antisecretory factor: synthesis, anatomical and cellular distribution, and biological action in experimental and clinical studies. Int Rev Cytol 210:39-75, 2001

147. Lonnroth I, Martinsson K, Lange S: Evidence of protection against diarrhoea in suckling piglets by a hormone-like protein in the sow's milk. Zentralbl Veterinarmed B 35:628-635, 1988

148. Bjorck S, Bosaeus I, Ek E, et al: Food induced stimulation of the antisecretory factor can improve symptoms in human inflammatory bowel disease: a study of a concept. Gut 46:824-829, 2000

149. Eriksson A, Shafazand M, Jennische E, et al: Effect of antisecretory factor in ulcerative colitis on histological and laborative outcome: a short period clinical trial. Scand J Gastroenterol 38:1045-1049, 2003

150. Hanson LA, Lonnroth I, Lange S, et al: Nutrition resistance to viral propagation. Nutr Rev 58:S31-S37, 2000

151. Svensson K, Lange S, Lonnroth I, et al: Induction of anti-secretory factor in human milk may prevent mastitis. Acta Paediatr 2004 (in press)

152. Ogundele MO: Inhibitors of complement activity in human breast-milk: a proposed hypothesis of their physiological significance. Mediators Inflamm 8:69-75, 1999

153. Labeta MO, Vidal K, Nores JE, et al: Innate recognition of bacteria in human milk is mediated by a milk-derived highly expressed pattern recognition receptor, soluble CD14. J Exp Med 191:1807-1812, 2000

154. Vidal K, Labeta MO, Schiffrin EJ, et al: Soluble CD14 in human breast milk and its role in innate immune responses. Acta Odontol Scand 59:330-334, 2001

155. LeBouder E, Rey-Nores JE, Rushmere NK, et al: Soluble forms of Toll-like receptor (TLR)2 capable of modulating TLR2 signaling are present in human plasma and breast milk. J Immunol 171:6680-6689, 2003

156. Filipp D, Alizadeh-Khiavi K, Richardson C, et al: Soluble CD14 enriched in colostrum and milk induces B cell growth and differentiation. Proc Natl Acad Sci USA 98:603-608, 2001

157. Baveye S, Elass E, Fernig DG, et al: Human lactoferrin interacts with soluble CD14 and inhibits expression of endothelial adhesion molecules, E-selectin and ICAM-1, induced by the CD14-lipopolysaccharide complex. Infect Immun 68:6519-6525, 2000

158. Brooker BE: The epithelial cells and cell fragments in human milk. Cell Tissue Res 210:321-332, 1980

159. Wirt DP, Adkins LT, Palkowetz KH, et al: Activated and memory T lymphocytes in human milk. Cytometry 13:282-290, 1992

160. Hawkes JS, Bryan DL, Gibson RA: Cytokine production by human milk cells and peripheral blood mononuclear cells from the same mothers. J Clin Immunol 22:338-344, 2002

161. Keeney SE, Schmalstieg FC, Palkowetz KH, et al: Activated neutrophils and neutrophil activators in human milk: increased expression of CD11b and decreased expression of L-selectin. J Leukoc Biol 54:97-104, 1993

162. Le Deist F, Saint-Basile G, Angeles-Cano E, et al: Prostaglandin E2 and plasminogen activators in human milk and their secretion by milk macrophages. Am J Reprod Immunol Microbiol 11:6-10, 1986

163. Cole FS, Schneeberger EE, Lichtenberg NA, et al: Complement biosynthesis in human breast-milk macrophages and blood monocytes. Immunology 46:429-441, 1982

164. Cameron PU, Lowe MG, Crowe SM, et al: Susceptibility of dendritic cells to HIV-1 infection in vitro. J Leukoc Biol 56:257-265, 1994

165. Granelli-Piperno A, Moser B, Pope M, et al: Efficient interaction of HIV-1 with purified dendritic cells via multiple chemokine coreceptors. J Exp Med 184:2433-2438, 1996

166. Ichikawa M, Sugita M, Takahashi M, et al: Breast milk macrophages spontaneously produce granulocyte-macrophage colony-stimulating factor and differentiate into dendritic cells in the presence of exogenous interleukin-4 alone. Immunology 108:189-195, 2003

167. Robinson G, Volovitz B, Passwell JH: Identification of a secretory IgA receptor on breast-milk macrophages: evidence for specific activation via these receptors. Pediatr Res 29:429-434, 1991

168. Honorio-Franca AC, Carvalho MP, Isaac L, et al: Colostral mononuclear phagocytes are able to kill enteropathogenic Escherichia coli opsonized with colostral IgA. Scand J Immunol 46:59-66, 1997

169. Nakajima S, Baba AS, Tamura N: Complement system in human colostrum: presence of nine complement components and factors of alternative pathway in human colostrum. Int Arch Allergy Appl Immunol 54:428-433, 1977

170. Bertotto A, Gerli R, Fabietti G, et al: Human breast milk T lymphocytes display the phenotype and functional characteristics of memory T cells. Eur J Immunol 20:1877-1880, 1990

171. Lindstrand A, Smedman L, Gunnlaugsson G, et al: Selective compartmentalization of gammadelta-T lymphocytes in human breastmilk. Acta Paediatr 86:890-891, 1997

172. Kunkel EJ, Campbell JJ, Haraldsen G, et al: Lymphocyte CC chemokine receptor 9 and epithelial thymus-expressed chemokine (TECK) expression distinguish the small intestinal immune compartment: Epithelial expression of tissue-specific chemokines as an organizing principle in regional immunity. J Exp Med 192:761-768, 2000

173. Keller MA, Kidd RM, Bryson YJ, et al: Lymphokine production by human milk lymphocytes. Infect Immun 32:632-636, 1981

174. Eglinton BA, Roberton DM, Cummins AG: Phenotype of T cells, their soluble receptor levels, and cytokine profile of human breast milk. Immunol Cell Biol 72:306-313, 1994

175. Beer AE, Billingham RE: Immunologic benefits and hazards of milk in maternal-perinatal relationship. Ann Intern Med 83:865-871, 1975

176. Weiler IJ, Hickler W, Sprenger R: Demonstration that milk cells invade the suckling neonatal mouse. Am J Reprod Immunol 4:95-98, 1983

177. Arvola M, Gustafsson E, Svensson L, et al: Immunoglobulin-secreting cells of maternal origin can be detected in B cell-deficient mice. Biol Reprod 63:1817-1824, 2000

178. Jain L, Vidyasagar D, Xanthou M, et al: In vivo distribution of human milk leucocytes after ingestion by newborn baboons. Arch Dis Child 64:930-933, 1989

179. Schnorr KL, Pearson LD: Intestinal absorption of maternal leucocytes by newborn lambs. J Reprod Immunol 6:329-337, 1984

180. Sheldrake RF, Husband AJ: Intestinal uptake of intact maternal lymphocytes by neonatal rats and lambs. Res Vet Sci 39:10-15, 1985

181. Siafakas C, Anderson W, Walker A, et al: Breast milk cells and their interaction with intestinal mucosa. In: Neonatal Hematology and Immunology III. Amsterdam, Elsevier Science Publishers, 1997

182. Tuboly S, Bernath S, Glavits R, et al: Intestinal absorption of colostral lymphoid cells in newborn piglets. Vet Immunol Immunopathol 20:75-85, 1988

183. Tuboly S, Bernath S, Glavits R, et al: Intestinal absorption of colostral lymphocytes in newborn lambs and their role in the development of immune status. Acta Vet Hung 43:105-115, 1995

184. Zhou L, Yoshimura Y, Huang Y, et al: Two independent pathways of maternal cell transmission to offspring: through placenta during pregnancy and by breast-feeding after birth. Immunology 101:570-580, 2000

185. Campbell DA, Jr., Lorber MI, Sweeton JC, et al: Breast feeding and maternal-donor renal allografts. Possibly the original donor-specific transfusion. Transplantation 37:340-344, 1984

186. Kois WE, Campbell DA, Jr., Lorber MI, et al: Influence of breast feeding on subsequent reactivity to a related renal allograft. J Surg Res 37:89-93, 1984

187. Zhang L, van Bree S, van Rood JJ, et al: Influence of breast feeding on the cytotoxic T cell allorepertoire in man. Transplantation 52:914-916, 1991

188. Deroche A, Nepomnaschy I, Torello S, et al: Regulation of parental alloreactivity by reciprocal F1 hybrids. The role of lactation. J Reprod Immunol 23:235-245, 1993

189. Ogra SS, Weintraub D, Ogra PL: Immunologic aspects of human colostrum and milk. III. Fate and absorption of cellular and soluble components in the gastrointestinal tract of the newborn. J Immunol 119:245-248, 1977

190. Schlesinger JJ, Covelli HD: Evidence for transmission of lymphocyte responses to tuberculin by breast-feeding. Lancet 2:529-532, 1977

191. Keller MA, Rodgriguez AL, Alvarez S, et al: Transfer of tuberculin immunity from mother to infant. Pediatr Res 22:277-281, 1987

6 Breastfeeding And Protection Against Disease

It is a difficult task to determine the clinical effects of breastfeeding by applying the modern requirements of ”evidence-based medicine”. It is, of course, not ethically possible to randomize breastfeeding studies deciding that some babies will be breastfed and some not for comparison. Instead, one study randomized breastfeeding promotion.[1]

Case-control studies are easier to perform. When trying to compensate for the many confounding factors involved, useful information may be obtained. Among the many factors complicating or confounding such studies are differences in living conditions for mother-child, differences in quality and quantity of food intake (both too little and too much), variations in microbial exposure, exposure to smoking and other toxic material, etc. In addition, many of the diseases studied have a complex background with geographic and genetic variations as to the mechanisms involved. For example, allergic diseases appear as a group of clinical patterns in different organ systems. These clinical patterns vary in different populations. It may be unrealistic to demand a simple answer about whether or not breastfeeding protects against “allergy” as you will see below. Against this complicated background, it remains important to be cautious about optimistic conclusions concerning the protective effects of breastfeeding in many conditions.

Breastfeeding And Infant Mortality

The infant mortality rate (IMR) is the number of infants per thousand dying during their first year of life. It varies from close to 3 deaths/1000 infants in Sweden to around 100 deaths/1000 in underprivileged populations.[2] The level of IMR says much about the living conditions in a particular country or a population group. Many factors influence the IMR. Infections, especially gastrointestinal and respiratory infections, are the leading causes of death in poor countries.

The strong contraceptive effect of breastfeeding was suggested to prevent more births than all the family planning programs in Third World countries.[3] The Lactational Amenorrhea Method (LAM) includes at least 10 short or 6 long breastfeeds within 24 hours and no more supplemental feeds than 30 ml/week during the first month, less than 60 ml/week during the second month, and less than 90 ml/week during the third month. This gave a contraceptive effect of 98.4% during the first 6 months and 92.2% during the first 12 months.[4] The lower fertility resulting from the lactation amenorrhea method plus the anti-infectious properties of breastmilk are very effective in decreasing IMR.[4-7] A spacing of less than 2 years between births increases the risk of dying before 5 years of age by 50%.[6]

There is a strong but complex link between high IMR and high fertility (Figure 14). Ninety-seven percent of the children are born in countries with the highest IMR and worst poverty.[8] Preventing childhood deaths by breastfeeding is an efficient way to reduce fertility.[9] Because contraceptives are not always available, promoting breastfeeding is beneficial as it reduces both IMR and fertility.

> The high IMR in poor countries is lowered both by the contraceptive and the anti-infectious effects of breastfeeding

According to the World Health Organization, a 40% increase in breastfeeding worldwide would reduce deaths from respiratory diseases by 50% and from diarrhea by 60% in children less than 18 months of age.[10] In a study in Pakistan, we found that even partial breastfeeding reduced the risk of neonatal septicemia with an odds ratio (OR, explained in Glossary) of 18 compared to no breastfeeding.[11] Since this very dangerous disease

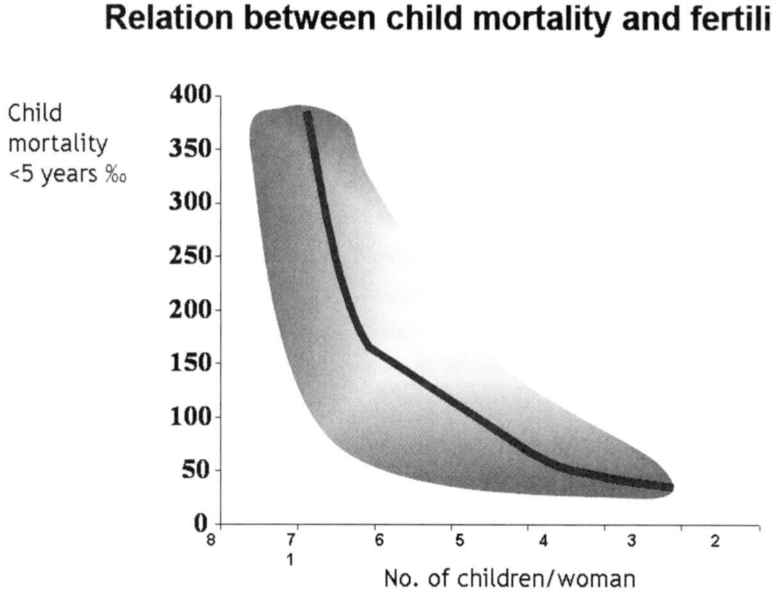

UNICEF and UN Population Division (adapted)

Figure 14. This graph correlates mortality for children less than 5 years old (expressed in ‰, with number of children born per woman, This graph illustrates the strong link between child mortality and fertility, Adapted from UNICEF and UN Population Division.

affects 2% of the births and has a mortality of 62% in that community, it is obvious that breastfeeding reduces infant mortality.[12] Similar findings were reported in another study from Pakistan.[13]

While the newborn is being colonized by bacteria, its immune system provides limited defense (Chapters 1 and 3). Colostrum and early milk play an important role in protecting the newborn. The milk SIgA antibodies directed against the microbes present in the mother's surrounding (Figure 10) along with the many other components in the milk (Chapter 5) provide this protection. It is likely that SIgA antibodies and the many forms of receptor analogues in the milk (Figure 3) bind and block the colonizing microbes so they cannot attach to the gut epithelium. Therefore, bacteria and viruses cannot easily enter the infant's tissues and cause infection in the blood and tissues.[14] It is quite likely that lactoferrin in the milk kills bacteria. It should be stressed that all of these defense factors work without inducing inflammation; they even counteract inflammation. The capacity to block inflammation is especially striking for lactoferrin (Chapter

5). Thus, protection is provided without induction of tissue-damaging, energy-consuming inflammation. Instead, the baby can use that energy for growth.

> Breastfeeding efficiently protects against neonatal septicemia, a very dangerous disease in the newborn. Several of the defense factors in milk such as the SIgA antibodies (Figure 10), the oligosaccharide receptor analogues (Figure 3), and, probably, the prominent milk protein, lactoferrin, help provide this protection. These are the reasons breastfeeding reduces IMR.

In poor countries, the risk of dying from diarrhea for non-breastfed babies is 25 times that of fully breastfed infants (Table 8).[15] A well controlled study from Brazil showed that babies on formula or cows' milk had a 4.2 times higher risk of dying from diarrhea than partially breastfed babies.[16] The infants fed formula or cow's milk had a 14.2 times higher risk of dying compared to an exclusively breastfed group.

Table 8

Reduction Of Mortality By Breastfeeding In Poor Countries

	Ratio between	
	Exclusive/no breastfeeding	Partial/no breastfeeding
Diarrhea	25[15]	
	14.2[16]	4.2[16]
Pneumonia	3.6[16]	1.6[16]
Infant mortality	1.8-2.6[18]	

The same study demonstrated that formula or cows' milk increased the risk of dying of a respiratory tract infection by 1.6 times compared with a partially breastfed group. Formula fed infants had a 3.6 times higher risk of dying than exclusively breastfed infants. The risk of dying of other infections increased by 2.5 times in fully weaned babies. An African study found breastfeeding to significantly diminish fatalities from diarrhea, measles, and acute lower respiratory infections.[17] Another investigation showed that each additional month of breastfeeding diminished IMR by 6.2 per 1000, whereas breastfeeding, together with supplements, resulted in a decrease of 3.8 per 1000. Artificial feeding increased mortality 1.8-2.6 times in this well controlled and large study (Table 8).[18]

It seems that breastfeeding not only prevents acute, but also prolonged, diarrhea. This is important because 80% of deaths from diarrhea are caused by prolonged diarrhea in poor areas like Pakistan.[19] Since deaths from diarrhea are so efficiently reduced by breastfeeding, it would seem that breastfeeding would prevent deaths from persistent diarrhea.[15;16] This is supported by two studies.[20;21]

Reduced neonatal deaths may result from the fact that breastfeeding helps prevent hypoglycemia and hypothermia in the newborn. This is especially important for low birth weight and premature babies.[22]

In poor countries, late neonatal deaths are mainly due to sepsis, acute respiratory infections, meningitis, omphalitis (infection of the umbilicus), and diarrhea. These diseases are potentially reduced by breastfeeding.

Exclusive breastfeeding in Bangladesh in early life gave a 2.23 times lower risk of deaths from all causes. For deaths from acute respiratory infections, the reduction was 2.40 fold and for diarrhea 3.94 fold.[23]

A recent review by a WHO collaborative team demonstrated that breastfeeding provides important protection against mortality for more than 8 million of the 12 million deaths yearly among children less than 5 years old in the world.[24] Pooled odds ratios from several sizable reports demonstrated significant protection ranging from 5.8 for infants less than 2 months of age to 1.4 for those 9-11 months of age. Girls were slightly better protected than boys. Up to 6 months of age, the protection was better against diarrhea than against acute respiratory infections with OR = 6.1 compared to 2.4. During the second half of the first year, the corresponding pooled figures were OR = 1.9 and 2.5. During the second year of life, the figures from the included studies ranged from OR = 1.6 – 2.1.

In an investigation from Latin America, 55% of infant deaths from acute respiratory infections and diarrhea could be prevented by exclusive breastfeeding during the first 3 months of life followed by partial breastfeeding during the first year.[25] Exclusive breastfeeding could protect against 32% of the deaths among infants 4-11 months of age. Taken together, 13.9% of infant deaths of all causes could be prevented by breastfeeding. This could impact 52,000 children yearly in Latin America. Against this background, it seems correct to suggest that not breastfeeding compromises infants' immune systems worldwide.[26] It emphasizes the importance of the WHO/UNICEF Baby Friendly Hospital initiative which strongly supports breastfeeding.[27] Recently a study from the USA showed that breastfeeding significantly reduced postneonatal deaths, that is, deaths between the ages of 28 days and 1 year of age.[28]

Breastfeeding protects against death from diarrhea and respiratory infections in poor as well as rich countries. Breastfeeding contributes greatly to the reduction of IMR .

It has been suggested that sudden infant death syndrome (SIDS) may be prevented by breastfeeding. This independent effect was seen in an investigation from New Zealand with an OR of 2.9, but not in other studies from England and Scotland.[29-31] A meta-analysis suggested a protective effect of breastfeeding, but the quality of the 23 studies reviewed were poor.[32] SIDS seemed twice as common among bottle-fed infants with an OR of 2.11 and a 95% Confidence Interval (CI, see Glossary for explanation) of 1.66-2.68. Not all confounding factors were excluded.

A collaborative study in Scandinavia took into consideration confounding factors like smoking during pregnancy, paternal employment, infant's age, and sleeping position (since sleeping on the stomach increases the risk of SIDS). It was found that breastfeeding had a weak but significant effect on reducing the incidence of SIDS.[33] Maternal smoking came out as the most important modifiable risk factor for SIDS if babies are not left to sleep on their stomach.[34] It has been suggested that passive smoking in the same room as the infant may eliminate the protective effect of breastfeeding.[35] Another cooperative British study noted that bottle-feeding was a risk factor.[36]

The mechanisms behind the effect of breastfeeding on SIDS are not clear. It may be possible that prevention of infections could be a factor including neutralization of bacterial toxins by milk SIgA antibodies.[37]

> Breastfeeding seems to have a protective effect against sudden infant death syndrome (SIDS), though the effect may be limited. To reduce the risk of SIDS, the baby should not be exposed to passive smoking, the mother should not smoke, and the baby should not sleep on its stomach.

In conclusion:

The infant mortality rate, IMR, varies enormously throughout the world from a low of approximately 3/1000 infants dying during the first year of life in Sweden to a high of around 100/1000 dying per year in poor countries. Breastfeeding can significantly reduce IMR both by its contraceptive effects and its anti-infectious capacities. Spacing less than 2 years between births in developing areas increases child mortality. Breastfeeding results in fewer and healthier children. Breastfeeding protects against deaths from infections like sepsis, diarrhea and pneumonia. According to WHO, an additional 40% increase in breastfeeding rates could result in a 50% reduction of IMR in poor areas.

There seems to be a weak effect of breastfeeding on the prevention of sudden infant death syndrome (SIDS), but many confounding factors make studies complicated. Smoking and leaving the baby to sleep on its stomach are important risk factors for SIDS.

Breastfeeding And Protection Against Specific Infections

Protection against diarrhea

There are significant methodological problems with studies of the protective capacity of breastfeeding because of the many confounding factors.[38-41] Several investigations provide good evidence that breastfeeding protects against diarrheal disease.[41-43] Some analyses relate the protective capacity of breastfeeding against certain diarrhea-causing microbes or their toxins to the level of specific SIgA antibodies in the milk of the mothers. This was demonstrated for milk SIgA antibodies against *V. cholerae*, enterotoxigenic *E. coli* (ETEC), *Campylobacter, Shigella and G. lamblia.*[44-49] The severity of *Shigella* diarrhea during the first three years of life in Bangladesh was determined by the extent of breastfeeding.[50] Protection by breastfeeding against *Campylobacter* was questioned in one investigation, but confirmed in another.[51;52]

> The SIgA antibodies in milk give significant protection against diarrhea-causing pathogens like *Campylobacter, Shigella*, enterotoxin-producing *E .coli, V. cholerae,* and the parasite, *G.lamblia.*

A large prospective 2 year follow-up study in Pakistan of four population groups showed significant protection against diarrhea by breastfeeding.[53] In the two poorest groups from a village and a periurban mud hut slum, the protection lasted through the first two years. It reached 70-80% during the first weeks of life; although, partial breastfeeding was most common. In the city slum with less poverty, partial breastfeeding gave significant protection during the first 9 months of life. In the upper middle class group, the protection lasted for 6 months. In this latter group, breastfeeding was least common.[54] The exclusively breastfed group was small but sufficient for a comparison with another group that was given extra water in addition to the breastfeeding during the hot season. It is a very common belief that babies needs extra water during the hot season: although, it has been clearly shown that this is unnecessary.[55] Giving extra water may be harmful because the babies nurse less often reducing milk supply and the water may be contaminated causing infant illness. In Pakistan, the extra water given during the hot season significantly increased the number of cases of diarrhea and impaired growth during that period of the year.[56]

> A breastfed baby does not need any extra water even in a hot, dry climate. Extra water may reduce suckling so less milk is produced. It may also increase the risk of infections.

Protection against diarrhea by breastfeeding has also been demonstrated in studies in the USA. The findings indicated a 50% reduction in diarrhea in breastfed infants compared to formula-fed groups.[57;58] Comparable results were reported from Scotland if breastfeeding continued beyond 13 weeks.[43] Hospital admissions were also reduced. The same results were noted in Canada. A more modest effect was seen in Holland.[59;60] A Cochrane review applying the strict rules of evidence-based medicine demonstrated that exclusive breastfeeding for six months compared to mixed feeding for 3 or 4 months led to less diarrhea.[61]

Breastfeeding in poor populations had positive effects in children who had severe wasting and stunting and protracted diarrhea as the only disease.[62] Comparing partially breastfed children to those weaned in Guinea-Bissau, the incidence of diarrhea was lower both at one and two years of age.[63] Even if the breastfed children were less well nourished, they had fewer diseases and lower mortality than the non-breastfed children and their duration of disease was shorter. Breastfeeding has been shown to reduce both the number and the volume of stools.[64]

A very extensive and well controlled study in Belarus demonstrated protection against diarrhea by breastfeeding during the first year of life.[1] Those exclusively breastfed for 6 months had significantly less gastrointestinal infections between 3-6 months of age compared to those exclusively breastfed for the first 3 months.[65]

Fully breastfed children in Mexico had five times less risk of infection from *G. lamblia* than non-breastfed.[66] Partially breastfed infants had a 1.8 times lower risk than non-breastfed infants of being infected. Although breastfed infants may be protected against infection, chronic carriage of remaining parasites was not prevented.

> Breastfeeding also seems to protect against infections from the parasite *Giardia lamblia.*

Infections caused by rotavirus are a major problem and result in high mortality in children. It seems surprising that breastfeeding may not provide efficient protection against this form of virus-induced diarrhea.[67;68]

Breastfeeding prevented severe diarrhea caused by rotavirus during the first year of life, but it seemed that this was followed by an increased risk of severe infection during the second year. Nicaraguan children had rotavirus infections at two months of age. The higher the levels of SIgA antibodies in the mother's milk against rotavirus, the later the virus appeared in the stools of the infant.[69] Asymptomatic infections tended to be related to long duration of breastfeeding.

In a large Italian investigation of nosocomial infections with rotavirus, there was significant protection from breastfeeding.[70] The breastfed infants who were infected did not develop any symptoms.

> Breastfeeding may have a protective effect against rotavirus infections. In some studies, it has been insufficient to prevent infections and symptoms.

Early colonization with *Helicobacter pylori* is common in children, especially in poor countries. A German investigation did not show any prevention of *H. pylori* infections by breastfeeding; although, κ-casein from human milk is known to prevent attachment of this microbe to human gastric mucosa presumably due to its fucose-containing moieties (Chapter 5).[71;72]

In conclusion:

Due to SIgA antibodies in milk, breastfeeding provides significant protection against diarrhea caused by *V. cholerae*, enterotoxin-producing *E. coli* (ETEC), *Shigella*, *Campylobacter*, and *G. lamblia*. Other defense factors in the milk may contribute to this protection, but since those factors are not specific for a certain infectious agent, it becomes very difficult to prove their role. The protection against diarrheal diseases by breastfeeding is striking in poor countries and it is significant in developed countries as well. However, for unknown reasons, protection against rotavirus infection is inadequate.

Protection against respiratory tract infections

There are many studies from industrialized countries suggesting that breastfeeding protects against otitis media – ear infections.[59;73-76] Other investigations have not confirmed this, have seen only a small effect, or have demonstrated that long term breastfeeding was required to get a protective effect.[43;77-79] A well planned study did find a 50% decrease in acute as well as recurrent otitis media in infants exclusively breastfed longer than 4 months.[80] The attacks of acute and prolonged ear infections were reduced by 20% during breastfeeding.[57] Compared with the formula group, the episodes of prolonged otitis were reduced by 80% in the breastfed group. Other studies support these findings.[58;81-83]

In children with cleft palate, effusions in the ears are a considerable problem. Feeding with human milk, mainly from the mother, efficiently protected against ear problems.[84;85]

> Breastfeeding protects against otitis media and recurrent otitis according to most studies.

Breastfeeding may prevent colonization in the nose and mouth from the potential pathogen, *H. influenzae*.[86] Milk SIgA antibodies against a surface protein on the bacteria were inversely related to the rate of colonization. Such bacterial colonization correlated to the risk of getting otitis media. However, colonization with the other major bacterial cause of middle ear infections, pneumococci, was not reduced by breastfeeding with milk containing antibodies against surface components of that bacteria.[87] In the pneumococci infected group, there was a reverse tendency towards increased colonization and no reduction in the rate of otitis media. There is no obvious explanation for these findings, but it should be noted that just as man tries to develop protective mechanisms, so do microorganisms. Their success as infecting agents depends on how well they can get around and how well they utilize the host's defense factors to their advantage.

Somewhat contradictory results have appeared in studies about the potential protection of breastfeeding against upper and lower respiratory tract infections. It has been suggested that confounding factors and a relatively weak effect against some forms of respiratory disease in developed countries may be the reasons for the contradictory results.[40;88-90] Breastfeeding may result in less severe disease.[91] In poor areas of Brazil, it was found that breastfeeding prevented many cases of death from pneumonia.[16] Another study by the same group demonstrated that non breastfed infants were 17 times more likely to need hospital care for pneumonia.[92] The relative risk was 61 times for infants less than 3 months old, diminishing to 10 times if older. Giving solids to these young ones gave a relative risk of 17.5 and 13.4 for all infants.

Breastfeeding protects against lower respiratory tract infections in underprivileged societies.

In developed countries, many studies have found that breastfeeding protects against various forms of respiratory tract infections.[43;59;60;83;89;93-95] There was no difference in the protection of exclusive breastfeeding for 3 or 6 months in a large study in Belarus.[65] An Italian study supported the findings that breastfeeding protects against lower respiratory tract infections.[96] A large investigation in the USA showed some protection against pneumonia, as well as middle ear infections.[97] Another extensive study in the USA found that breastfeeding protects against wheezing respiratory tract infections during the first four months of life.[90] Such infections are usually virus-induced. In one study, breastfeeding protected against some community-transmitted respiratory infections during the first month of life. This effect was only seen in girls, not in boys. No reason for this sex difference could be found.[98] The protection against lower respiratory infections by breastfeeding was especially evident if the mother smoked.[99] A recent study from Australia showed that predominant breastfeeding for less than 2 months, or partial breastfeeding for less than 6 months was related to more frequent visits to health care services for upper respiratory tract infections. Predominant breastfeeding for less than 6 months was associated with an increased risk for two or more such visits caused by lower respiratory illness with wheezing. Breastfeeding for less than 8 months significantly increased the risk of two or more instances of wheezing lower respiratory tract infections. The authors concluded that predominant breastfeeding for at least 6 months and partial breastfeeding for up to a year reduces respiratory illnesses in infancy.[100]

Breastfeeding protects against lower respiratory tract infections, including infections with wheezing, not only in poor countries but also in countries like the USA and Australia. A large study from Belarus comparing the effect of exclusive breastfeeding for 3 and 6 months on respiratory tract infections did not show any difference. Prolonged breastfeeding in an Australian study showed enhanced protection during the first year. If the mother smokes, the protective effect of breastfeeding may become more evident. There is also evidence that breastfeeding protects against upper respiratory infections.

Studies of a Navajo population in the USA demonstrated that increasing rates of breastfeeding resulted in a decrease in pneumonia and gastroenteritis, 32.2% and 14.6% respectively. Feeding with formula from birth resulted in increased rates of croup and bronchiolitis.[90] These latter infections may have originated from a viral epidemic that did not affect the exclusively breastfed infants.

In conclusion:

In several studies, breastfeeding has been shown to protect against otitis media, although some studies did not show this effect. There also seems to be protection against recurrent otitis. The problems with prolonged ear infections in children with cleft palate were counteracted by feeding with human milk.

In poor populations, breastfeeding seems to offer protection against various forms of respiratory tract infections. Such infections with wheezing were prevented by breastfeeding in studies in the USA and Australia. In a recent study in the USA, protection against community-transmitted respiratory tract infections was noted in girls, but not in boys. No apparent explanation could be provided. A Norwegian study suggested that breastfeeding was especially protective against lower respiratory infections if the mother smoked.

Protection against neonatal septicemia

It has already been mentioned that breastfeeding prevents deaths from neonatal septicemia in poor countries.[11;13] Protection against this severe condition was also noted in Sweden.[101] Feeding expressed human milk to low birth weight babies had the same effect as breastfeeding.[102] In a study in the USA, giving very low birth weight babies human milk diminished significantly any infection including sepsis/meningitis.[103]

In conclusion:

Breastfeeding protects against neonatal septicemia/meningitis, a very dangerous disease. There is good evidence that breastfeeding reduces infant mortality from this condition, especially in poor countries.

Protection against urinary tract infections

It has been suggested that breastfeeding can prevent urinary tract infections.[104;105] These observations were recently substantiated in a prospective case-control study of 200 consecutive cases presenting with first-time febrile urinary tract infections. It was found that ongoing breastfeeding resulted in a significantly lower risk of infection. Longer duration of breastfeeding resulted in a lower risk of infection after weaning, suggesting long-term protection. Breastfeeding until 7 months of age resulted in protection lasting until 2 years of age. This was more evident in girls than boys.[106] These results can presumably be explained by the information in Chapter 5 about immediate and long term protective components in human milk. The likely mechanisms behind such long term effects are discussed below in this chapter. The reason for the better protection in girls than boys is not clear, but may be related to the anatomical differences in the urinary tract between the sexes.

> Breastfeeding protects against urinary tract infections. This protection is more evident in girls than in boys.

The bacteria causing urinary tract infections usually originate from the patient's intestinal microflora. Since the lymphoid cells in the mammary glands which produce the milk SIgA antibodies have migrated there from the mother's gut, the milk will likely contain antibodies against the gut flora of the infant, normally colonized with microbes from the mother or family members (Figure 10). Therefore, the microbes in the gut of a breastfed baby are coated by the specific SIgA antibodies from the milk (Chapter 5). These antibody-covered bacteria cannot easily enter the gut mucosa and cause a blood-born infection in the kidneys. Likewise, they are prevented by these milk antibodies from infecting the urinary tract through the urethra and ureters.[107] Furthermore, breastfeeding favors a less pathogenic gut microflora with lower counts of potentially pathogenic bacteria, diminishing the risk of infection. Lactoferrin and fragments thereof originating from the milk lactoferrin in the gut are absorbed and transported into the urine via the kidneys (Chapter 5). In a mouse model, lactoferrin and the fragments have been shown to protect against experimental urinary tract infections.[108] These studies also showed that lactoferrin efficiently turns off inflammatory responses while killing bacteria.[109] As a result, symptoms of infection like fever, tiredness, and loss of appetite are prevented via this protective mechanism. This saves pain, tissue damage, and energy in the infant. Another protective mechanism is due to milk oligosaccharides. They appear in the urine of breastfed babies and prevent the attachment of bacteria to the urinary tract epithelium (Figure 3).[110] This defense mechanism was discussed in some detail in Chapter 5.

In conclusion:

There is good evidence that breastfeeding prevents febrile urinary tract infections. Breastfeeding up to 7 months resulted in reduced risk of infection up to 2 years of age. The effect was more evident in girls than boys, possibly because of the difference in the anatomy of the genito-urinary tracts between the sexes. The protection is presumably due to the effect of the milk SIgA antibodies on the bacteria in the gut microflora which is the common origin of such infections. Furthermore, the milk protein lactoferrin and fragments thereof are found in urine. They have been shown to significantly reduce inflammation and infection in the urinary tract of mice with experimental urinary tract infections involving the kidneys.

Protection against necrotizing enterocolitis (NEC)

NEC is a severe disease mainly occurring in small premature infants. NEC is linked to enteral feeding, intestinal hypoxia, and bacterial colonization. A strong inflammatory response to the colonizing bacteria caused by the lack of an efficient host defense may be a major factor. Several studies have indicated that human milk may have a protective effect.[111-113]

> Human milk seems to protect against necrotizing enterocolitis (NEC) an often lethal condition in premature infants.

The platelet-activating factor (PAF) has been mentioned as one of the components important for the inflammation appearing in the gut mucosa. The inflammation may even result in perforation. Human milk contains an enzyme, PAF-acetylhydrolase, which degrades PAF.[114] Exaggerated production of IL-8 by fetal human gut epithelial cells may also be part of the pathogenesis.[115] IL-8 is a strong chemokine that brings in neutrophils which are part of the inflammatory mechanisms in NEC. In a rat model, it was shown that maternal milk could reduce the severity of NEC. This effect was associated with induced production of IL-10 at the site of injury in the gut.[116] This cytokine is anti-inflammatory and often plays a key role in balancing inflammatory host responses. Most likely, the milk SIgA antibodies and the oligosaccharide receptor analogues that prevent bacteria from attaching to the gut epithelium (Figure 3) are also important in blocking the bacteria colonizing the intestine of the small premature infant who has very little defense on its own.

In conclusion:

Necrotizing enterocolitis (NEC) in small premature infants is a very dangerous condition. Human milk seems to protect against NEC. This protection may be due to the many anti-inflammatory components in milk and its capacity to control the early bacterial colonization of the gut via the SIgA antibodies directed against the colonizing bacteria. The oliogosaccharide receptor analogues in the milk also help prevent the bacteria from attaching to the gut mucosa, causing disease (Figure 3).

Protection against other infections

It has been suggested that breastfeeding prevents botulism.[117] Some retrospective studies proposed that children with acute appendicitis, hypertrophic pyloric stenosis, or who have had tonsillectomies are less likely to have been breastfed.[118-120] One study indicated that breastfeeding may delay early intestinal colonization with *H. pylori*.[121] That effect may result from the fact that κ-casein in human milk prevents attachment of *H. pylori* to the gastric mucosa.[72] All these reports need confirmation.

Long-term Effects Of Breastfeeding

Breastfeeding and vaccinations

Infants vaccinated with tetanus and diphtheria toxoid and live oral poliovirus have higher antibody responses if they were breastfed rather than formula-fed.[122] There was an increase in IgG antibodies in serum, IgM antibodies in stool, and SIgA antibodies in saliva against all the vaccines indicating that there was likely protection via the blood and the mucosal membranes. The antibodies remained at a similar level 1-2 years later. Similar enhancement by breastfeeding was seen in another study using the *H. influenzae* type b (Hib) polysaccharide-conjugate vaccine.[123] These positive effects on the primary vaccine response were present months after breastfeeding was terminated.

The enhancing effects of breastfeeding on the serum antibody response to the live oral poliovirus vaccine was also seen in a study where the infants had been exclusively breastfed for 2 months and then were given mixed feeding or formula.[124] One of the control groups received a nucleotide-enriched formula. The other group received an iron-enriched formula. The group receiving the nucleotide-enriched formula had higher antibody levels to the Hib vaccine than the other two groups at 7 months of age.

The BCG vaccine induces a response in the T cell-mediated part of the immune system (Figure 5). One study suggested that the BCG vaccination given before 1 month of age gave a stronger T lymphocyte response if the babies had been breastfed, even if they were only breastfed for 2 weeks.[125]

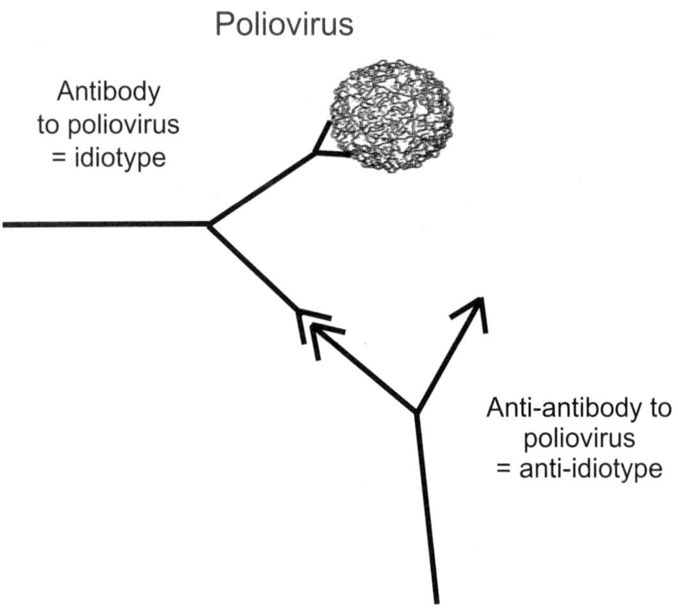

Figure 15. The binding site of an antibody is specific for a particular virus and is able to bind and neutralize that virus, e.g. poliovirus. The binding site for the antigen, e.g. a bacterial peptide, is recognized as an antigen by the immune system. The immune system produces antibodies specific for that binding site. Antibodies against an antibody are called anti-antibodies or anti-idiotypes. Both antibodies and anti-antibodies are present in human milk and may help induce the corresponding antibody in the breastfed baby.

Breastfeeding may enhance vaccine responses against some vaccines, but this finding is not consistently obtained.

Other vaccine studies have not confirmed the enhancing effect of breastfeeding, especially not for live virus vaccines against influenza, rotavirus, and poliovirus. This finding may be due to the fact that these viruses are common in many societies and one would expect to find antibodies against them in the serum and milk. These antibodies may have inhibited the vaccine responses.[126-128] Sabin, who made the first live oral vaccine against poliomyelitis, noted that breastfeeding close to the time of giving live oral poliovirus vaccine neutralizes the vaccine virus and prevents the planned effect of the vaccination. This effect has been confirmed in a recent study by WHO.[129] It may not be safe to breastfeed within a half hour before or after giving a dose of oral poliovirus vaccine. This problem is avoided by using inactivated, killed poliovirus vaccines but they are more expensive.

> An oral dose of a live virus vaccine, like the poliovirus vaccine, must not be given too close to the time of breastfeeding because the antibodies in the milk will neutralize the vaccine virus and make it ineffective.

There are studies that show that tetanus toxoid and Hib vaccines do not give better responses in breastfeeding infants.[130-133] Such outcomes are probably due to variations in the definition of breastfeeding and its extent and duration. It is also clear that the infant may have antibodies before the vaccination that were acquired via the placenta during pregnancy. Such transplacental antibodies may inhibit vaccine responses as discussed in Chapter 4. More complicated is the fact that an antibody against a specific antigen in an individual has a unique structure in its binding site, and antibodies against that binding site called anti-antibodies can be formed (Figure 15). The anti-antibodies can either stimulate the production of the antibody or inhibit its production. We have demonstrated that human milk contains both antibodies and anti-antibodies against poliovirus.[134] As discussed later in this chapter, these antibodies transferred via the milk to the offspring may immunize the offspring. In experimental animals, we have shown that effects of such antibody transfers may even go from one generation to the next two subsequent ones.[135]

The fact that breastfed infants produce more IFN-γ than non-breastfed infants during an infection with respiratory syncytial virus (RSV) could be due to an enhancing effect of one or a few of the many components in the milk described in Chapter 5.[136] It has also been indicated that the levels of SIgA antibodies and lactoferrin in the urine are enhanced by breastfeeding. This may be helpful in the prevention of urinary tract infections as discussed above in this chapter. Finally, it was noted that the levels of SIgA antibodies in saliva during the first 6 months of life increased more among breastfed than non-breastfed infants. This could be related to the presence of enhancing factors in the milk and possible exposure to bacteria from the mother while breastfeeding.[137]

In conclusion:

Some studies have shown that breastfeeding enhances vaccine responses. Other studies do not show this. The variations may be due to differences in the mothers' immune responses which are transferred to the baby via the placenta. They may also be influenced by immune factors like antibodies, lymphocytes, cytokines, growth factors, etc. which are transferred via the milk.

Long term protection against infections

In Saarinen's study of the effect of breastfeeding on recurrent otitis media, it was noted that an enhanced protection lasted during a 3 year follow up.[74] Howie et al found that breastfeeding for more than 13 weeks resulted in a reduction in attacks of gastroenteritis through the first year of life.[43] Follow up of these children in Dundee suggested that they had enhanced protection against respiratory tract infections at the age of 7 years.[138] Breastfeeding also resulted in significantly better protection against dangerous invasive infections caused by *H. influenzae* type b (Hib), like meningitis. This effect lasted up to 10 years.[139] This enhanced protection of the infant may occur because breastfeeding promotes production of IgG2 antibodies against the Hib bacteria.[140] The duration of breastfeeding was found to relate to the levels of antibodies against Hib through pre-school age.[141]

> There is evidence that the enhanced protection against certain infections afforded by breastfeeding may continue for some years after termination of breastfeeding.

Prevention of wheezing was enhanced by breastfeeding during a 6-7 year follow up.[78] Most likely, this was because breastfeeding prevents respiratory tract infections causing wheezing. This effect is mainly seen in nonatopic children.[90;142;143] This is further discussed in the section on breastfeeding and allergy.

Children breastfed through 6 months of age were better protected against respiratory tract infections, diarrhea, skin infections and urogenital infections until the age of 3 years in a study from the Netherlands.[60] The effects reviewed above were supported in a recent critical review of the

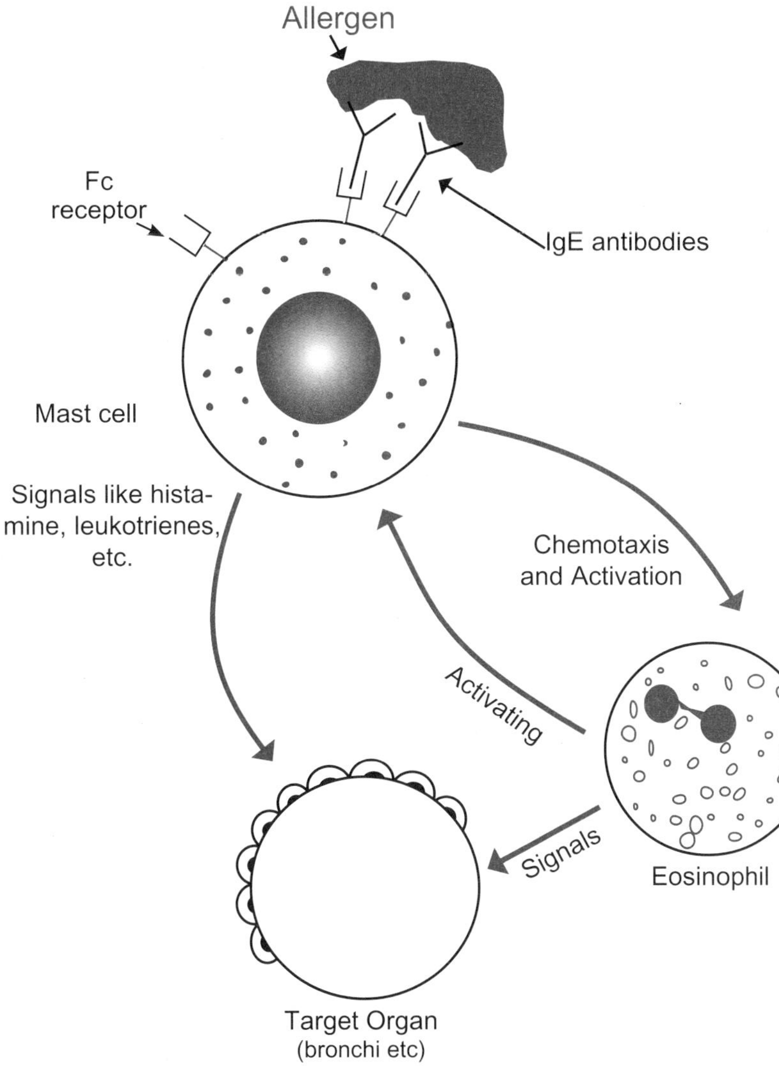

Figure 16. This figure shows the mechanisms behind the immediate hypersensitivity reaction. IgE antibody-mediated allergic reactions cause atopic dermatitis or eczema, hayfever, and asthma. Two IgE antibodies bound next to each other via Fc receptors on mast cells release this reaction when they bind to their antigen (allergen). The allergen may be pollen, mites, foods, etc. The binding causes the mast cell to release numerous active substances which cause many of the allergic symptoms. Eosinophil and basophil leucocytes migrate into the site of the reaction. Active mediators are released from these cells, adding to the atopic inflammatory process. The symptoms differ depending on the organ affected - asthma in the lungs, hayfever in the nose and eyes, and eczema in the skin.

evidence for long-term protection against infections in the gastrointestinal and respiratory tracts by breastfeeding.[144] Another recent study shows that breastfeeding provides enhanced protection against urinary tract infections through the second year of life.[106]

In conclusion:

Breastfeeding results in enhanced protection against infections like otitis media, respiratory infections with or without wheezing, urinary tract infections, and invasive infections with H. influenzae type b. This protection may last several years after termination of breastfeeding. We do not know which factors determine whether, or to what extent, this will happen. However, ongoing research indicates that several possible mechanisms are involved.

Breastfeeding and allergy

About allergic diseases

Allergic diseases make up a group of related conditions. These conditions usually occur in individuals with a genetic tendency to react by producing IgE antibodies (Figures 5 and 6) against the antigen which causes the disease.[145] Such allergy-inducing antigens are called *allergens*. The allergen may come from pollen, mites, or foods. An inflammation with many special characteristics is induced when the allergen binds its IgE antibodies (Figure 16). Individuals reacting to the allergens are called *atopic*.

IgE antibodies are normally produced in defense against large parasites. In atopic individuals, control of IgE production has failed and IgE antibodies are directed against allergens like pollen. Such IgE antibodies attach to mast cells which have the capacity to release several active substances like histamine, leukotrienes, and Platelet Activating Factor (PAF). These mediators of the allergic symptoms are secreted by the mast cell when two close IgE antibodies attached to the mast cell bind to their specific allergen as shown in Figure 16. Among the active factors released, some are chemotactic and bring in eosinophil and basophil leucocytes. In this way, many such cells appear at the site. They are activated and release further pro-inflammatory substances, normally aimed at destroying parasites. This inflammation is called an immediate hypersensitivity reaction and takes place in the lungs of a patient with asthma, in the skin of an eczematous patient, in the gut of a food allergic individual, etc. Other forms of inflammation may be added at later stages.

The immediate hypersensitivity reaction is seen as a positive skin test when a patient is allergic to an allergen. It proves that the patient has IgE antibodies against that allergen. Allergic disease, especially in the form of asthma, is becoming more common. Seven - fifteen percent of school children in some regions have asthma. In some countries, it is twice as common.[145;146]

> Allergic diseases are mostly due to an abnormal response of *IgE antibodies* against harmless components like food, pollen, mites, etc. Such antibodies, which are really for defense against parasites, induce a special inflammation, the immediate hypersensitivity reaction. This reaction is what gives the typical allergic symptoms of asthma in the lungs, eczema in the skin, hayfever in the nose, etc. A positive skin test has the same mechanism and demonstrates that the reacting individual has IgE antibodies against the applied allergen.

Children often start with food allergies in early life, and usually recover from them spontaneously. Later, they may get allergies in the airways such as hay fever and asthma. This course of events is called the "allergy march".[147] Against this background, it is of great interest to find out whether breastfeeding can prevent or lessen allergic diseases.

> Allergic diseases like asthma, are a growing problem among children in many parts of the world. It is of great interest to determine whether breastfeeding can have preventive effects on some, or several, of the different forms of allergic diseases.

Breastfeeding and allergy: food allergy in infancy and early childhood

In early life, the initial symptoms of allergy are often in the form of a food allergy. In many cases, the allergies are caused by cow's milk. Some cases are also caused by other foods such as soy proteins. It has been frequently debated whether food allergies can be prevented by breastfeeding.[148;149]

Infants normally respond with antibodies against cow's milk proteins (CMP). Producing IgE antibodies may result in allergy. A low risk of cow's milk allergy is related to high IgA in the mother's milk. This suggests that the milk antibodies may decrease exposure to the CMPs.[150;151] A higher risk of developing eczema noted in an 18 month follow up was related to low IgA in mothers' milk and high blood eosinophils in breastfed babies.[152] The risk of allergy in the offspring is related to the number of eosinophils in the milk, to the number of B lymphocytes, and their expression of a receptor for IgE.

Although it has been questioned in a large study, it seems that CMP may be transferred to the offspring via the maternal milk.[153;154] It has been debated whether an early, temporary feeding with CMPs increases the risk of the baby to develop cow's milk allergy. Some studies suggest that there is such a risk, and that the timing and amount of the exposure are important.[155-157] Pre-term babies were found to develop cow's milk allergy more often after early exposure if there was a family history of allergic diseases.[158] Increased permeability of the mammary epithelium can be measured by an increased sodium/potassium (Na/K) ratio in the milk. This condition has been linked to sub-clinical mastitis and is further discussed in Chapter 7. Recently, it was found that increased ratios of Na/K in milk from atopic mothers were associated with a significantly increased risk of development of positive skin prick tests and atopic disease in their babies.[159] A possible explanation may be an increased load of allergens via the milk from the mother to her baby.

Milk factors possibly involved in protection against or development of allergy, in the child.

Studies of chemokines in the milk (Chapter 5) suggested that IL-8 and RANTES were higher in the milk of allergic mothers.[160] Such chemokines may bring about the transfer and stimulation of inflammatory cells. Obviously, many factors in the mother's milk may determine whether the baby will be protected by breastfeeding, or even the reverse.

Allergic mothers have significantly more IL-4 in their milk. This cytokine is needed for the production of the allergy-mediating IgE antibodies. The major cytokine in milk, TGF-β, down-regulates inflammation.[161;162] Lower levels of TGF-β1 in the milk was related to increased IgE antibody production against CMP by the B lymphocytes in the CMP allergic child.[162] Similar observations were made in a prospective study of infants from atopic families suggesting that the high levels of TGF-β may help prevent or delay atopic disease.[163] Another study did not show any major effects of levels of cytokines, chemokines, or SIgA in mother's milk on the development of positive skin tests, measuring presence of IgE to allergens, or atopic symptoms during the first two years.[164] Breastfeeding protected against wheezing in still another study. A linear relationship was found between lower levels of TGF-β in the mother's milk and the risk of the infant developing wheezing.[165] These reports agree with previous findings that TGF-β is a factor which down-regulates IgE production but up-regulates production of protective SIgA antibodies.

> Whether breastfeeding prevents cow's milk allergy is still being debated. Many factors in the milk may affect the outcome

The Hygiene hypothesis of allergy development

The "Hygiene hypothesis" claims that exposure, at least during the first year of life, to certain microbes may help prevent allergic diseases. It agrees with observations that early exposure to lipopolysaccharides (LPS), the surface structure in Gram negative bacteria also called endotoxin (Chapter 1), may decrease the risk of developing allergic diseases. Having dogs or cats in the household, living on a farm with animals, or drinking un-pasteurized milk seems to be preventive. It has been suggested that the common factor is inhalation or ingestion of endotoxin-containing material.[166] Soluble CD14 binds LPS from Gram negative bacteria so they can activate phagocytes (see Chapter 2). Soluble CD14 was significantly reduced in the milk at 3 months postpartum in mothers whose infants developed eczema by 6 months of age.[167] The soluble CD14 may enhance exposure of the young infant's immune system to the bacteria, including Gram negatives which normally colonize the gut from birth on (Chapter 1). They may help the baby develop the capacity to become immunologically tolerant (Chapter 2) to food and other potential allergens. This very likely relates to the differences shown to occur in the intestinal microflora in neonates who developed atopic disease compared to those who did not.[168] In agreement with such a mechanism, it seems that early colonization of the infant with certain probiotic bacteria may prevent allergic diseases.[169]

Birth order and larger number of siblings, possibly affecting the degree of microbial exposure, have been claimed to decrease the risk of developing allergy.[170-172] Excluding lower respiratory tract infections, it has been suggested that repeated viral infections in early life reduce the risk of developing asthma before school age.[173] Another study has cast doubts about these findings.[172] Vaginal colonization with *Ureoplasma urealyticum* of the mother during pregnancy was associated with infant wheezing, but not with asthma during the fifth year of life.[174] Maternal colonization with *Staphylococcus aureus* and the use of antibiotics during pregnancy were linked to an increased risk of asthma during the fifth year of life. The presence of *S. aureus* in the stool flora has been related to the appearance of allergic disease.[175;176] The appearance of staphylococci among the gut bacteria is regarded as a sign of a disturbed microflora. In agreement with the Hygiene hypothesis, a large study from Brazil suggested that there was a significant link between increased risk for asthma in adolescents and high socioeconomic status, living in an uncrowded household, and being breastfed for 9 months or longer.[177] This can be assumed to show that the risk for asthma increases with decreased exposure to a normal bacterial flora in early life due to hygienic measures applied in a well-to-do group. In that situation, breastfeeding may not have the capacity to protect against asthma or may even contribute to it as discussed below.

In agreement with the Hygiene hypothesis, the use of broad-spectrum antibiotics in babies, which affect the gut microflora, has been linked to an increased risk of allergy in some studies. Recently, studies have found this link to be doubtful.[178;179] The link may have been due to reverse causation: the tendency to seek more medical help and to be prescribed antibiotics more often in the presence of allergic disease.

One might consider that caesarean section interferes with the normal bacterial colonization of the newborn. Its effect on the development of allergy has been studied and it has been shown that the procedures increase the risk of allergy.[180-183]

During the first year, the continuous exposure to cats decreases the risk of developing asthma.[184] This may be due to increased exposure to bacteria from cat stools. It may also be due to the fact that a cat allergen, like endotoxin, binds to CD14 and induces production of the pro-inflammatory cytokines IL-1β, TNF-α, and IL-6 from monocytes.[185] Although the cat allergen does not seem to bind the TLR–2 and -4 receptors, it may be that this kind of stimulation of innate immunity serves to induce potentially protective regulatory T cells (Treg).[185] It is of some interest that human milk contains a large amount of CD14.[186] These various observations illustrate that many factors determine whether a child develops allergy and that breastfeeding can play many roles in this process. This will be further discussed below.

> According to the Hygiene hypothesis, early colonization of the infant's gut with a normal bacterial flora helps the infant become immunologically tolerant to allergens so that it does not react against them. Gram negative bacteria may be especially important for the education of the immune system in early life. Normally, there should be no harmful immune response against food, pollen, mites, etc., thanks to this immunological tolerance, but only protective immune responses against microbes which may cause infections. By erroneous hygienic measures at delivery and afterwards, infants are prevented from picking up a normal bacterial flora. This could be one important factor behind the drastic increase in allergic diseases in many current societies.

A relationship has been demonstrated between serum IgE levels in the mother and the child.[187] Breastfeeding mothers with low serum IgE levels had children who at the age of 6 years had lower serum IgE than children who had never been breastfed. A child who had been breastfed for 4 months or longer by a mother with a high IgE concentration had more IgE than those not breastfed, or those breastfed for less than 4 months. Experimental studies have shown similar results.[188;189] This illustrates still another factor that complicates the relationship between mother and child when discussing allergy. It makes us see the multiplicity and complexity of factors that influence whether a baby develop allergies and what role the mother may play.

Review of studies investigating whether breastfeeding protects against various forms of allergic diseases

It is difficult to define the exact role of breastfeeding as a single factor in the protection against various forms of allergic disease. The development of allergic diseases is dependent on genetics (allergic diseases in the family) and age, as well as form and dose of allergen at initial and subsequent exposures, and the infant's capacity to become immunologically tolerant to foods, pollen, and other allergens as discussed above.

A meta-analysis of whether or not breastfeeding protects against atopic eczema in infants showed a positive effect in those with a family history of atopy. There was less effect in the general population. The effect was negligible among those infants without first order atopic relatives.[190] A Japanese study using questionnaires suggested an increased risk for atopic eczema among adolescents without a family history of allergy who had been breastfed.[191] Their prevalence of wheeze and allergic rhino-conjunctivitis (hayfever) was not affected by mode of early feeding. However, the method of feeding was recalled long after it happened. It should be noted that wheezing in early life is often a symptom of lower respiratory infection. Later in life, wheezing is usually linked to asthma.

At 2 years of age, a large group of Swedish children had less atopic dermatitis if they had been exclusively breastfed for 4 months.[192] A Danish investigation of 15,430 mother-infant pairs suggested that current breastfeeding was not linked to the appearance of atopic dermatitis.[193] Interestingly, exclusive breastfeeding for at least 4 months was related to an increased risk of dermatitis if no parent was allergic, but not if one or both of the parents were allergic. With both parents having allergy and a sibling with atopic dermatitis, breastfeeding was protective. German children had more atopic eczema if there was parental eczema. Breastfeeding was longer in that group. Each additional month of breastfeeding added to the prevalence of the child to develop eczema.[194] However, many of these infants received formula during the first days of life. Finnish children with atopic heredity had long-term protection from breastfeeding, whereas those without a family history showed the reverse.[195] Infants with atopic diseases in the family were reported in a large German study to have had a reduced risk for developing eczema at 1 year of age if they had been breastfed exclusively for 4 months, compared with a partially or fully formula fed group (OR=0.47,95% CI 0.30-0.74).[196] In the large study by Kramer et al in Belarus, the participants were randomized as to breastfeeding promotion.[1] The prevalence of eczema was ½ – ¼ of that in the German study and significant reduction of eczema was obtained in the group where breastfeeding was promoted. When comparing infants exclusively breastfed for 3 months with those exclusively breastfed for 6 months, there was no difference in the prevalence of eczema.[65]

Recently, another large, well controlled study showed that exclusive breastfeeding was not associated with an increased risk of atopic dermatitis even if there was a family history of the disease.[314] It was proposed that such findings previously were due to reverse causation in observational studies. Instead, the authors in this study found exclusive breastfeeding to protect against atopic dermatitis with an adjusted OR of 0.64 (95% CI 0.45-0.90) regardless of family history.

> Some studies seem to indicate that breastfeeding reduces the risk of developing atopic eczema, but the effect was small or absent. Allergies in the family increased the risk in some studies and decreased it in others. A recent, well controlled study suggests that some findings may be due to reverse causation in observational studies and that there could be significant protection whether or not there is a family history of eczema.

There are numerous studies of the possible effects of breastfeeding on the appearance of wheezing and asthma in the offspring. In a 4 year follow up of 4,089 Swedish children, it was found that exclusive breastfeeding for 4 months or more reduced the risk of asthma with an OR of 0.72 (95%

CI 0.53-0.97). This was unaffected by sensitization to airborne allergens shown by skin tests reflecting the presence of IgE antibodies.[197] If children with wheezing were excluded, the risk estimate was further reduced with OR= 0.64 (0.46-0.88). Exclusive breastfeeding for 3-4 months followed by partial breastfeeding for 3 months or more gave an OR of 0.44 (95% CI 0.21-0.87). In this study, there was no obvious interaction between breastfeeding and heredity for asthma.

A systematic meta-analysis based on 12 studies showed that exclusive breastfeeding during the first months of life resulted in lower rates of asthma during childhood.[198] A critical review of all studies on breastfeeding and allergy during 1966-2001 analyzed 132 in detail.[199] Of these, 56 were regarded as conclusive. The conclusion was that breastfeeding seems to protect against allergic diseases with a stronger effect in children with atopic disease in the family. Using cow's milk proteins which are degraded or hydrolyzed so extensively that the immune system no longer recognizes them is a way to avoid allergic reactions in CMP-allergic infants. Giving extensively hydrolyzed formula instead of un-hydrolyzed or partially hydrolyzed formula seemed preferable for decreasing the risk of attracting allergic symptoms if mother's milk was unavailable or insufficient.

A large prospective study in New Zealand showed that among those who had been breastfed initially, there was more asthma and a higher presence of IgE antibodies by skin test against cats, mites, and grass pollen in individuals between the ages of 9-26 years. This was unrelated to parental history of hay fever or asthma.[200] This study has been greatly debated. Among other aspects, it has been mentioned that extra nightly formula feeds were given to the newborns to let the mother sleep and that the attitudes towards breastfeeding at that time were unsupportive. Thus, breastfeeding was only permitted for a limited time at certain hours. The mother and newborn were separated outside of feeding times. The breastfeeding recorded may not have been optimal. The data on breastfeeding was documented retrospectively at the age of 3 years and the information about allergy in the family was deficient. These and other problems with definitions and variables involved in such studies have recently been discussed.[201]

A recent review of breastfeeding, asthma, and atopic diseases using the strict criteria of Kramer concentrated on prospective studies.[148;202] This report by Oddy and Peat is helpful because of its critical approach and careful analysis of the difficulties involved in studies of such a complex group of diseases in growing individuals. Children have a continuously developing immune system which is the mediator of the various patterns of the allergic diseases. Summarizing the adequate population and cohort studies remaining after review, the ORs were in agreement with a limited positive effect in the range of 1.2 – 1.5. The disagreements found in the rather extensive literature related to that different aspects of allergic diseases had been studied using different modes of measuring the outcomes. A meta-analysis for children breastfed for at least 3 months gave an estimated OR of 0.80 (95% CI, 0.66-0.97). For those breastfed for less than 3 months, an increased OR of 1.25 was obtained (95% CI, 1.03-1.52). An increased risk of 1.2-1.3 was obtained for breastfeeding for less than 4 months compared to 4 months or more. Even the relatively weak protective effects may be of public health importance since breastfeeding is such a frequently used mode of feeding and many of the allergic diseases studied are very common and seem to be becoming even more common. Asthma now occurs in more than 30% of children in some areas.[146]

Critically reviewing prospective studies of breastfeeding in children with a family history of asthma, Oddy and Peat found 5 investigations meeting the criteria. Variable outcomes were noted which agrees with other recent reports. Some authors found that the breastfed child was at an increased risk of developing the different atopic diseases if the parents were not atopic, but were protected if the parents were atopic.[193;195] A report on breastfeeding and atopic eczema showed the reverse.[194] The outcome of children's asthma or recurrent wheeze in relation to breastfeeding varied with the mother's status as to asthma and the age of the child. Breastfeeding protected against recurrent wheeze in early life, but was related to an increased risk of recurrent wheeze and asthma after the age of 6 years, but only in atopic children who had asthmatic mothers.[203] Such differing observations may have several explanations. The definition of the disease states studied is important and the various atopic diseases differ in many respects. Thus, wheezing can be caused by infection or can be part of asthmatic disease. This relationship changes with age.[143]

Numerous studies have investigated whether breastfeeding protects against asthma. Recent critical reviews have indicated that breastfeeding may be protective, although at a low level. Since breastfeeding is so common in many societies and asthma is becoming such a common disease, this limited, positive effect is of public health importance. A family history of allergic disease makes breastfeeding have quite variable effects on asthma as well as eczema in different studies.

Nutrients, breastfeeding, and allergic diseases

Another aspect of allergic diseases is the effect of Body Mass Index (BMI). In a study of 12-year-old Swedish children, current wheeze and high Body Mass Index (BMI) were significantly linked after adjusting for confounders.[204] Asthma severity and presence of eczema, but not hay fever, were also linked to a high BMI. Breastfeeding may help prevent obesity as discussed in Chapter 6.

The ratio of n-6/n-3 long chain polyunsaturated fatty acid in human milk varies. It is lower in milk from Australian mothers compared to European mothers.[205] Low levels of n-3 fatty acids have been found in milk and were linked to the development of atopy in children.[206-208] On the other hand, there was no difference between the levels of n-6 and n-3 long chain fatty acids in the milk from mothers with or without allergy.[209] Another investigation noted a significant positive association between TGF-β2 in milk and the proportion of polyunsaturated fatty acids and a negative association between TGF-β2 and saturated fatty acids.[210] The mothers with atopic dermatitis had less TGF-β2 in their milk. This cytokine normally enhances the development of the SIgA antibodies which may protect mucosal membranes in the breastfed infant. SIgA also protects against the uptake of un-degraded proteins. A recent report showed that supplementation with fish oil, rich in n-3 fatty acids, tended to reduce allergy in the breastfed offspring.[211]

In an experimental model in rats, we gave mother rats a diet varying in the ratio between n-6/n-3 fatty acids from late pregnancy through lactation. During early lactation, we gave the mother rats ovalbumin to drink so that the offspring would be exposed to this foreign food protein via the milk. We found in a first study that the offspring of the mother rats that were given diets that differed in the content of essential fatty acids also differed in their reaction to the food protein they were exposed via the milk. In a second study we could confirm that the essential factor was the ratio of n-6/n-3 fatty acids in the mother's diet. With a ratio of 9 which is common in many diets today the offspring did not become tolerant. Those whose mothers obtained a diet with an n-6/n-3 ratio below 1, became tolerant. The offspring developing tolerance to the foreign protein responded with significantly less IgG, IgM and IgE antibodies and T cells than the offspring of the mothers given the higher ratio of n-6/n-3 fatty acids.[212;213] The tolerance was due to production of TGF-β shown in local lymph glands. But another mechanism of tolerance, presumably due to elimination of specifically responding T lymphocytes, so called anergy, was also noted. These observations agree with the low n-6/n-3 ratio in milk from Australian mothers and the protection seen against allergy by breastfeeding in a well controlled Australian study.[214]

Another confounding factor may be that smoking affects the airways of children exposed to smoke. It seems as if breastfeeding would protect against the adverse effects of smoking, including increased risk of respiratory tract infections and wheezing.[215;216]

In atopic families, mothers have tried to adhere to a strict diet that avoids common food allergens during late pregnancy.[217] A 5 year follow up did not show any effect. The same diet applied during the first 3 months of lactation did diminish the appearance of atopic dermatitis in the babies.[218] This effect remained at the age of 4 years.[219] Another similar large prophylaxis study using a diet during the third trimester of pregnancy and through lactation gave a significant reduction of atopic dermatitis, urticaria and/or gastrointestinal disease during the first year of life.[220] At 2 years of age, the prevalence of allergic rhinitis, asthma, and positive skin tests to inhalant allergens were unaffected. A recent critical Cochrane analysis applying the rules of scrutiny of "evidence-based medicine" summarized that an antigen avoidance diet eaten by high-risk women during pregnancy is unlikely to protect her baby from atopic disease. Antigen avoidance diets during lactation may decrease the risk for her baby to attract atopic eczema but better studies are needed.[221]

In conclusion:

Allergic disease makes up a group of conditions caused by a deficient control of the immune system so that individuals with a certain genetic background erroneously produce IgE antibodies against food, pollen, mites, etc. Such antibodies induce a special inflammation at the site where they come in contact with their antigen which may be in the skin, the gut, the nose, the eyes, or the respiratory tract. It seems that if the infant is not colonized with the proper microbes in the gut from delivery on (see Chapter 1), then the infant's immune system is not educated to develop the capacity to become immunologically tolerant to foods, pollen, mites, etc. The child should not react against such harmless materials.

Allergic diseases, which mostly start in childhood, are becoming increasingly common in many societies. These diseases are no longer restricted to well-to-do communities as it seemed initially.

The role of breastfeeding in the prevention or, in some instances, the promotion of allergic diseases is very complex due to the large number of components in the milk which can affect the immune system of the infant.

The evidence that breastfeeding may prevent early food allergy is somewhat conflicting. As to the effect on atopic eczema or dermatitis, the outcome is quite variable in different studies. Some show protection, a few show weak protection, and some no protection. With allergy in the family, breastfeeding protects in some analyses and promotes in others. A recent critical study suggests that some of the confusion may be due to observational studies which cannot detect the protection they could show. As for asthma, it seems that there is a protective effect by breastfeeding which is rather weak but of public health importance since asthma is becoming such a common disease and breastfeeding is so widely practiced. Again, with allergy in the family, the effect becomes more complex with some studies indicating protection.

The intake of unsaturated fatty acids by the mother and specifically the ratio between n-6/n-3 fatty acids may be important. This is

supported by animal studies. It seems that a high BMI correlates with the incidence of asthma. This is interesting because breastfeeding may protect against obesity as described in Chapter 6.

Breastfeeding, autoimmune, and other inflammatory diseases

Breastfeeding may reduce the risk of developing type 1 diabetes according to some studies.[97;222;223] An additional investigation suggested that after adjustment for possible confounding factors like birth year, maternal age, socioeconomic situation, sex, and race, breastfeeding was protective as compared to controls with an OR of 0.70.[224] Breastfeeding for more than 12 months reduced the risk of insulin-dependent diabetes even further with an OR of 0.54.

Exclusive breastfeeding for 2-3 months was reported to significantly reduce the risk of developing juvenile diabetes in Finnish studies. The risk was less if supplementary feeding was not introduced until the infants were 4 months or older.[225;226] This form of protection is proposed to be more important in children genetically predisposed to type 1 diabetes.[227] Such an effect may be due to breastfeeding limiting the exposure to a cow's milk peptide which triggers type 1 diabetes.[228]

Formation of auto-antibodies against the insulin-producing β–cells in the pancreas islets has been considered a likely important mechanism behind type1 diabetes. Reduced exclusive breastfeeding did not increase the risk of producing such auto-antibodies, but food supplementation with gluten-containing food significantly enhanced that risk.[229] Other studies disagree and it is still being debated whether or not early introduction of cow's milk or gluten plays any role in the risk of attracting type 1 diabetes.[230;231]

Non-insulin dependent diabetes and obesity is very common among Pima Indians. Exclusive breastfeeding for 2 months reduced their risk of diabetes with an OR of 0.41 (CI 0.18-0.93).[232] Obesity was also reduced. However, the very long recall of the mothers as to the history of breastfeeding is a problem in that study. A study of limited size of type 2 diabetics among Canadian natives showed significant protection by breastfeeding greater than 12 months with an OR of 0.24 (95% CI 0.13-0.99).[233]

A few studies suggest that breastfeeding may protect against multiple sclerosis and rheumatoid arthritis.[234;235] These observations need confirmation. A recent retrospective study of rheumatoid arthritis showed that initiation of breastfeeding was among the perinatal factors influencing the risk of contracting the disease.[236] The protective effect gave an OR of 0.2 (95% CI 0.1-0.7).

It has also been proposed in three out of eight studies that breastfeeding may prevent Crohn's disease.[237-239] Similarly, three out of eight studies of ulcerative colitis suggest protection by breastfeeding.[239-241] It is not easy to produce conclusive results with such relatively uncommon diseases where many factors may be involved. The incidence of colitis appearing in IL-10 deficient mice was reduced by foster feeding by normal mothers producing IL-10.[242] This cytokine, which is present in human milk, is efficiently anti-inflammatory. On the other hand, this mechanism does not explain the long term effects of breastfeeding. Chapter 5 gives examples of numerous additional factors in human milk which can have long lasting effects on the immune system of the offspring. Clearly more studies are needed both at the experimental and the clinical levels.

It was suggested that celiac disease was more frequent in children who had been breastfed for a shorter period than the controls.[243;244] Other studies did not agree with this.[245;246] More support for protection by breastfeeding was presented in two interesting studies.[247;248] In one of these, there was evidence that protection may be attained if gluten was introduced during breastfeeding possibly optimizing the protective effect.[248]

It may be that breastfeeding protects against symptomatic celiac disease, but not asymptomatic. This may explain the findings of another study of siblings of children with celiac disease who carried the genes DQAI#0501-DQBI#02 which increase susceptibility to the disease.[249] Diagnosing their silent celiac disease not on symptoms but on food recording, small intestinal biopsy, and interviews revealed no relation to the duration of breastfeeding or age at introduction of cow's milk or gluten. Also, we do not know how long breastfeeding may protect against symptomatic celiac disease, which is life long.

There is evidence that introduction of gluten during breastfeeding prevents symptomatic celiac disease during childhood.

We now know that celiac disease is initiated by an autoimmune reaction against the enzyme transglutaminase.[250] The cases with the typical gastrointestinal problems are becoming less common while less typical patterns are more prevalent with neurological symptoms, gastrointestinal and hematological cancers, secondary autoimmune diseases, etc.[250]

In conclusion:

Some studies suggest that breastfeeding may protect against type 1 and type 2 diabetes but further confirmation is needed. This is also true for the reports suggesting that breastfeeding may protect against other autoimmune diseases like multiple sclerosis and rheumatoid arthritis. Confirmation is also required for a few similar studies concerning ulcerative colitis and Crohn's disease.

One interesting study shows that introduction of gluten during breastfeeding may decrease the risk of symptomatic celiac disease.

Breastfeeding, obesity, and other metabolic conditions

It has been proposed that breastfeeding may have effects on metabolic conditions. This appears especially in studies showing that breastfeeding may have long-term preventive effects on obesity into adolescence.[251-256] The risk of obesity was decreased by breastfeeding with adjusted ORs of 0.75-0.84 in several large studies.[252;253] Increased duration of breastfeeding predicted lower rates of future obesity. One of the large studies following children from 6-14 years showed a continued protective effect of breastfeeding in a socio-economically homogenous population suggesting that there was no confounding by socio-economic status.[255] The OR for breastfeeding protecting against overweight was 0.80 (95% CI, 0.71-0.90) and for breastfeeding and obesity was 0.80 (95% CI. 0.66-0.96). In a large representative group of Swedish adolescents, a higher BMI was significantly related to exclusive breastfeeding for less than 3 months ($p<0.04$).[257]

A large study from the USA confirmed that breastfeeding in non-Hispanic white children followed up to 4 years of age decreased the risk of becoming obese with an adjusted OR of 0.70 (95% CI, 0.50-0.99) compared to those breastfed for 6-12 months with no breastfeeding.[258] No such association was found among Hispanics and non-Hispanic blacks. In a sizable longitudinal birth cohort study, breastfeeding for more than 3 months was studied as to its effect on overweight and obesity at the age of 6 years. There was one group with no breastfeeding or breastfeeding for less than 3 months named BO and another group with breastfeeding for more than 3 months named BF.[259] At 3 months of age, there was already a significantly higher BMI in the BO group. Comparing the BO infants to the BF infants at 6 months of age, the former had consistently higher proportions of BMI above the 90th and 97th percentile. From the age of 4 to 6 years, the prevalence of obesity almost tripled in the BO group. The difference in BMI and skin fold thickness between the two groups became significant. The important risk factors for obesity at the age of 6 years were bottle-feeding, a maternal BMI above 27, maternal smoking during pregnancy, and low social status. Early bottle-feeding predicted later obesity.

Other recent studies from Brazil and the UK have not confirmed that breastfeeding can prevent obesity into adolescence and adulthood.[260-262] A recent editorial lists a number of problems with many of the reviewed studies. They are often retrospective and lack a priory hypothesis. In many instances, there is a long recall for the data on breastfeeding which is also often poorly defined as to exclusivity and duration.[263]

> There is evidence from several large studies that breastfeeding prevents obesity in childhood and adolescence at least in white populations. However, recently discordant studies of effects into adolescence and adulthood have been published.

The proposed link between breastfeeding and prevention of obesity could have many explanations. For instance, breastfeeding affects insulin production which can have effects on long-term energy metabolism.[264;265] Cytokines present in milk can influence insulin levels since IL-1β can inhibit insulin production while TNF-α may block insulin receptors.[266-268] IL-6 increases release of insulin, cortisol, and glucagon as well as oxidation of glucose and fatty acids.[269-271]

Another milk component that can be important in this connection is leptin which is a hormone of cytokine structure. It regulates appetite as discussed in Chapter 5 and is found in higher concentration in breastfed than formula-fed infants. Some of the leptin may come from mother's milk.[272] In a rat model, we found that we could modify the leptin levels in rat offspring by changing the n-6/n-3 fatty acid levels in the maternal diet.[273] With a low ratio of n-6/n-3 in the mother's diet, the leptin levels in the offspring were lower than in those whose mothers had had a higher ratio in their diet. However, it may be that the leptin levels in the milk is of no importance for appetite regulation in the offspring.[274-276]

Leptin is present in milk fat globules and mammary gland epithelial cells and is produced by fat cells.[277] The pro-inflammatory cytokines IL-1β, TNF-α, and IL-6 increase during infections and make blood leptin increase. This is one reason that it is common to loose your appetite during infections and why repeated or long term infections may cause undernutrition. Leptin has further links to the immune system and is considered to enhance reactivity of Th1 lymphocytes which reflect cell-mediated immunity (Figure 5). Leptin levels are low during starvation. Leptin levels in the thymus are also low during starvation. The thymus and lymph glands get smaller during starvation and cell-mediated immunity is impaired. In starved animals, the sensitivity to septic shock is increased with exposure to LPS and TNF-α as important factors. Leptin counteracts this sensitivity.[278] Thus, it is possible that the leptin in milk supports the immune system of the breastfed baby.

There have been suggestions that breastfeeding may reduce blood pressure in later life. This was claimed on the basis of a randomized prospective follow up of premature infants, controlling for several confounding factors.[279] Recently, a systematic review and meta-analysis indicated that breastfeeding, at most, has a modest effect on blood pressure. This effect is of limited public health importance.[280] It may be that prolonged breastfeeding can have a protective effect.[281]

There is also data to indicate that breastfeeding increases serum total cholesterol and low-density lipoproteins in infancy, but lowers them in adult life.[282] An interesting report studied the effect in adolescence of banked breastmilk or formula on premature infants. At the age of 13-16 years, the breastfed group showed a significantly lower ratio of low to high density lipoproteins and other parameters suggesting long term benefits of human milk on risk factors for arteriosclerosis.[283] One study indicated that breastfeeding is related to decreased arterial distensibility in adult life.[282]

In conclusion:

Several large investigations provide evidence that breastfeeding may prevent obesity. Some studies have followed the participants through adolescence. Many factors in milk may be involved in preventing obesity. One factor may be the appetite-regulating hormone leptin. Recent studies do not confirm a protective effect against obesity into adolescence and adulthood. Several of these studies have been questioned. There is some evidence that breastfeeding may reduce the ratio of low to high density lipoproteins and may modestly reduce blood pressure in later life.

Breastfeeding and tumors

There are many factors involved in whether a child will contract a malignant disease. It becomes very difficult to determine the possible role of one factor like breastfeeding which contains many components with possible relevant effects. Davis recently reviewed several case-control studies which have suggested that there may be an increased risk of childhood cancers in relation to artificial feeding.[284] Other investigations do not confirm this. Important determinants of effect, like the duration or extent of breastfeeding, were often not included. In the positive reports, the significant ORs for all cancers ranged from 1.75 (1.08-2.83) to 7.0 (3.6-13.5).[284;285] Three studies of Hodgkin's disease showed effects from 1.47 (1.06-2.0) to 2.5 ($p=0.02$).[286;287] Only one report showed protection against non-Hodgkin lymphoma with an OR of 6.8 (1.0-59.0).[287] The ORs given for acute leukemia were 1.27 (1.09-1.43) and 9.2 (3.1-28.1).[287-289] A recent analysis of acute lymphoblastic and acute myeloblastic leukemia in children did not show any protective effect of breastfeeding.[290]

> Some studies suggest that breastfeeding protects against malignancies in children including Hodgkin's disease, Hodgkin's lymphoma, and acute leukemia. Other studies do not confirm this. One of the major milk proteins, α-lactalbumin, can take a form called HAMLET which can kill various tumor cells as discussed in Chapter 5.

Breastfeeding reduces the risk of breast cancer. Mothers who breastfed more than 3 children had a 50% reduction in the risk of getting breast cancer compared to controls who had never breastfed. Mothers who breastfed their first child for more than 13 months had the same reduction.[291] A critical review of a large number of studies from many countries showed that in addition to the 7% reduction in breast cancer induced by each pregnancy, there is a 4.3% reduction for each year of breastfeeding. This effect of breastfeeding is present in developed as well as developing countries and in various ethnic groups.[292] A recent study of Mormon women showed that high parity and breastfeeding was linked to comparatively low breast cancer incidence rates.[293]

> Breastfeeding significantly protects against breast cancer.

One of the major milk proteins, α-lactalbumin, may turn into another form called HAMLET (human α–lactalbumin made lethal to tumor cells) as described in Chapter 5. It is possible, but not yet studied, that this structure from human milk which has been shown to destroy many forms of human malignancies plays a role in the prevention of tumors in the mammary glands and in the gut of the infant. It may be of interest that ⅔ of the whole immune system is present in the intestine and that the fast turnover of lymphoid and other cells in the gut adds to the risk that some cells may become malignant.

In conclusion:

There is some evidence, although, not fully convincing, that breastfeeding may prevent cancers like leukemia and Hodgkin's disease in children. Breastfeeding has a significant preventive effect on breast cancer.

Recently a milk protein, α-lactalbumin, has been found to have the capacity to take another form, named HAMLET, which has anti-tumor activity. It is still not known whether it can prevent breast cancer and tumors in children.

Mechanisms behind possible long term effects of breastfeeding

Besides antibodies, milk has been shown to contain anti-antibodies described in Chapter 6 and shown in Figure 15. Such anti-antibodies, or anti-idiotypes, can induce production of antibodies. They have been demonstrated in human milk.[134] In neonatal animals, such anti-antibodies given via the mother's milk enhanced antibody responses to a bacterial polysaccharide capsule and to a virus.[294;295] There is evidence in man that breastfeeding may enhance vaccine responses. The transfer of anti-antibodies via the milk could be one explanation for such enhanced vaccine response.[122]

> Anti-antibodies, shown in Figure 15, are present in human milk and can stimulate the immune system of the offspring to respond more efficiently to vaccines and, probably, to infectious agents.

Another possible form of immunologically specific effects of milk components on the infant's immune system may be the transfer of lymphocytes carrying immunological capacities from the mother. There is much experimental evidence that this happens both in experimental animals and in man, as was reviewed in Chapter 5. It seems very surprising that immunologically active cells like lymphocytes from another individual and like T and B lymphocytes in the milk from the mother are absorbed by the baby. Still, this seems to happen. It may offer a way to transfer immunological capacity to the offspring potentially enhancing immune responses to infecting microbes as well as against vaccines. This is supported by animal experiments that show that radioactive isotope-labeled human colostral cells given to premature baboons resulted in radioactivity in the gut mucosa, spleen, and liver.[296] Human milk cells were infused into human fetal small intestine that had been transplanted into nude mice who lack an immune system and cannot reject the human tissue. Most of the milk cells were found in the gut wall 20-72 hours later.[297] A few of the cells were present intact in the spleen and lungs. The transfer experiment in sheep, mentioned in Chapter 5, showed that the milk cells from a vaccinated mother sheep transferred to the lamb. This transfer resulted in a better vaccine response when vaccinating the lamb.[298]

The transfer of tuberculin sensitivity via the milk, suggested by some studies, would also agree with an uptake of maternal T lymphocytes from the milk.[299;300] The T lymphocytes in human milk twice as often carry the Tγδ rcccptor as T cells from the peripheral blood. The milk from tuberculin-positive mothers had higher specific responses among their Tγδ lymphocytes than those from tuberculin-negative mothers.[301] The animal experiments showing a transfer of antibody-producing B lymphocytes via the milk support the possibility of transfer of specific immunological capacity via the milk.[302]

As reviewed in Chapter 5, the appearance of tolerance to the mother's HLA antigen, or tissue type, after breastfeeding is another reason to believe that maternal milk cells are absorbed and may induce this tolerance. That a kidney allograft from a mother to her offspring survives and functions better if the offspring has been breastfed supports this concept.[303] It also agrees with the finding that breastfeeding decreased the number of lymphocytes directed against the maternal HLA.[304]

> Quite surprisingly, T and B lymphocytes present in milk seem to be absorbed by the offspring judging from various animal experiments. The studies suggest that, in this way, capacity to respond with the immune system may be transferred to the offspring.

Thus, anti-antibodies and T as well as B lymphocytes may be transferred via the milk supporting, in an immunologically specific manner, the immune system of the breastfed infant. There are numerous additional factors in milk which may non-specifically enhance the immunological capacity of the offspring. The milk contains numerous cytokines, growth factors, and hormones many of which may have effects on the immune system (Tables 6 and 7). The appetite-regulating hormone leptin has a broad influence which also effects the immune system including the thymus and the T lymphocytes (Chapter 5).

The effects can be more specific like that of IFN-γ in milk. This cytokine may be responsible for the observation that breastfeeding selectively increases the production of IgG2 antibodies against the polysaccharide capsule of *H. influenzae* type b (Hib) bacteria.[140] The cytokine IFN-γ selectively supports the production of IgG2 antibodies. The IgG2 antibodies provide optimal protection against this microbe which can cause severe invasive infections in children. Such activity of the IFN-γ in the milk may explain why children 18 months or older showed a significant relation between the duration of exclusive breastfeeding and the level of IgG2 antibodies against the Hib polysaccharide, the critical component of Hib vaccines.[141]

Breastfed infants have been reported to express surface markers on their lymphocytes not shown on the lymphocytes of non-breastfed infants. This is also noted after vaccination of breast- and formula-fed infants.[305] It seems that breastfeeding enhances Th1 type immune responses (Chapter 2, Figure 5).

The striking expansion of the size of the thymus in response to breastfeeding, discussed in Chapter 5, is probably mediated by the IL-7 present in milk, possibly in cooperation with other cytokines like IL-2.[306;307] Directly related to the size of the thymus is the number of T lymphocytes in the blood of the baby.[308] Thus, it seems that breastfeeding results in a larger thymus which may directly support a more capable immune system. Also, the leptin present in milk may play a role by stimulating the proliferation and survival of T cells in the thymus.[309] The regulatory T lymphocytes (Treg) which control and down-regulate autoimmune and allergic reactivity come from the thymus in early life. Removing the thymus in rodents in early life before these cells had left the thymus, strikingly inhibited the capacity of the rodents to become tolerant to their own tissues.[310;311] Against this background, it is possible that breastfeeding enhances the development and expansion of the thymus. This may help protect against the appearance of autoimmune diseases and may affect the appearance of allergic diseases as discussed in this chapter.

The nucleotides present in human milk may enhance vaccine responses and stimulate the killer cell activity of NK cells.[124;312;313]

> Human milk contains numerous signals like cytokines, hormones, growth factors, etc., which may have short and long term effects on the immune system of the breastfed baby. One example is that the thymus, the central organ of the immune system, expands to twice its size in exclusively breastfed babies compared to non-breastfed babies. As a result, breastfed babies have more blood T lymphocytes presumably coming from the larger thymus. It is likely that these mechanisms give the breastfed infant a larger, more efficient immune system.

In conclusion:

There are some findings which suggest that breastfeeding may have long term stimulating effects on the immune system of the baby. These effects include enhancement of some vaccine responses and improved protection against certain infections that continue after the termination of breastfeeding. This can be partly explained by the observation that anti-antibodies (Figure 15) are transferred via the milk and may enhance the responsiveness of the immune system of the baby.

Similar effects may appear from the surprising capacity of offspring in various experimental models to absorb lymphocytes from their mother's milk. The immune system usually eliminates foreign cells as potentially dangerous, but breastfed babies develop tolerance towards the mother's tissue type, or HLA, which seems to permit them to absorb maternal lymphocytes from the milk. In experimental models, such cells have been shown to stimulate the immune response of the offspring. Their eventual role in man is not yet known.

Further, milk contains numerous signals from the mother which can act on the baby's immune system with short and long term effects. These signals include cytokines, hormones, growth factors, etc. One or more of those seem to explain how the breastfed baby can have a much larger thymus and more T lymphocytes in the circulation than the non-breastfed baby.

Some of these many components with immunological capacities in milk may be involved in the suggested effects of breastfeeding on certain allergic diseases, autoimmune and inflammatory diseases, and metabolic conditions like obesity.

Reference List

1. Kramer MS, Chalmers B, Hodnett ED, et al: Promotion of Breastfeeding Intervention Trial (PROBIT): a randomized trial in the Republic of Belarus. JAMA 285:413-420, 2001

2. Costello A, White H: Reducing global inequalities in child health. Arch Dis Child 84:98-102, 2001

3. Rosa FW: Breast feeding in family planning. PAG Bull 5-10, 1975

4. Labbok MH, Hight-Laukaran V, Peterson AE, et al: Multicenter study of the Lactational Amenorrhea Method (LAM): I. Efficacy, duration, and implications for clinical application. Contraception 55:327-336, 1997

5. Aaby P, Bukh J, Lisse IM, et al: Overcrowding and intensive exposure as determinants of measles mortality. Am J Epidemiol 120:49-63, 1984

6. Hobcraft JN, McDonal JW, Rutstein SO: Demographic determinants of infant and early child mortality: A comparative analysis. Population Studies 363-385, 1985

7. Reves R: Declining fertility in England and Wales as a major cause of the twentieth century decline in mortality. The role of changing family size and age structure in infectious disease mortality in infancy. Am J Epidemiol 122:112-126, 1985

8. Hanson LA, Ashraf R, Zaman S, et al: Breast feeding is a natural contraceptive and prevents disease and death in infants, linking infant mortality and birth rates. Acta Paediatr 83:3-6, 1994

9. Hanson LA, Bergstrom S: The link between infant mortality and birth rates--the importance of breastfeeding as a common factor. Acta Paediatr Scand 79:481-489, 1990

10. WHO: Breastfeeding, Science and Society. Pontific Acad Scient Doc 28:1-33, 1996

11. Ashraf RN, Jalil F, Zaman S, et al: Breast feeding and protection against neonatal sepsis in a high risk population. Arch Dis Child 66:488-490, 1991

12. Khan SR, Jalil F, Zaman S, et al: Early child health in Lahore, Pakistan: X. Mortality. Acta Paediatr Suppl 82 Suppl 390:109-117, 1993

13. Bhutta ZA, Yusuf K: Neonatal sepsis in Karachi: factors determining outcome and mortality. J Trop Pediatr 43:65-70, 1997

14. Hanson LA, Korotkova M, Telemo E: Human milk, its components and their immunobiological function, in J Mestecky JB, Lamm ME, Mayer L, et al (eds): Mucosal Immunology. 3rd Edition. San Diego, Academic Press, 2004 (In press)

15. Feachem RG, Koblinsky MA: Interventions for the control of diarrhoeal diseases among young children: promotion of breast-feeding. Bull World Health Organ 62:271-291, 1984

16. Victora CG, Smith PG, Vaughan JP, et al: Evidence for protection by breast-feeding against infant deaths from infectious diseases in Brazil. Lancet 2:319-322, 1987

17. Lepage P, Munyakazi C, Hennart P: Breastfeeding and hospital mortality in children in Rwanda. Lancet 2:409-411, 1981

18. Habicht JP, DaVanzo J, Butz WP: Does breastfeeding really save lives, or are apparent benefits due to biases? Am J Epidemiol 123:279-290, 1986

19. Zaman S, Jalil F, Karlberg J: Early child health in Lahore, Pakistan: IV. Child care practices. Acta Paediatr Suppl 82 Suppl 390:39-46, 1993

20. Sazawal S, Bhan MK, Bhandari N: Type of milk feeding during acute diarrhoea and the risk of persistent diarrhoea: a case control study. Acta Paediatr Suppl 381:93-97, 1992

21. Victora CG, Huttly SR, Fuchs SC, et al: Deaths due to dysentery, acute and persistent diarrhoea among Brazilian infants. Acta Paediatr Suppl 381:7-11, 1992

22. Huffman SL, Zehner ER, Victora C: Can improvements in breast-feeding practices reduce neonatal mortality in developing countries? Midwifery 17:80-92, 2001

23. Arifeen S, Black RE, Antelman G, et al: Exclusive breastfeeding reduces acute respiratory infection and diarrhea deaths among infants in Dhaka slums. Pediatrics 108:E67, 2001

24. WHO: Effect of breastfeeding on infant and child mortality due to infectious diseases in less developed countries: a pooled analysis. WHO Collaborative Study Team on the Role of Breastfeeding on the Prevention of Infant Mortality. Lancet 355:451-455, 2000

25. Betran AP, de Onis M, Lauer JA, et al: Ecological study of effect of breast feeding on infant mortality in Latin America. BMJ 323:303-306, 2001

26. Hanson LA: Non-breastfeeding - The most common immunodeficiency. HK Paediatr J 3:5-8, 1998

27. Nicoll A, Williams A: Breastfeeding. Arch Dis Child 87:91-92, 2002

28. Chen A, Rogan WJ: Breastfeeding and the risk of postneonatal death in the United States. Pediatrics 113:e435-e439, 2004

29. Ford RP, Taylor BJ, Mitchell EA, et al: Breastfeeding and the risk of sudden infant death syndrome. Int J Epidemiol 22:885-890, 1993

30. Fleming PJ, Blair PS, Bacon C, et al: Environment of infants during sleep and risk of the sudden infant death syndrome: results of 1993-5 case-control study for confidential inquiry into stillbirths and deaths in infancy. Confidential Enquiry into Stillbirths and Deaths Regional Coordinators and Researchers. BMJ 313:191-195, 1996

31. Brooke H, Gibson A, Tappin D, et al: Case-control study of sudden infant death syndrome in Scotland, 1992-5. BMJ 314:1516-1520, 1997

32. McVea KL, Turner PD, Peppler DK: The role of breastfeeding in sudden infant death syndrome. J Hum Lact 16:13-20, 2000

33. Alm B, Wennergren G, Norvenius SG, et al: Breast feeding and the sudden infant death syndrome in Scandinavia, 1992-95. Arch Dis Child 86:400-402, 2002

34. Chong DS, Yip PSF, Karlberg J: Maternal smoking: an increasing unique risk factor for sudden infant death syndrome in Sweden. Acta Paediatrica 93:471-478, 2004

35. Klonoff-Cohen HS, Edelstein SL, Lefkowitz ES, et al: The effect of passive smoking and tobacco exposure through breast milk on sudden infant death syndrome. JAMA 273:795-798, 1999

36. Fleming PJ, Blair PS, Ward PM, et al: Sudden infant death syndrome and social deprivation: assessing epidemiological factors after post-matching for deprivation. Paediatr Perinat Epidemiol 17:272-280, 2003

37. Gordon AE, Saadi AT, MacKenzie DA, et al: The protective effect of breast feeding in relation to sudden infant death syndrome (SIDS): III. Detection of IgA antibodies in human milk that bind to bacterial toxins implicated in SIDS. FEMS Immunol.Med Microbiol. 25:175-182, 1999

38. Jalil F, Adlerberth I, Ashraf R, et al: Methodological problems in assessment of long-term health outcomes in breast-fed versus bottle-fed infants, in Atkinson SA, Hanson LA, Chandra RK (eds): Breastfeeding, Nutrition, Infection and Infant Growth in Developed and Emerging Countries. St. John's Newfoundland, Canada, ARTS Biomedical Publishers 381-394, 1990

39. Jason JM, Nieburg P, Marks JS: Mortality and infectious disease associated with infant-feeding practices in developing countries. Pediatrics 74:702-727, 1984

40. Kovar MG, Serdula MK, Marks JS, et al: Review of the epidemiologic evidence for an association between infant feeding and infant health. Pediatrics 74:615-638, 1984

41. Victora CG: Case-control studies of the influence of breast-feeding on child morbidity and mortality: methodological issues, in Atkinson S, Hanson L, Chandra RK (eds): Breastfeeding, Nutrition, Infection and Infant Growth in Develped and Emerging Countries. St. John's Newfoundland, Canada, ARTS Biomedical Publisher. 405-418, 1990

42. Glass RI, Stoll BJ: The protective effect of human milk against diarrhea. A review of studies from Bangladesh. Acta Paediatr Scand Suppl 351:131-136, 1989

43. Howie PW, Forsyth JS, Ogston SA, et al: Protective effect of breast feeding against infection. BMJ 300:11-16, 1990

44. Cruz JR, Gil L, Cano F, et al: Breast milk anti-Escherichia coli heat-labile toxin IgA antibodies protect against toxin-induced infantile diarrhea. Acta Paediatr Scand 77:658-662, 1988

45. Glass RI, Svennerholm AM, Stoll BJ, et al: Protection against cholera in breast-fed children by antibodies in breast milk. N Engl J Med 308:1389-1392, 1983

46. Hayani KC, Guerrero ML, Morrow AL, et al: Concentration of milk secretory immunoglobulin A against Shigella virulence plasmid-associated antigens as a predictor of symptom status in Shigella-infected breast-fed infants. J Pediatr 121:852-856, 1992

47. Long K, Vasquez-Garibay E, Mathewson J, et al: The impact of infant feeding patterns on infection and diarrheal disease due to enterotoxigenic Escherichia coli. Salud Publica Mex 41:263-270, 1999

48. Ruiz-Palacios GM, Calva JJ, Pickering LK, et al: Protection of breast-fed infants against Campylobacter diarrhea by antibodies in human milk. J Pediatr 116:707-713, 1990

49. Walterspiel JN, Morrow AL, Guerrero ML, et al: Secretory anti-Giardia lamblia antibodies in human milk: protective effect against diarrhea. Pediatrics 93:28-31, 1994

50. Clemens JB, Stanton B, Stoll B, et al: Breastfeeding as a determinant of severity in shigellosis: evidence for protection throughout the first three years of life in Bangladeshi children. Am J Epidemiol 123:710-720, 1986

51. Glass RI, Stoll BJ, Blaser MJ, et al: Effect of breast-feeding on protection against diarrhea associated with Campylobacter jejuni, in Pearson A, Skirrow M, Lior H, et al (eds): Campylobacter III. London, Publick Health Laboratory Service. 130-141, 1985

52. Megraud F, Boudraa G, Bessaoud K, et al: Incidence of Campylobacter infection in infants in western Algeria and the possible protective role of breast feeding. Epidemiol Infect 105:73-78, 1990

53. Jalil F, Lindblad BS, Hanson LA, et al: Early child health in Lahore, Pakistan: IX. Perinatal events. Acta Paediatr Suppl 82 Suppl 390:95-107, 1993

54. Ashraf, R: The epidemiology of breastfeeding and its impact compared to other modes of feeding on infections and growth in a poor population. University of Goteborg, Sweden. PhD Thesis. 1993

55. Ashraf RN, Jalil F, Aperia A, et al: Additional water is not needed for healthy breast-fed babies in a hot climate. Acta Paediatr 82:1007-1011, 1993

56. Ashraf RN, Jalil F, Hanson LA, et al: Giving additional water during breastfeeding affects diarrhoeal incidence, and early short term growth in a poor environment. Pakistan Paediatr J 27:1-7, 2003

57. Dewey KG, Heinig MJ, Nommsen-Rivers LA: Differences in morbidity between breast-fed and formula-fed infants. J Pediatr 126:696-702, 1995

58. Scariati PD, Grummer-Strawn LM, Fein SB: A longitudinal analysis of infant morbidity and the extent of breastfeeding in the United States. Pediatrics 99:E5, 1997

59. Chandra RK: Prospective studies of the effect of breast feeding on incidence of infection and allergy. Acta Paediatr Scand 68:691-694, 1979

60. van den Bogaard BC, van den Hoogen HJ, Huygen FJ, et al: The relationship between breast-feeding and early childhood morbidity in a general population. Fam Med 23:510-515, 1991

61. Kramer MS, Kakuma R: Optimal duration of exclusive breastfeeding. Cochrane Database Syst Rev CD003517, 2002

62. Sachdev HP, Kumar S, Singh KK, et al: Does breastfeeding influence mortality in children hospitalized with diarrhoea? J Trop Pediatr 37:275-279, 1991

63. Molbak K, Gottschau A, Aaby P, et al: Prolonged breast feeding, diarrhoeal disease, and survival of children in Guinea-Bissau. BMJ 308:1403-1406, 1994

64. Khin MU, Nyunt NW, Myo K, et al: Effect on clinical outcome of breast feeding during acute diarrhoea. BMJ (Clin Res Ed) 290:587-589, 1985

65. Kramer MS, Guo T, Platt RW, et al: Infant growth and health outcomes associated with 3 compared with 6 mo of exclusive breastfeeding. Am J Clin Nutr 78:291-295, 2003

66. Morrow AL, Reves RR, West MS, et al: Protection against infection with Giardia lamblia by breast-feeding in a cohort of Mexican infants. J Pediatr 121:363-370, 1992

67. Duffy LC, Byers TE, Riepenhoff-Talty M, et al: The effects of infant feeding on rotavirus-induced gastroenteritis: a prospective study. Am J Public Health 76:259-263, 1986

68. Clemens J, Rao M, Ahmed F, et al: Breast-feeding and the risk of life-threatening rotavirus diarrhea: prevention or postponement? Pediatrics 92:680-685, 1993

69. Espinoza F, Paniagua M, Hallander H, et al: Rotavirus infections in young Nicaraguan children. Pediatr Infect.Dis J 16:564-571, 1997

70. Gianino P, Mastretta E, Longo P, et al: Incidence of nosocomial rotavirus infections, symptomatic and asymptomatic, in breast-fed and non-breast-fed infants. J Hosp Infect 50:13-17, 2002

71. Rothenbacher D, Bode G, Brenner H: History of breastfeeding and Helicobacter pylori infection in pre-school children: results of a population-based study from Germany. Int J Epidemiol 31:632-637, 2002

72. Stromqvist M, Falk P, Bergstrom S, et al: Human milk kappa-casein and inhibition of Helicobacter pylori adhesion to human gastric mucosa. J Pediatr Gastroenterol Nutr 21:288-296, 1995

73. Owen MJ, Baldwin CD, Swank PR, et al: Relation of infant feeding practices, cigarette smoke exposure, and group child care to the onset and duration of otitis media with effusion in the first two years of life. J Pediatr 123:702-711, 1993

74. Saarinen UM: Prolonged breast feeding as prophylaxis for recurrent otitis media. Acta Paediatr Scand 71:567-571, 1982

75. Teele DW, Klein JO, Rosner B: Epidemiology of otitis media during the first seven years of life in children in greater Boston: a prospective, cohort study. J Infect Dis 160:83-94, 1989

76. Timmermans FJ, Gerson S: Chronic granulomatous otitis media in bottle-fed Inuit children. Can Med Assoc J 122:545-547, 1980

77. Kero P, Piekkala P: Factors affecting the occurrence of acute otitis media during the first year of life. Acta Paediatr Scand 76:618-623, 1987

78. Porro E, Indinnimeo L, Antognoni G, et al: Early wheezing and breast feeding. J Asthma 30:23-28, 1993

79. Sipila M, Karma P, Pukander J, et al: The Bayesian approach to the evaluation of risk factors in acute and recurrent acute otitis media. Acta Otolaryngol 106:94-101, 1988

80. Duncan B, Ey J, Holberg CJ, et al: Exclusive breast-feeding for at least 4 months protects against otitis media. Pediatrics 91:867-872, 1993

81. Aniansson G, Alm B, Andersson B, et al: A prospective cohort study on breast-feeding and otitis media in Swedish infants. Pediatr Infect Dis J 13:183-188, 1994

82. Duffy LC, Faden H, Wasielewski R, et al: Exclusive breastfeeding protects against bacterial colonization and day care exposure to otitis media. Pediatrics 100:E7, 1997

83. Cushing AH, Samet JM, Lambert WE, et al: Breastfeeding reduces risk of respiratory illness in infants. Am J Epidemiol 147:863-870, 1998

84. Paradise JL, Elster BA, Tan L: Evidence in infants with cleft palate that breast milk protects against otitis media. Pediatrics 94:853-860, 1994

85. Aniansson G, Svensson H, Becker M, et al: Otitis media and feeding with breast milk of children with cleft palate. Scand J Plast Reconstr Surg Hand Surg 36:9-15, 2002

86. Harabuchi Y, Faden H, Yamanaka N, et al: Human milk secretory IgA antibody to nontypeable Haemophilus influenzae: possible protective effects against nasopharyngeal colonization. J Pediatr 124:193-198, 1994

87. Rosen IA, Hakansson A, Aniansson G, et al: Antibodies to pneumococcal polysaccharides in human milk: lack of relationship to colonization and acute otitis media. Pediatr Infect.Dis J 15:498-507, 1996

88. Bauchner H, Leventhal JM, Shapiro ED: Studies of breast-feeding and infections. How good is the evidence? JAMA 256:887-892, 1986

89. Woodward A, Douglas RM, Graham NM, et al: Acute respiratory illness in Adelaide children: breast feeding modifies the effect of passive smoking. J Epidemiol Community Health 44:224-230, 1990

90. Wright AL, Holberg CJ, Martinez FD, et al: Breast feeding and lower respiratory tract illness in the first year of life. Group Health Medical Associates. BMJ 299:946-949, 1989

91. Frank AL, Taber LH, Glezen WP, et al: Breast-feeding and respiratory virus infection. Pediatrics 70:239-245, 1982

92. Cesar JA, Victora CG, Barros FC, et al: Impact of breast feeding on admission for pneumonia during postneonatal period in Brazil: nested case-control study. BMJ 318:1316-1320, 1999

93. Downham MA, Scott R, Sims DG, et al: Breast-feeding protects against respiratory syncytial virus infections. BMJ 2:274-276, 1976

94. Watkins CJ, Leeder SR, Corkhill RT: The relationship between breast and bottle feeding and respiratory illness in the first year of life. J Epidemiol Community Health 33:180-182, 1979

95. Pullan CR, Toms GL, Martin AJ, et al: Breast-feeding and respiratory syncytial virus infection. BMJ 281:1034-1036, 1980

96. Pisacane A, Graziano L, Zona G, et al: Breast feeding and acute lower respiratory infection. Acta Paediatr 83:714-718, 1994

97. Ford K, Labbok M: Breast-feeding and child health in the United States. J Biosoc Sci 25:187-194, 1993

98. Sinha A, Madden J, Ross-Degnan D, et al: Reduced risk of neonatal respiratory infections among breastfed girls but not boys. Pediatrics 112:e303, 2003

99. Nafstad P, Jaakkola JJ, Hagen JA, et al: Breastfeeding, maternal smoking and lower respiratory tract infections. Eur Respir J 9:2623-2629, 1996

100. Oddy WH, Sly PD, de Klerk NH, et al: Breast feeding and respiratory morbidity in infancy: a birth cohort study. Arch Dis Child 88:224-228, 2003

101. Winberg J, Wessner G: Does breast milk protect against septicaemia in the newborn? Lancet 1:1091-1094, 1971

102. Narayanan I, Prakash K, Prabhakar AK, et al: A planned prospective evaluation of the anti-infective property of varying quantities of expressed human milk. Acta Paediatr Scand 71:441-445, 1982

103. Hylander MA, Strobino DM, Dhanireddy R: Human milk feedings and infection among very low birth weight infants. Pediatrics 102:E38, 1998

104. Marild S, Jodal U, Hanson LA: Breastfeeding and urinary-tract infection. Lancet 336:942, 1990

105. Pisacane A, Graziano L, Mazzarella G, et al: Breast-feeding and urinary tract infection. J Pediatr 120:87-89, 1992

106. Marild S, Hansson S, Jodal U, et al: Protective effect of breastfeeding against urinary tract infection. Acta Paediatr 93:164-168, 2004

107. Hanson LA: Protective effects of breastfeeding against urinary tract infection. Acta Paediatr 93:154-156, 2004

108. Haversen LA, Engberg I, Baltzer L, et al: Human lactoferrin and peptides derived from a surface-exposed helical region reduce experimental Escherichia coli urinary tract infection in mice. Infect Immun 68:5816-5823, 2000

109. Haversen L, Ohlsson BG, Hahn-Zoric M, et al: Lactoferrin down-regulates the LPS-induced cytokine production in monocytic cells via NF-kappa B. Cell Immunol 220:83-95, 2002

110. Coppa GV, Gabrielli O, Giorgi P, et al: Preliminary study of breastfeeding and bacterial adhesion to uroepithelial cells. Lancet 335:569-571, 1990

111. Lucas A, Cole TJ: Breast milk and neonatal necrotising enterocolitis. Lancet 336:1519-1523, 1990

112. Buescher ES: Host defense mechanisms of human milk and their relations to enteric infections and necrotizing enterocolitis. Clin Perinatol 21:247-262, 1994

113. Schanler RJ: The use of human milk for premature infants. Pediatr Clin North Am 48:207-219, 2001

114. Furukawa M, Narahara H, Yasuda K, et al: Presence of platelet-activating factor-acetylhydrolase in milk. J Lipid Res 34:1603-1609, 1993

115. Claud EC, Savidge T, Walker WA: Modulation of human intestinal epithelial cell IL-8 secretion by human milk factors. Pediatr Res 53:419-425, 2003

116. Dvorak B, Halpern MD, Holubec H, et al: Maternal milk reduces severity of necrotizing enterocolitis and increases intestinal IL-10 in a neonatal rat model. Pediatr Res 53:426-433, 2003

117. Arnon SS, Damus K, Thompson B, et al: Protective role of human milk against sudden death from infant botulism. J Pediatr 100:568-573, 1982

118. Pisacane A, de Luca U, Impagliazzo N, et al: Breast feeding and acute appendicitis. BMJ 310:836-837, 1995

119. Pisacane A, de Luca U, Criscuolo L, et al: Breast feeding and hypertrophic pyloric stenosis: population based case-control study. BMJ 312:745-746, 1996

120. Pisacane A, Impagliazzo N, De Caprio C, et al: Breast feeding and tonsillectomy. BMJ 312:746-747, 1996

121. Thomas JE, Austin S, Dale A, et al: Protection by human milk IgA against Helicobacter pylori infection in infancy. Lancet 342:121, 1993

122. Hahn-Zoric M, Fulconis F, Minoli I, et al: Antibody responses to parenteral and oral vaccines are impaired by conventional and low protein formulas as compared to breast-feeding. Acta Paediatr Scand 79:1137-1142, 1990

123. Pabst HF, Spady DW: Effect of breast-feeding on antibody response to conjugate vaccine. Lancet 336:269-270, 1990

124. Pickering LK, Granoff DM, Erickson JR, et al: Modulation of the immune system by human milk and infant formula containing nucleotides. Pediatrics 101:242-249, 1998

125. Pabst HF, Godel J, Grace M, et al: Effect of breast-feeding on immune response to BCG vaccination. Lancet 1:295-297, 1989

126. Pichichero ME: Effect of breast-feeding on oral rhesus rotavirus vaccine seroconversion: a meta-analysis. J Infect Dis 162:753-755, 1990

127. Ceyhan M, Kanra G, Secmeer G, et al: Take of rhesus-human reassortant tetravalent rotavirus vaccine in breast-fed infants. Acta Paediatr 82:223-227, 1993

128. Karron RA, Steinhoff MC, Subbarao EK, et al: Safety and immunogenicity of a cold-adapted influenza A (H1N1) reassortant virus vaccine administered to infants less than six months of age. Pediatr Infect Dis J 14:10-16, 1995

129. WHO: Factors affecting the immunogenicity of oral poliovirus vaccine: a prospective evaluation in Brazil and the Gambia. World Health Organization Collaborative Study Group on Oral Poliovirus Vaccine. J Infect Dis 171:1097-1106, 1995

130. Stephens S, Kennedy CR, Lakhani PK, et al: In-vivo immune responses of breast- and bottle-fed infants to tetanus toxoid antigen and to normal gut flora. Acta Paediatr.Scand. 73:426-432, 1984

131. Watemberg N, Dagan R, Arbelli Y, et al: Safety and immunogenicity of Haemophilus type b-tetanus protein conjugate vaccine, mixed in the same syringe with diphtheria-tetanus-pertussis vaccine in young infants. Pediatr Infect Dis J 10:758-763, 1991

132. Decker MD, Edwards KM, Bradley R, et al: Comparative trial in infants of four conjugate Haemophilus influenzae type b vaccines. J Pediatr 120:184-189, 1992

133. Scheifele D, Bjornson GJ, Guasparini R, et al: Breastfeeding and antibody responses to routine vaccination in infants. Lancet 340:1406, 1992

134. Hahn-Zoric M, Carlsson B, Jeansson S, et al: Anti-idiotypic antibodies to poliovirus antibodies in commercial immunoglobulin preparations, human serum, and milk. Pediatr Res 33:475-480, 1993

135. Lundin BS, Dahlman-Hoglund A, Pettersson I, et al: Antibodies given orally in the neonatal period can affect the immune response for two generations: evidence for active maternal influence on the newborn's immune system. Scand J Immunol 50:651-656, 1999

136. Chiba Y, Minagawa T, Mito K, et al: Effect of breast feeding on responses of systemic interferon and virus-specific lymphocyte transformation in infants with respiratory syncytial virus infection. J Med Virol 21:7-14, 1987

137. Avanzini MA, Plebani A, Monafo V, et al: A comparison of secretory antibodies in breast-fed and formula-fed infants over the first six months of life. Acta Paediatr 81:296-301, 1992

138. Wilson AC, Forsyth JS, Greene SA, et al: Relation of infant diet to childhood health: seven year follow up of cohort of children in Dundee infant feeding study. BMJ 316:21-25, 1998

139. Silfverdal SA, Bodin L, Olcen P: Protective effect of breastfeeding: an ecologic study of Haemophilus influenzae meningitis and breastfeeding in a Swedish population. Int J Epidemiol 28:152-156, 1999

140. Silfverdal SA, Bodin L, Ulanova M, et al: Long term enhancement of the IgG2 antibody response to Haemophilus influenzae type b by breast-feeding. Pediatr Infect Dis J 21:816-821, 2002

141. Silverdal, S. A., Bodin, L., Ulanova, M., Hahn-Zoric, M, Hanson, L. A., and Olce'n, P. Duration of breastfeeding in relation to antibodies against Haemophilus influenzae type b in pre-school children. In manuscript 2004

142. Burr ML, Limb ES, Maguire MJ, et al: Infant feeding, wheezing, and allergy: a prospective study. Arch Dis Child 68:724-728, 1993

143. Wright AL: Analysis of epidemiological studies: facts and artifacts. Paediatr Respir Rev 3:198-204, 2002

144. Chien PF, Howie PW: Breast milk and the risk of opportunistic infection in infancy in industrialized and non-industrialized settings. Adv Nutr Res 10:69-104, 2001

145. Hanson, L. A. Allergy. In: Nature Encyclopedia of Life Scinces. London: Nature Publishing Group. www.els.net 2003

146. Soto-Quiros ME, Soto-Martinez M, Hanson LA: Epidemiological studies of the very high prevalence of asthma and related symptoms among school children in Costa Rica from 1989 to 1998. Pediatr Allergy Immunol 13:342-349, 2002

147. Bergmann RL, Edenharter G, Bergmann KE, et al: Atopic dermatitis in early infancy predicts allergic airway disease at 5 years. Clin Exp Allergy 28:965-970, 1998

148. Kramer MS: Does breast feeding help protect against atopic disease? Biology, methodology, and a golden jubilee of controversy. J Pediatr 112:181-190, 1988

149. Hanson LA: Breastfeeding provides passive and likely long-lasting active immunity. Ann Allergy Asthma Immunol 81:523-533, 1998

150. Savilahti E, Tainio VM, Salmenpera L, et al: Low colostral IgA associated with cow's milk allergy. Acta Paediatr Scand 80:1207-1213, 1991

151. Jarvinen KM, Laine ST, Jarvenpaa AL, et al: Does low IgA in human milk predispose the infant to development of cow's milk allergy? Pediatr Res 48:457-462, 2000

152. Calbi M, Giacchetti L: Low breast milk IgA and high blood eosinophil count in breast-fed newborns determine higher risk for developing atopic eczema after an 18-month follow-up. J Investig Allergol Clin Immunol 8:161-164, 1998

153. Restani P, Gaiaschi A, Plebani A, et al: Evaluation of the presence of bovine proteins in human milk as a possible cause of allergic symptoms in breast-fed children. Ann Allergy Asthma Immunol 84:353-360, 2000

154. Jarvinen KM, Makinen-Kiljunen S, Suomalainen H: Cow's milk challenge through human milk evokes immune responses in infants with cow's milk allergy. J Pediatr 135:506-512, 1999

155. Saarinen KM, Juntunen-Backman K, Jarvenpaa AL, et al: Supplementary feeding in maternity hospitals and the risk of cow's milk allergy: A prospective study of 6209 infants. J Allergy Clin Immunol 104:457-461, 1999

156. Saarinen KM, Juntunen-Backman K, Jarvenpaa AL, et al: Breast-feeding and the development of cows' milk protein allergy. Adv Exp Med Biol 478:121-130, 2000

157. Stintzing G, Zetterstrom R: Cow's milk allergy, incidence and pathogenetic role of early exposure to cow's milk formula. Acta Paediatr Scand 68:383-387, 1979

158. Lucas A, Brooke OG, Morley R, et al: Early diet of preterm infants and development of allergic or atopic disease: randomised prospective study. BMJ 300:837-840, 1990

159. Benn CS, Bottcher MF, Pedersen BV, et al: Mammary epithelial paracellular permeability in atopic and non-atopic mothers versus childhood atopy. Pediatr Allergy Immunol 15:123-126, 2004

160. Bottcher MF, Jenmalm MC, Bjorksten B, et al: Chemoattractant factors in breast milk from allergic and nonallergic mothers. Pediatr Res 47:592-597, 2000

161. Cummins AG, Thompson FM: Postnatal changes in mucosal immune response: a physiological perspective of breast feeding and weaning. Immunol Cell Biol 75:419-429, 1997

162. Saarinen KM, Vaarala O, Klemetti P, et al: Transforming growth factor-beta1 in mothers' colostrum and immune responses to cows' milk proteins in infants with cows' milk allergy. J Allergy Clin Immunol 104:1093-1098, 1999

163. Kalliomaki M, Ouwehand A, Arvilommi H, et al: Transforming growth factor-beta in breast milk: a potential regulator of atopic disease at an early age. J Allergy Clin Immunol 104:1251-1257, 1999

164. Bottcher MF, Jenmalm MC, Bjorksten B: Cytokine, chemokine and secretory IgA levels in human milk in relation to atopic disease and IgA production in infants. Pediatr Allergy Immunol 14:35-41, 2003

165. Oddy WH, Halonen M, Martinez FD, et al: TGF-beta in human milk is associated with wheeze in infancy. J Allergy Clin Immunol 112:723-728, 2003

166. Liu AH: Endotoxin exposure in allergy and asthma: reconciling a paradox. J Allergy Clin Immunol 109:379-392, 2002

167. Jones CA, Holloway JA, Popplewell EJ, et al: Reduced soluble CD14 levels in amniotic fluid and breast milk are associated with the subsequent development of atopy, eczema, or both. J Allergy Clin Immunol 109:858-866, 2002

168. Kalliomaki M, Kirjavainen P, Eerola E, et al: Distinct patterns of neonatal gut microflora in infants in whom atopy was and was not developing. J Allergy Clin Immunol 107:129-134, 2001

169. Kalliomaki M, Salminen S, Poussa T, et al: Probiotics and prevention of atopic disease: 4-year follow-up of a randomised placebo-controlled trial. Lancet 361:1869-1871, 2003

170. Karmaus W, Eneli I: Maternal atopy and the number of offspring: is there an association? Pediatr Allergy Immunol 14:470-474, 2003

171. Bernsen RM, de Jongste JC, van der Wouden JC: Birth order and sibship size as independent risk factors for asthma, allergy, and eczema. Pediatr Allergy Immunol 14:464-469, 2003

172. Benn CS, Melbye M, Wohlfahrt J, et al: Cohort study of sibling effect, infectious diseases, and risk of atopic dermatitis during the first 18 months of life. BMJ 2004 (in press)

173. Illi S, von Mutius E, Lau S, et al: Early childhood infectious diseases and the development of asthma up to school age: a birth cohort study. BMJ 322:390-395, 2001

174. Benn CS, Thorsen P, Jensen JS, et al: Maternal vaginal microflora during pregnancy and the risk of asthma hospitalization and use of antiasthma medication in early childhood. J Allergy Clin Immunol 110:72-77, 2002

175. Bjorksten B, Naaber P, Sepp E, et al: The intestinal microflora in allergic Estonian and Swedish 2-year-old children. Clin Exp Allergy 29:342-346, 1999

176. Bjorksten B, Sepp E, Julge K, et al: Allergy development and the intestinal microflora during the first year of life. J Allergy Clin Immunol 108:516-520, 2001

177. da Costa LR, Victora CG, Menezes AM, et al: Do risk factors for childhood infections and malnutrition protect against asthma? A study of Brazilian male adolescents. Am J Public Health 93:1858-1864, 2003

178. Bremner SA, Carey IM, DeWilde S, et al: Early-life exposure to antibacterials and the subsequent development of hayfever in childhood in the UK: case-control studies using the General Practice Research Database and the Doctors' Independent Network. Clin Exp Allergy 33:1518-1525, 2003

179. Cullinan P, Harris J, Mills P, et al: Early prescriptions of antibiotics and the risk of allergic disease in adults: a cohort study. Thorax 59:11-15, 2004

180. Benn CS, Jeppesen DL, Hasselbalch H, et al: Thymus size and head circumference at birth and the development of allergic diseases. Clin Exp Allergy 31:1862-1866, 2001

181. Kero J, Gissler M, Gronlund MM, et al: Mode of delivery and asthma -- is there a connection? Pediatr Res 52:6-11, 2002

182. Eggesbo M, Botten G, Stigum H, et al: Is delivery by cesarean section a risk factor for food allergy? J Allergy Clin Immunol. 112:420-426, 2003

183. Hakansson S, Kallen K: Caesarean section increases the risk of hospital care in childhood for asthma and gastroenteritis. Clin Exp Allergy 33:757-764, 2003

184. Oberle D, von Mutius E, von Kries R: Childhood asthma and continuous exposure to cats since the first year of life with cats allowed in the child's bedroom. Allergy 58:1033-1036, 2003

185. Andersson AC, Grindebacke H, Karlsson H, et al: Cat allergen extract and Fel d 1 stimulate innate immunity responses from human monocytes through CD14. In manuscript 2004

186. Labeta MO, Vidal K, Nores JE, et al: Innate recognition of bacteria in human milk is mediated by a milk-derived highly expressed pattern recognition receptor, soluble CD14. J Exp Med 191:1807-1812, 2000

187. Wright AL, Sherrill D, Holberg CJ, et al: Breast-feeding, maternal IgE, and total serum IgE in childhood. J Allergy Clin Immunol 104:589-594, 1999

188. Jarrett EE, Hall E: IgE suppression by maternal IgG. Immunology 48:49-58, 1983

189. Bednar-Tantscher E, Mudde GC, Rot A: Maternal antigen stimulation downregulates via mother's milk the specific immune responses in young mice. Int Arch Allergy Immunol 126:300-308, 2001

190. Gdalevich M, Mimouni D, David M, et al: Breast-feeding and the onset of atopic dermatitis in childhood: a systematic review and meta-analysis of prospective studies. J Am Acad Dermatol 45:520-527, 2001

191. Miyake Y, Yura A, Iki M: Breastfeeding and the prevalence of symptoms of allergic disorders in Japanese adolescents. Clin Exp Allergy 33:312-316, 2003

192. Kull I, Wickman M, Lilja G, et al: Breast feeding and allergic diseases in infants-a prospective birth cohort study. Arch Dis Child 87:478-481, 2002

193. Benn CS, Wohlfahrt J, Aabye P, et al: Breastfeeding and risk of atopic dermatitis during the first 18 months of life by parental history of allergy. Am J Epidemiol 2004 (in press)

194. Bergmann RL, Diepgen TL, Kuss O, et al: Breastfeeding duration is a risk factor for atopic eczema. Clin Exp Allergy 32:205-209, 2002

195. Siltanen M, Kajosaari M, Poussa T, et al: A dual long-term effect of breastfeeding on atopy in relation to heredity in children at 4 years of age. Allergy 58:524-530, 2003

196. Schoetzau A, Filipiak-Pittroff B, Franke K, et al: Effect of exclusive breast-feeding and early solid food avoidance on the incidence of atopic dermatitis in high-risk infants at 1 year of age. Pediatr Allergy Immunol 13:234-242, 2002

197. Kull I, Almqvist C, Lilja G, et al: Breastfeeding reduces the risk of asthma during the first four years of life. J Allergy Clin Immunol 2004 (In press)

198. Gdalevich M, Mimouni D, Mimouni M: Breast-feeding and the risk of bronchial asthma in childhood: a systematic review with meta-analysis of prospective studies. J Pediatr 139:261-266, 2001

199. van Odijk J, Kull I, Borres MP, et al: Breastfeeding and allergic disease: a multidisciplinary review of the literature (1966-2001) on the mode of early feeding in infancy and its impact on later atopic manifestations. Allergy 58:833-843, 2003

200. Sears MR, Greene JM, Willan AR, et al: Long-term relation between breastfeeding and development of atopy and asthma in children and young adults: a longitudinal study. Lancet 360:901-907, 2002

201. Halken S: Early sensitisation and development of allergic airway disease - risk factors and predictors. Paediatr Respir Rev 4:128-134, 2003

202. Oddy WH, Peat JK: Breastfeeding, asthma, and atopic disease: an epidemiological review of the literature. J Hum Lact 19:250-261, 2003

203. Wright AL, Holberg CJ, Taussig LM, et al: Factors influencing the relation of infant feeding to asthma and recurrent wheeze in childhood. Thorax 56:192-197, 2001

204. Mai XM, Nilsson L, Axelson O, et al: High body mass index, asthma and allergy in Swedish schoolchildren participating in the International Study of Asthma and Allergies in Childhood: Phase II. Acta Paediatr 92:1144-1148, 2003

205. Fidler N, Koletzko B: The fatty acid composition of human colostrum. Eur J Nutr 39:31-37, 2000

206. Businco L, Ioppi M, Morse NL, et al: Breast milk from mothers of children with newly developed atopic eczema has low levels of long chain polyunsaturated fatty acids. J Allergy Clin Immunol 91:1134-1139, 1993

207. Duchen K, Casas R, Fageras-Bottcher M, et al: Human milk polyunsaturated long-chain fatty acids and secretory immunoglobulin A antibodies and early childhood allergy. Pediatr Allergy Immunol 11:29-39, 2000

208. Yu G, Duchen K, Bjorksten B: Fatty acid composition in colostrum and mature milk from non-atopic and atopic mothers during the first 6 months of lactation. Acta Paediatr 87:729-736, 1998

209. Wijga A, Houwelingen AC, Smit HA, et al: Fatty acids in breast milk of allergic and non-allergic mothers: The PIAMA birth cohort study. Pediatr Allergy Immunol 14:156-162, 2003

210. Laiho K, Lampi AM, Hamalainen M, et al: Breast milk fatty acids, eicosanoids, and cytokines in mothers with and without allergic disease. Pediatr Res 53:642-647, 2003

211. Dunstan JA, Mori TA, Barden A, et al: Maternal fish oil supplementation in pregnancy reduces interleukin-13 levels in cord blood of infants at high risk of atopy. Clin Exp Allergy 33:442-448, 2003

212. Korotkova M, Telemo E, Hanson LA, et al: Modulation of neonatal immunological tolerance to ovalbumin by maternal essential fatty acid intake. Pediatr Allergy Immunol 15:112-122, 2004

213. Korotkova M, Telemo E, Hanson LA, et al: The ratio of n-6 to n-3 fatty acids in maternal diet influences the induction of neonatal immunological tolerance to ovalbumin. Clin Exp Immunol 2004 (In press)

214. Oddy WH, Holt PG, Sly PD, et al: Association between breast feeding and asthma in 6 year old children: findings of a prospective birth cohort study. BMJ 319:815-819, 1999

215. Nafstad P, Jaakkola JJ: Breast-feeding, passive smoking, and asthma and wheeze in children. J Allergy Clin Immunol 112:807-808, 2003

216. Chulada PC, Arbes SJ, Jr., Dunson D, et al: Breast-feeding and the prevalence of asthma and wheeze in children: analyses from the Third National Health and Nutrition Examination Survey, 1988-1994. J Allergy Clin Immunol 111:328-336, 2003

217. Falth-Magnusson K, Kjellman NI: Allergy prevention by maternal elimination diet during late pregnancy--a 5-year follow-up of a randomized study. J Allergy Clin Immunol 89:709-713, 1992

218. Hattevig G, Kjellman B, Sigurs N, et al: The effect of maternal avoidance of eggs, cow's milk, and fish during lactation on the development of IgE, IgG, and IgA antibodies in infants. J Allergy Clin Immunol 85:108-115, 1990

219. Sigurs N, Hattevig G, Kjellman B: Maternal avoidance of eggs, cow's milk, and fish during lactation: effect on allergic manifestations, skin-prick tests, and specific IgE antibodies in children at age 4 years. Pediatrics 89:735-739, 1992

220. Zeiger RS, Heller S, Mellon MH, et al: Effect of combined maternal and infant food-allergen avoidance on development of atopy in early infancy: a randomized study. J Allergy Clin Immunol 84:72-89, 1989

221. Kramer MS, Kakuma R: Maternal dietary antigen avoidance during pregnancy and/or lactation for preventing or treating atopic disease in the child. Cochrane Database Syst Rev CD000133, 2003

222. Borch-Johnsen K, Joner G, Mandrup-Poulsen T, et al: Relation between breast-feeding and incidence rates of insulin-dependent diabetes mellitus. A hypothesis. Lancet 2:1083-1086, 1984

223. Fort P, Lanes R, Dahlem S, et al: Breast feeding and insulin-dependent diabetes mellitus in children. J Am Coll Nutr 5:439-441, 1986

224. Mayer EJ, Hamman RF, Gay EC, et al: Reduced risk of IDDM among breast-fed children. The Colorado IDDM Registry. Diabetes 37:1625-1632, 1988

225. Virtanen SM, Rasanen L, Aro A, et al: Infant feeding in Finnish children less than 7 yr of age with newly diagnosed IDDM. Childhood Diabetes in Finland Study Group. Diabetes Care 14:415-417, 1991

226. Virtanen SM, Rasanen L, Aro A, et al: Feeding in infancy and the risk of type 1 diabetes mellitus in Finnish children. The 'Childhood Diabetes in Finland' Study Group. Diabet Med 9:815-819, 1992

227. Kimpimaki T, Erkkola M, Korhonen S, et al: Short-term exclusive breastfeeding predisposes young children with increased genetic risk of Type I diabetes to progressive beta-cell autoimmunity. Diabetologia 44:63-69, 2001

228. Dosch HM, Martin JM, Robinson BH, et al: An immunological basis for disproportionate diabetes risks in children with a type I diabetic mother or father. Diabetes Care 16:949-951, 1993

229. Ziegler AG, Schmid S, Huber D, et al: Early infant feeding and risk of developing type 1 diabetes-associated autoantibodies. JAMA 290:1721-1728, 2003

230. Hummel M, Fuchtenbusch M, Schenker M, et al: No major association of breast-feeding, vaccinations, and childhood viral diseases with early islet autoimmunity in the German BABYDIAB Study. Diabetes Care 23:969-974, 2000

231. Couper JJ: Environmental triggers of type 1 diabetes. J Paediatr Child Health 37:218-220, 2001

232. Pettitt DJ, Forman MR, Hanson RL, et al: Breastfeeding and incidence of non-insulin-dependent diabetes mellitus in Pima Indians. Lancet 350:166-168, 1997

233. Young TK, Martens PJ, Taback SP, et al: Type 2 diabetes mellitus in children: prenatal and early infancy risk factors among native canadians. Arch Pediatr Adolesc Med 156:651-655, 2002

234. Pisacane A, Impagliazzo N, Russo M, et al: Breast feeding and multiple sclerosis. BMJ 308:1411-1412, 1994

235. Brun JG, Nilssen S, Kvale G: Breast feeding, other reproductive factors and rheumatoid arthritis. A prospective study. Br J Rheumatol 34:542-546, 1995

236. Jacobsson LT, Jacobsson ME, Askling J, et al: Perinatal characteristics and risk of rheumatoid arthritis. BMJ 326:1068-1069, 2003

237. Bergstrand O, Hellers G: Breast-feeding during infancy in patients who later develop Crohn's disease. Scand J Gastroenterol. 18:903-906, 1983

238. Koletzko S, Sherman P, Corey M, et al: Role of infant feeding practices in development of Crohn's disease in childhood. BMJ 298:1617-1618, 1989

239. Corrao G, Tragnone A, Caprilli R, et al: Risk of inflammatory bowel disease attributable to smoking, oral contraception and breastfeeding in Italy: a nationwide case-control study. Cooperative Investigators of the Italian Group for the Study of the Colon and the Rectum (GISC). Int J Epidemiol 27:397-404, 1998

240. Acheson E, True Love S: Early weaning in the aetiology of ulcerative colitis. A study of feeding in infancy in cases and controls. BMJ 5257:929-933, 1961

241. Whorwell PJ, Holdstock G, Whorwell GM, et al: Bottle feeding, early gastroenteritis, and inflammatory bowel disease. Br Med J 1:382, 1979

242. Madsen KL, Fedorak RN, Tavernini MM, et al: Normal Breast Milk Limits the Development of Colitis in IL-10-Deficient Mice. Inflamm Bowel Dis 8:390-398, 2002

243. Auricchio S, Follo D, de Ritis G, et al: Does breast feeding protect against the development of clinical symptoms of celiac disease in children? J Pediatr Gastroenterol Nutr 2:428-433, 1983

244. Greco L, Auricchio S, Mayer M, et al: Case control study on nutritional risk factors in celiac disease. J Pediatr Gastroenterol Nutr 7:395-399, 1988

245. Anderson CM, Brueton MJ: Does breast feeding protect against development of clinical symptoms of celiac disease in children? J Pediatr Gastroenterol Nutr 4:507-508, 1985

246. Peters U, Schneeweiss S, Trautwein EA, et al: A case-control study of the effect of infant feeding on celiac disease. Ann Nutr Metab 45:135-142, 2001

247. Falth-Magnusson K, Franzen L, Jansson G, et al: Infant feeding history shows distinct differences between Swedish celiac and reference children. Pediatr Allergy Immunol 7:1-5, 1996

248. Ivarsson A, Hernell O, Stenlund H, et al: Breast-feeding protects against celiac disease. Am J Clin Nutr 75:914-921, 2002

249. Ascher H, Krantz I, Rydberg L, et al: Influence of infant feeding and gluten intake on coeliac disease. Arch Dis Child 76:113-117, 1997

250. Schuppan D, Esslinger B, Dieterich W: Innate immunity and coeliac disease. Lancet 362:3-4, 2003

251. Kramer MS: Do breast-feeding and delayed introduction of solid foods protect against subsequent obesity? J Pediatr 98:883-887, 1981

252. von Kries R, Koletzko B, Sauerwald T, et al: Breast feeding and obesity: cross sectional study. BMJ 319:147-150, 1999

253. Gillman MW, Rifas-Shiman SL, Camargo CA, Jr., et al: Risk of overweight among adolescents who were breastfed as infants. JAMA 285:2461-2467, 2001

254. Hediger ML, Overpeck MD, Kuczmarski RJ, et al: Association between infant breastfeeding and overweight in young children. JAMA 285:2453-2460, 2001

255. Toschke AM, Vignerova J, Lhotska L, et al: Overweight and obesity in 6- to 14-year-old Czech children in 1991: protective effect of breast-feeding. J Pediatr 141:764-769, 2002

256. Armstrong J, Reilly JJ: Breastfeeding and lowering the risk of childhood obesity. Lancet 359:2003-2004, 2002

257. Tulldahl J, Pettersson K, Andersson SW, et al: Mode of infant feeding and achieved growth in adolescence: early feeding patterns in relation to growth and body composition in adolescence. Obes Res 7:431-437, 1999

258. Grummer-Strawn LM, Mei Z: Does breastfeeding protect against pediatric overweight? Analysis of longitudinal data from the Centers for Disease Control and Prevention Pediatric Nutrition Surveillance System. Pediatrics 113:e81-e86, 2004

259. Bergmann KE, Bergmann RL, von Kries R, et al: Early determinants of childhood overweight and adiposity in a birth cohort study: role of breast-feeding. Int J Obes Relat Metab Disord 27:162-172, 2003

260. Parsons TJ, Power C, Manor O: Infant feeding and obesity through the lifecourse. Arch Dis Child 88:793-794, 2003

261. Victora CG, Barros F, Lima RC, et al: Anthropometry and body composition of 18 year old men according to duration of breast feeding: birth cohort study from Brazil. BMJ 327:9012003

262. Eriksson J, Forsen T, Osmond C, et al: Obesity from cradle to grave. Int J Obes Relat Metab Disord 27:722-727, 2003

263. Clifford TJ: Breast feeding and obesity. BMJ 327:879-880, 2003

264. Lucas A, Sarson DL, Blackburn AM, et al: Breast vs bottle: endocrine responses are different with formula feeding. Lancet 1:1267-1269, 1980

265. Lucas A, Boyes S, Bloom SR, et al: Metabolic and endocrine responses to a milk feed in six-day-old term infants: differences between breast and cow's milk formula feeding. Acta Paediatr Scand 70:195-200, 1981

266. Hauner H, Petruschke T, Russ M, et al: Effects of tumour necrosis factor alpha (TNF alpha) on glucose transport and lipid metabolism of newly-differentiated human fat cells in cell culture. Diabetologia 38:764-771, 1995

267. Hotamisligil GS, Peraldi P, Budavari A, et al: IRS-1-mediated inhibition of insulin receptor tyrosine kinase activity in TNF-alpha- and obesity-induced insulin resistance. Science 271:665-668, 1996

268. Mauricio D, Mandrup-Poulsen T: Apoptosis and the pathogenesis of IDDM: a question of life and death. Diabetes 47:1537-1543, 1998

269. Shimizu H, Sato N, Tanaka Y, et al: Interleukin-6 stimulates insulin secretion in HIT-T 15 cells. Horm Metab Res 27:37-38, 1995

270. van Zaanen HC, Koopmans RP, Aarden LA, et al: Endogenous interleukin 6 production in multiple myeloma patients treated with chimeric monoclonal anti-IL6 antibodies indicates the existence of a positive feed-back loop. J Clin Invest 98:1441-1448, 1996

271. Keller C, Steensberg A, Pilegaard H, et al: Transcriptional activation of the IL-6 gene in human contracting skeletal muscle: influence of muscle glycogen content. FASEB J 15:2748-2750, 2001

272. Savino F, Costamagna M, Prino A, et al: Leptin levels in breast-fed and formula-fed infants. Acta Paediatr. 91:897-902, 2002

273. Korotkova M, Gabrielsson B, Lonn M, et al: Leptin levels in rat offspring are modified by the ratio of linoleic to alpha-linolenic acid in the maternal diet. J Lipid Res 43:1743-1749, 2002

274. Locke R: Preventing obesity: the breast milk-leptin connection. Acta Paediatr 91:891-894, 2002

275. Singhal A, Farooqi IS, O'Rahilly S, et al: Early nutrition and leptin concentrations in later life. Am J Clin Nutr 75:993-999, 2002

276. Uysal FK, Onal EE, Aral YZ, et al: Breast milk leptin: its relationship to maternal and infant adiposity. Clin Nutr 21:157-160, 2002

277. Smith-Kirwin SM, O'Connor DM, De Johnston J, et al: Leptin expression in human mammary epithelial cells and breast milk. J Clin Endocrinol Metab 83:1810-1813, 1998

278. Takahashi N, Waelput W, Guisez Y: Leptin is an endogenous protective protein against the toxicity exerted by tumor necrosis factor. J Exp Med 189:207-212, 1999

279. Singhal A, Cole TJ, Lucas A: Early nutrition in preterm infants and later blood pressure: two cohorts after randomised trials. Lancet 357:413-419, 2001

280. Owen CG, Whincup PH, Gilg JA, et al: Effect of breast feeding in infancy on blood pressure in later life: systematic review and meta-analysis. BMJ 327:1189-1195, 2003

281. Taittonen L, Nuutinen M, Turtinen J, et al: Prenatal and postnatal factors in predicting later blood pressure among children: cardiovascular risk in young Finns. Pediatr Res 40:627-632, 1996

282. Owen CG, Whincup PH, Odoki K, et al: Infant feeding and blood cholesterol: a study in adolescents and a systematic review. Pediatrics 110:597-608, 2002

283. Singhal A, Cole TJ, Fewtrell M, et al: Breastmilk feeding and lipoprotein profile in adolescents born preterm: follow-up of a prospective randomized study. Lancet 363:1571-1578, 2004

284. Davis MK: Breastfeeding and chronic disease in childhood and adolescence. Pediatr Clin North Am 48:125-41, ix, 2001

285. Davis MK, Savitz DA, Graubard BI: Infant feeding and childhood cancer. Lancet 2:365-368, 1988

286. Schwartzbaum JA, George SL, Pratt CB, et al: An exploratory study of environmental and medical factors potentially related to childhood cancer. Med Pediatr Oncol 19:115-121, 1991

287. Smulevich VB, Solionova LG, Belyakova SV: Parental occupation and other factors and cancer risk in children: I. Study methodology and non-occupational factors. Int J Cancer 83:712-717, 1999

288. Shu XO, Clemens J, Zheng W, et al: Infant breastfeeding and the risk of childhood lymphoma and leukaemia. Int J Epidemiol 24:27-32, 1995

289. Shu XO, Linet MS, Steinbuch M, et al: Breast-feeding and risk of childhood acute leukemia. J Natl Cancer Inst 91:1765-1772, 1999

290. Jourdan-Da Silva N, Perel Y, Mechinaud F, et al: Infectious diseases in the first year of life, perinatal characteristics and childhood acute leukaemia. Br J Cancer 90:139-145, 2004

291. Zheng T, Holford TR, Mayne ST, et al: Lactation and breast cancer risk: a case-control study in Connecticut. Br J Cancer 84:1472-1476, 2001

292. Collaborative Group on Hormonal Factors in Breast Cancer: Breast cancer and breastfeeding: collaborative reanalysis of individual data from 47 epidemiological studies in 30 countries, including 50,302 women with breast cancer and 96,973 women without the disease. Lancet 360:187-195, 2002

293. Daniels M, Merrill RM, Lyon JL, et al: Associations between breast cancer risk factors and religious practices in Utah. Prev Med 38:28-38, 2004

294. Okamoto Y, Tsutsumi H, Kumar NS, et al: Effect of breast feeding on the development of anti-idiotype antibody response to F glycoprotein of respiratory syncytial virus in infant mice after post-partum maternal immunization. J Immunol 142:2507-2512, 1989

295. Stein KE, Soderstrom T: Neonatal administration of idiotype or antiidiotype primes for protection against Escherichia coli K13 infection in mice. J Exp Med 160:1001-1011, 1984

296. Jain L, Vidyasagar D, Xanthou M, et al: In vivo distribution of human milk leucocytes after ingestion by newborn baboons. Arch Dis Child 64:930-933, 1989

297. Siafakas C, Anderson W, Walker A, Xanthou M: Breast milk cells and their interaction with intestinal mucosa Amsterdam, Elsevier Science Publishers, 121-6, 1997

298. Tuboly S, Bernath S, Glavits R, et al: Intestinal absorption of colostral lymphocytes in newborn lambs and their role in the development of immune status. Acta Vet Hung 43:105-115, 1995

299. Ogra SS, Weintraub D, Ogra PL: Immunologic aspects of human colostrum and milk. III. Fate and absorption of cellular and soluble components in the gastrointestinal tract of the newborn. J Immunol 119:245-248, 1977

300. Schlesinger JJ, Covelli HD: Evidence for transmission of lymphocyte responses to tuberculin by breast-feeding. Lancet 2:529-532, 1977

301. Bertotto A, Gerli R, Castellucci G, et al: Mycobacteria-reactive gamma/delta T cells are present in human colostrum from tuberculin-positive, but not tuberculin-negative nursing mothers. Am J Reprod Immunol 29:131-134, 1993

302. Arvola M, Gustafsson E, Svensson L, et al: Immunoglobulin-secreting cells of maternal origin can be detected in B cell-deficient mice. Biol Reprod 63:1817-1824, 2000

303. Campbell DA, Jr., Lorber MI, Sweeton JC, et al: Breast feeding and maternal-donor renal allografts. Possibly the original donor-specific transfusion. Transplantation 37:340-344, 1984

304. Zhang L, van Bree S, van Rood JJ, et al: Influence of breast feeding on the cytotoxic T cell allorepertoire in man. Transplantation 52:914-916, 1991

305. Pabst HF, Spady DW, Pilarski LM, et al: Differential modulation of the immune response by breast- or formula-feeding of infants. Acta Paediatr 86:1291-1297, 1997

306. Hasselbalch H, Engelmann MD, Ersboll AK, et al: Breast-feeding influences thymic size in late infancy. Eur J Pediatr 158:964-967, 1999

307. Ngom PT, Collinson A, Pido-Lopez J, et al: Improved thymic function in exclusively breast-fed babies is associated with higher breast milk IL-7. Am J Clin Nutr 2004 (in press)

308. Jeppesen DL, Hasselbalch H, Lisse IM, et al: T-lymphocyte subsets, thymic size and breastfeeding in infancy. Pediatr Allergy Immunol 15:127-132, 2004

309. Lord G: Role of leptin in immunology. Nutr Rev 60:S35-S38, 2002

310. Stephens LA, Mottet C, Mason D, et al: Human CD4(+)CD25(+) thymocytes and peripheral T cells have immune suppressive activity in vitro. Eur J Immunol 31:1247-1254, 2001

311. Suri-Payer E, Amar AZ, Thornton AM, et al: CD4+CD25+ T cells inhibit both the induction and effector function of autoreactive T cells and represent a unique lineage of immunoregulatory cells. J Immunol 160:1212-1218, 1998

312. Carver JD, Pimentel B, Cox WI, et al: Dietary nucleotide effects upon immune function in infants. Pediatrics 88:359-363, 1991

313. Pickering LK, Granoff DM, Erickson J, et al: Dietary modulation of the immune system by human milk (HM) and infant formula containing HM levels of nucleotides. Pediatr Res 37:131A, 1995

314. Laubereau B, Brockow I, Zirngibl A, et al: Effect of breast-feeding on the development of atopic dermatitis J Pediatr 144: 602-7, 2004

7 Infectious Agents In Milk

Bacteria

Human milk received by the baby is not sterile. Normally occurring bacteria like *Staph. epidermidis, Strep. salivarius,* and *Strep. mitis* were the predominant species found in 30-60% of the milk samples in a recent Finnish study.[1] *Enterococcus faecalis*, enterococci, and lactic acid producing bacteria like *Lactobacillus rhamnosus, L. crispatus, Lactococcus lactis,* and *Leuconostoc mesenteroides* were present in 12.5% of the samples. Several of these bacteria inhibited the growth of *Staph. aureus* which was uncommon in the milk samples. Human milk from Spanish mothers seemed to provide a significant source of potentially probiotic lactic acid bacteria like *Lactobacillus gasseri* and *Enterococcus faecium*.[2]

Swedish infants today are colonized with *S. aureus* in the gut. Up to 73% of the infants had this bacterium in their gut by the age of 2-6 months. Sixteen percent had *S. aureus* bacteria in their gut by 3 days after delivery.[3] These staphylococci originated mainly from their mother's breast, nose, and skin, but babies can also get them from their father's skin. None of these breastfed infants had any symptoms from the presence of these bacteria.[4] Most likely, they were rendered harmless by the many protective factors in milk (Chapter 5) and by the competition with the normal flora. The fact that staphylococci appear in the intestinal flora of infants probably signifies a changed balance in the microbial ecology today. There is decreased competition from the harmless anaerobic bacterial flora that normally take over in the gut of the infant as discussed in Chapter 1 (Figure 2). This changing microbial ecology was also discussed in Chapter 6 in connection with the "Hygiene hypothesis" and the increase in allergic diseases among children.

In addition to *S. aureus,* pathogens like group B streptococci, *Campylobacter, Salmonellae, Mycobacterium tuberculosis,* and *Borrelia burgdorferi* have been found in some instances in human milk.[5;6]

In conclusion:

Human milk normally contains a harmless bacterial flora which may depress the growth of potential pathogens like *S. aureus*. Today, Swedish mothers often have *S. aureus* in their nose, on their skin, and on their nipples without any untoward effects in their infants. The common presence of these microbes may signify a change in microbes in the environment of infants in today's society as discussed in Chapters 1 and 6. Pathogenic bacteria have been found in human milk in a few studies.

Mastitis

This condition is caused by an inflammation in the mammary gland. It appears in 24 - 33% of lactating women.[7] It ranges from a relatively short-lasting but painful inflammatory process in the breast to a more intense long-lasting inflammation with severe symptoms. Milk stasis may induce an influx of leucocytes that release pro-inflammatory cytokines in the mammary gland.[8] In the worst cases, there is also an infection usually caused by *S. aureus*. In those instances, antibiotic treatment is needed. Such treatment, together with anti-inflammatory measures, are often not immediately effective and the process of breastfeeding may be interrupted. As mentioned in Chapter 5, preliminary results suggest that induction of anti-secretory factor in mother's milk may prevent mastitis.[9] This effect is most likely due to the anti-inflammatory and anti-infectious activities of the anti-secretory factor.

In the dairy industry, the condition *sub-clinical mastitis* is well known. There may be no obvious symptoms but milk production can be impaired. Sub-clinical mastitis is detected by an increase in the Na/K ratio in the milk. This is also found in man.[10] The increase relates to the content of IL-8. This cytokine is a strong chemokine signal for neutrophils. It reveals the presence of an inflammatory process in the mammary glands associated with neutrophils which probably promote the inflammation. This agrees with the fact that sub-clinical mastitis is followed by an increase in cell counts in the milk and potential transfer of HIV-1.[11] Filteau and coworkers found that the presence of sub-clinical mastitis relates to poor infant growth.[12] It is relatively easy to demonstrate the presence of subclinical mastitis by determining the Na/K ratio in the mother's milk. It may be that sub-clinical mastitis is part of a more generalized inflammation. Dietary intake of vitamin E-rich sunflower oil was helpful in reducing this inflammation whereas postpartum vitamin A supplementation had no effect.[12;13]

The fact that sub-clinical mastitis seems to lead to an increased infectious load of HIV-1 in the milk from HIV-infected mothers is further discussed in the next section.

In conclusion:

Mastitis is an inflammation in the mammary gland. At its worst, there is an infection usually caused by *S. aureus*. It is a common and painful condition which may interfere with breastfeeding. Preliminary data suggest that mastitis may be prevented by induction of the anti-secretory factor in the milk.

Sub-clinical mastitis has been linked to an increased risk of transfer of HIV-1 from mother to offspring via the milk.

Viruses

HIV-1 and 2

The HIV-1/AIDS epidemic has one additional tragic component: the transfer of the virus from an infected mother to her offspring. This may take place during pregnancy, during delivery, or via breastfeeding. The HIV-1 may occur in the cell free portion of the milk as well as in the cellular components.[14] Various studies of the risk of children becoming infected via breastfeeding have recently been summarized in a Technical Report from the American Academy of Pediatrics.[15] Postnatal transmission after 2.5 months of age is 3.2 per 100 child years of breastfeeding but earlier postnatal transfer of infections may be more common.[16;17] The HIV-1 transmission due to breastfeeding seems to range from 4 - 22% in prospective cohorts. Mothers with chronic HIV-1 infections have an additional risk of 14% of infecting their children (95% CI, 7 - 22%) while mothers infected after delivery have a risk of 29% (95% CI, 16 - 42%). Presumably, the presence of the virus in the blood during the primary infection increases the number of virus particles transferred via the milk.

A meta-analysis of prospective cohort studies of HIV-1-infected women and their babies indicated that the estimated risk of infection via breastfeeding was 16% (95% CI, 9 - 22%). Of the infants with HIV-1 infection, 47% were infected via the maternal milk.[18] Of those breastfed for 3 months or more, 21% became infected. Thirteen percent (95% CI, 4 - 21%) of those breastfed for less than 2 months became infected.

Numerous risk factors for increased HIV-1 transfer via the milk have been defined (Table 9). They include maternal factors like younger age, more pregnancies, more advanced disease with low blood lymphocyte count, and more virus particles in the blood. Breast abscess and mastitis as well as nipple lesions are obvious risk factors that increase the infants' exposure to the virus. Sub-clinical mastitis, reflected by an increased Na/K ratio in the milk, may add to the risk of milk-mediated exposure to HIV-1.[19] In women with sub-clinical mastitis, HIV-1 was present in the milk in 75% of the cases. HIV-1 was present in only 35% of the women without sub-clinical mastitis. During the first 14 weeks of lactation in South African women, the viral load was associated with sub-clinical mastitis and severe immunosuppression of the mother. There were several contributors to the viral load since multivariate models had limited predictive value.

Partial breastfeeding may be one reason sub-clinical mastitis causes a higher risk of HIV transfer. Coutsoudis et al suggested that exclusive breastfeeding may protect against HIV-1 infection in the baby. Exclusive breastfeeding may decrease the risk of sub-clinical mastitis.[20] Exclusive breastfeeding is uncommon in many traditional societies.[21;22] Lactation counseling significantly reduced the appearance of sub-clinical mastitis as measured by the Na/K ratio in the milk of Bangladeshi women.[23] As described in Chapter 5, induction of the anti-secretory factor in milk seems to prevent mastitis.[9]

The longer the duration of breastfeeding by an infected mother, the higher the risk of infecting the baby with HIV-1. An important risk factor is a high viral load in the milk which parallels a high load in the blood. Further risk factors are low concentrations of the many potentially anti-viral components in the milk such as SIgA, IgG and IgM antibodies, lactoferrin, lysozyme, epidermal growth factor, etc..[15;24]

Table 9

Potential Risk Factors For Transfer Of HIV-1 To The Baby Via Breastfeeding

- **Maternal factors**
  - Young age
  - Many deliveries
  - High virus load in blood
  - Low number of blood lymphocytes
  - Mastitis, sub-clinical mastitis, breast abscess, nipple lesions
- **Milk factors**
  - High viral load
  - Long duration of breastfeeding
  - Mixed feeding
  - Low levels of anti-viral factors, such as cytotoxic T lymphocytes, SIgA, IgG and IgM antibodies, lactoferrin, lysozyme, etc.
- **Infant factor**
  - Oral candidiasis

HIV-1 is a virus which has the capacity to vary its structure to avoid host defense mechanisms. For instance, when HIV-1 virus is exposed to specific antibodies with the capacity to neutralize it, the virus changes its glycosylation of surface structures providing itself with a "glycan shield".[25] In this way, it may avoid the effects of the protective antibodies. Oral candidiasis in the child is a risk factor for HIV-1 presumably by providing a port of entry for the virus in the damaged mucosa (Table 9).

> The HIV-1 virus may be transferred from the mother to her offspring during pregnancey, at delivery, or during breastfeeding. There are a number of factors increasing the risk of transfer via the milk such as a young mother, more pregnancies, advanced disease with severe immunosuppression to the mother, and a higher viral load in the milk. Long-term and partial breastfeeding seem to increase the risk. Some data suggest that exclusive breastfeeding may protect aginst HIV-1. Ongoing studies are investigating this further. Prevention of sub-clinical mastitis by exclusive breastfeeding may possibly decrease the risk of transfer of HIV-1.

Countries which have infant mortality rates 10 - 20 times higher than developed countries may see a doubling of infant and child mortality due to HIV-1.[26] Between 200,000-350,000 infants in the world may be infected every year with HIV-1 via breastfeeding. According to UNICEF, some 1.5 million non-HIV-1 related deaths can be prevented each year by breastfeeding. WHO estimates that infants in poor areas who are given formula or something similar and not their mother's milk have a 6-fold increased risk of dying in the first 2 months of life.[27] A study from Kenya randomized babies to formula or breastfeeding groups and found that at 2 years there was similar mortality rates and incidence of diarrhea and pneumonia in both groups. But HIV-1 free survival was significantly more common in the formula group.[28] The conclusion was that formula feeding can be safe providing adequate education and access to clean water is provided. More recently, a review article concluded that HIV-1 transmission after birth via the milk was best prevented by the use of exclusive replacement feeds or exclusive breastfeeding for a limited period (4-6 months).[29] However, the latter procedure has not yet been fully tested.

Studies are being performed to analyze whether exclusive breastfeeding for a certain period of time may be protective.

For the premature infant, the possibility exists of inactivating any HIV-1 present in the mother's milk before giving it to the baby. Oral candidiasis in the infant and any mammary gland inflammation or nipple erosions should be treated. The possibility of elective caesarean section, providing antiretroviral prophylaxis and/or treatment to mother and offspring, and inactivation of HIV-1 in mother's expressed milk should be considered.[15;30] Formula feeding is a safe alternative in well-to-do countries.

While 200,000-350,000 infants may become infected with HIV-1 via breastfeeding every year, 1,500,000 infants deaths may be prevented by breastfeeding in poor areas of the world. However, if formula feeding is provided with clean water and adequate health education, the mortality rate was similar to the breastfed group at two years. HIV-1 free survival was more common in the formula group. Without such supportive measures, a six times higher mortality rate could be expected in the non-breastfed group. Ongoing studies will hopefully discover whether exclusive breastfeeding really enhances protection and which approach gives optimal protection against HIV transfer via the mothers' milk. In developed areas, formula feeding is safe.

HIV is present in the fluid phase of the milk as well as in milk cells. HIV-infected milk cells can be detected throughout lactation. In HIV-1-infected mothers, 0.1 - 1% of T cells and macrophages contained the virus.[31] Ninety-seven percent of the infected cells were macrophages.

It is assumed that the port of entry of HIV infection in the infant may be the lympho-epithelial tissues of the tonsils, gut epithelium, M cells which cover the Peyer's patches in the gut, and other lymphoid tissues in the gut (Fig. 10).[17] HIV-1 binds to certain chemokine receptors called CCR5 which are present on the microvilli in the gut mucosa. These receptors efficiently absorb the virus. This process is enhanced by the presence of infected macrophages in the gut lumen.[32]

Milk SIgA and SIgM antibodies against HIV-1 may be protective.[33] A more detailed investigation of the effect of milk SIgA and IgG antibodies against 3 different peptides from HIV-1 found no difference between mothers transmitting the virus via their milk and those who did not.[34] There are high levels of 90K(Mac-2BP) protein in the serum of HIV-1 infected mothers and their babies. The level of this protein related to less transfer of the virus.[35] This component is known to activate NK cells which then become capable of killing viruses. It is also present in the milk and has been proposed to neutralize certain viruses and counteract acute respiratory tract infections.[36]

At this time, there is no data to suggest that the much less virulent HIV-2 can be transferred via the milk.[37]

In conclusion:

The spread of HIV-1 causing AIDS is an enormous catastrophe for mankind. It is a further tragedy that infected women may transfer the infection to their offspring by breastfeeding. Formula feeding is safe in developed areas with clean water and informed mothers. In poor areas, breastfeeding may still save more lives than are lost by the transfer of HIV-1 to infants via the milk. Ongoing studies will, hopefully, define alternatives so that factors increasing the risk of transfer can be avoided or prevented possibly by treating the mother and infant with anti-retroviral drugs. Exclusive breastfeeding for a defined period of time with prevention of clinical and sub-clinical mastitis may be proven optimal especially in poor areas.

Human T cell leukemia virus (HTLV)

HTLV-1 is the cause of adult T cell leukemia-lymphoma. In one region of southwest Japan, approximately 60% of the new cases each year result from the transfer of the virus via breastfeeding, sexual contact, and transfusions with infected blood.[38] More than 85% of mothers of children carrying the HTLV-1 are also carriers and 21% of the children of carrier mothers become infected. It has not been proven that those infected by breastfeeding develop T cell malignancies in adulthood. Still, breastfeeding has been discouraged in southern Japan with the hope that the epidemic will be interrupted. Bottle-feeding Japanese infants of HTLV-1 sero-positive mothers reduced, but did not fully prevent HTLV-1 infection.[39]

HTLV-1 is also found in the Caribbean, parts of Africa, South America, and the Middle East. It causes HTLV-1–associated myelopathy or "tropical spastic paraparesis".[40] In Jamaica, it was found that trans-placental antibodies from the mother may protect the infant (see Chapter 4). A mother with a high load of provirus should avoid breastfeeding. In Delhi, antibodies to HTLV-1 was found in 10.6% of a high risk population.[41] In an African population, the viral transfer from mother to infant was 9.7%.[42] In Brazil, HTLV-1 infected banked milk was found to originate from mothers with family cases of adult T cell leukemia/lymphoma.[43]

The related retrovirus HTLV-2 can be transferred via the milk to the offspring similarly to HTLV-1.[44]

In conclusion:

HTLV-1 is transferred to the baby via the milk in areas of Japan and may cause adult T cell leukemia-lymphoma in adults. Bottle-feeding can reduce but not fully prevent the infection. The virus also exists in the Caribbean, parts of Africa, India, the Middle East, and South America causing HTLV-1 associated myelopathy.

Cytomegalovirus (CMV)

The most common cause of congenital and perinatal infection in man is cytomegalovirus.[45;46] In the mother, a primary infection with CMV induces an immune response and then becomes latent. Reactivation during pregnancy is common and the virus may infect the infant via the placenta or during delivery. The virus also appears in milk in about 25% of the cases, more often in mature milk than colostrum. The virus is mainly found in the fluid portion of the milk, less often in the milk cells. In one study, CMV infected milk resulted in an infection in 69% of the infants. The risk increased if breastfeeding continued for more than one month.[47] The infection has been reported not to cause any symptoms and it is not clear if there are later consequences.

In a sizable prospective German study of very low birth weight babies (<1500 grams), sero-positive mothers transmitted the virus in 37% of the cases.[48;49] Half of those infected had symptoms such as thrombocytopenia, neutropenia, and hepatopathy. In four cases, there was a sepsis-like picture. In very low birth weight babies, the risk of symptomatic CMV infection postnatally via the milk was considerable. A Japanese study of preterm infants weighing less than 2000 grams noted that in spite of a high rate of CMV DNA in the mothers' milk there were no clinical symptoms of CMV infection in any of the babies.[50] Differences in handling the milk or differences in the studied populations were considered as possible explanations for this contrasting outcome.

Lactoferrin kills CMV in vitro. However, the risk of virus transfer to preterm babies is related to the load of CMV DNA in milk, but not to the level of lactoferrin in the milk.[51] Obviously, several factors in milk determine whether an infective virus is transferred via the milk.

A study of congenital CMV infection in the USA suggested that the presence of serum IgG antibodies against CMV during a previous pregnancy decreased the risk of fetal infection during the next pregnancy from 3% to 1%. In the group of mothers who were infected between pregnancies, there were congenital infections in 12.7%.[52] A vaccine against CMV would be helpful, but will not be available in the near future.

It seems that, at least in full term infants, the CMV infection results in a latent infection without any obvious consequences. As to very preterm infants, further studies may be needed to determine when preventive measures, such as pasteurization of the mother's milk, need to be taken.

In conclusion:

Infections with CMV are very common in man, but mostly remain latent without any symptoms. The infection is often reactivated during pregnancy and the virus is transferred during pregnancy, at delivery, or, in about 25% of the cases, via the mother's milk. The transfer via the milk results in a latent infection in the infant, possibly due to protective IgG antibodies received during pregnancy as described in

Chapter 4. CMV exposure via the milk may be riskier for low birth weight babies than for full term babies; although, there are only few studies on this topic.

Hepatitis viruses

Hepatitis viruses A, B, and C can be present in mother's milk, but transmissions are reported to be uncommon.[53] Although there is no evidence that the hepatitis B virus (HBV) is transferred via the milk, it may be that transfer can occur via cracked or bleeding nipples.[54-56] Breastfeeding does not interfere with successful vaccination of the baby against HBV.[57]

Hepatitis C virus (HCV) was suggested to be present in milk from infected mothers who had antibodies in the milk but did not transfer the virus.[58] In another series of 76 HCV-infected mothers, no milk sample contained HCV RNA in spite of the fact that 60% of the mothers had viremia.[59] An Italian study mentions that transfer of HCV from mother to offspring may occur in utero (5 - 6%), during labour, or after birth.[60] If the mother had both HIV-1 and HCV infections, the risk of transfer of HCV increased 3-4 times. Caesarian section and no breastfeeding was recommended for these mothers.[61] In the absence of HIV infection, there was no transfer of HCV via breastfeeding according to multivariate analysis of 1,474 HCV infected mothers, 35% of whom also had HIV-1 infection.

In conclusion:

Hepatitis A, B, and C viruses may be present in milk, but transmission is rare. The hepatitis B virus may, however, be transferred via bleeding nipples. Most data suggest that hepatitis C virus is not transferred via the milk.

Rubella and other viruses

Neonatal rubella is rarely seen in infants breastfed by mothers with a rubella infection after delivery.[62;63] Vaccinating women with attenuated rubella vaccine after delivery made the virus appear in 70% of their milk. Fifty percent of the infants picked up the virus from the milk, none developed the disease.[64;65] Such exposure to the virus did not inhibit later vaccine responses of the children against rubella.[66]

Other viruses like parvovirus and herpes viruses may also appear in the milk but transmission is rare.[53] The only contraindication for breastfeeding in relation to herpes infection would be if the mother has nipple lesions.[56] A study from an area in Japan with endemic HTLV-1 infection (see above) investigated the prevalence of antibodies to two herpes viruses, HHV-6 and Epstein-Barr virus.[67] No evidence was found for the transfer of these viruses via breast milk.

In conclusion:

Rubella virus from infected mothers rarely causes infection in breastfed infants. Rubella virus appeared in the milk from many mothers vaccinated with attenuated virus. The rubella virus caused no disease in the infant and did not impair later vaccine responses in the baby. Parvovirus and herpes viruses rarely appear in milk, but herpes lesions of the nipples are a contraindication to breastfeeding.

Parasites

There is little or no evidence that parasites reaching the infant via the milk cause disease.[68] Some protozoa as well as trypanosomes and schistosomes have occasionally been found in milk.

Reference List

1. Heikkila MP, Saris PE: Inhibition of Staphylococcus aureus by the commensal bacteria of human milk. J Appl Microbiol 95:471-478, 2003

2. Martin R, Langa S, Reviriego C, et al: Human milk is a source of lactic acid bacteria for the infant gut. J Pediatr 143:754-758, 2003

3. Lindberg E, Nowrouzian F, Adlerberth I, et al: Long-time persistence of superantigen-producing Staphylococcus aureus strains in the intestinal microflora of healthy infants. Pediatr Res 48:741-747, 2000

4. Lindberg E, Adlerberth I, Hesselmar B, et al: High rate of transfer of Staphylococcus aureus from parental skin to infant gut flora. J Clin Microbiol 42:530-534, 2004

5. Law BJ, Urias BA, Lertzman J, et al: Is ingestion of milk-associated bacteria by premature infants fed raw human milk controlled by routine bacteriologic screening? J Clin Microbiol 27:1560-1566, 1989

6. Sharp JCM: Milk-born infection. J Med Microbiol 29:1989

7. Fetherston CM, Lee CS, Hartmann PE: Mammary gland defense: the role of colostrum, milk and involution secretion. Adv Nutr Res 10:167-198, 2001

8. Thomsen AC, Hansen KB, Moller BR: Leukocyte counts and microbiologic cultivation in the diagnosis of puerperal mastitis. Am J Obstet Gynecol 146:938-941, 1983

9. Svensson K, Lange S, Lonnroth I, et al: Induction of anti-secretory factor in human milk may prevent mastitis. Acta Paediatr 2004 (in press)

10. Filteau S: The influence of mastitis on antibody transfer to infants through breast milk. Vaccine 21:3377-3381, 2003

11. Semba RD, Kumwenda N, Hoover DR, et al: Human immunodeficiency virus load in breast milk, mastitis, and mother-to-child transmission of human immunodeficiency virus type 1. J Infect Dis 180:93-98, 1999

12. Filteau SM, Rice AL, Ball JJ, et al: Breast milk immune factors in Bangladeshi women supplemented postpartum with retinol or beta-carotene. Am J Clin Nutr 69:953-958, 1999

13. Filteau SM, Lietz G, Mulokozi G, et al: Milk cytokines and subclinical breast inflammation in Tanzanian women: effects of dietary red palm oil or sunflower oil supplementation. Immunology 97:595-600, 1999

14. Hoffman IF, Martinson FE, Stewart PW, et al: Human immunodeficiency virus type 1 RNA in breast-milk components. J Infect Dis 188:1209-1212, 2003

15. Read JS: Human milk, breastfeeding, and transmission of human immunodeficiency virus type 1 in the United States. American Academy of Pediatrics Committee on Pediatric AIDS. Pediatrics 112:1196-1205, 2003

16. Nduati R, John G, Mbori-Ngacha D, et al: Effect of breastfeeding and formula feeding on transmission of HIV-1: a randomized clinical trial. JAMA 283:1167-1174, 2000

17. Van de Perre P: Breast milk transmission of HIV-1. Laboratory and clinical studies. Ann N Y Acad Sci 918:122-127, 2000

18. John GC, Richardson BA, Nduati RW, et al: Timing of breast milk HIV-1 transmission: a meta-analysis. East Afr Med J 78:75-79, 2001

19. Willumsen JF, Filteau SM, Coutsoudis A, et al: Breastmilk RNA viral load in HIV-infected South African women: effects of subclinical mastitis and infant feeding. AIDS 17:407-414, 2003

20. Coutsoudis A: Influence of infant feeding patterns on early mother-to-child transmission of HIV-1 in Durban, South Africa. Ann N Y Acad Sci 918:136-144, 2000

21. Ashraf RN, Jalil F, Khan SR, et al: Early child health in Lahore, Pakistan: V. Feeding patterns. Acta Paediatr Suppl 82 Suppl 390:47-61, 1993

22. Bland RM, Rollins NC, Coutsoudis A, et al: Breastfeeding practices in an area of high HIV prevalence in rural South Africa. Acta Paediatr 91:704-711, 2002

23. Flores M, Filteau S: Effect of lactation councelling on subclinical mastitis among Bangladeshi women. Ann Trop Paediatr 22:85-88, 2004

24. Kourtis AP, Butera S, Ibegbu C, et al: Breast milk and HIV-1: vector of transmission or vehicle of protection? Lancet Infect Dis 3:786-793, 2003

25. Wei X, Decker JM, Wang S, et al: Antibody neutralization and escape by HIV-1. Nature 422:307-312, 2003

26. Goldenberg RL, Stringer JS, Sinkala M, et al: Perinatal HIV transmission: developing country considerations. J Matern Fetal Neonatal Med 12:149-158, 2002

27. Coutsoudis A, Goga AE, Rollins N, et al: Free formula milk for infants of HIV-infected women: blessing or curse? Health Policy Plan 17:154-160, 2002

28. Mbori-Ngacha D, Nduati R, John G, et al: Morbidity and mortality in breastfed and formula-fed infants of HIV-1-infected women: A randomized clinical trial. JAMA 286:2413-2420, 2001

29. Rollins N, Meda N, Becquet R, et al: Preventing postnatal transmission of HIV-1 through breast-feeding: modifying infant feeding practices. J Acquir Immune Defic Syndr 35:188-195, 2004

30. Newell ML: Prevention of mother-to-child transmission of HIV: challenges for the current decade. Bull World Health Organ 79:1138-1144, 2001

31. Southern SO: Milk-borne transmission of HIV. Characterization of productively infected cells in breast milk and interactions between milk and saliva. J Hum Virol 1:328-337, 1998

32. Bomsel M, David V: Mucosal gatekeepers: selecting HIV viruses for early infection. Nat Med 8:114-116, 2002

33. Van de Perre P, Simonon A, Hitimana DG, et al: Infective and anti-infective properties of breastmilk from HIV-1-infected women. Lancet 341:914-918, 1993

34. Becquart P, Hocini H, Levy M, et al: Secretory anti-human immunodeficiency virus (HIV) antibodies in colostrum and breast milk are not a major determinant of the protection of early postnatal transmission of HIV. J Infect Dis 181:532-539, 2000

35. Pelliccia P, Galli L, De Martino M, et al: Lack of mother-to-child HIV-1 transmission is associated with elevated serum levels of 90 K immune modulatory protein. AIDS 14:F41-F45, 2000

36. Fornarini B, Iacobelli S, Tinari N, et al: Human milk 90K (Mac-2 BP): possible protective effects against acute respiratory infections. Clin Exp Immunol 115:91-94, 1999

37. Michie CA, Gilmour J: Breastfeeding and the risks of viral transmission. Arch Dis Child 84:381-382, 2001

38. Tsuji Y, Doi H, Yamabe T, et al: Prevention of mother-to-child transmission of human T-lymphotropic virus type-I. Pediatrics 86:11-17, 1990

39. Ando Y, Matsumoto Y, Nakano S, et al: Long-term follow-up study of HTLV-I infection in bottle-fed children born to seropositive mothers. J Infect 46:9-11, 2003

40. Hisada M, Maloney EM, Sawada T, et al: Virus markers associated with vertical transmission of human T lymphotropic virus type 1 in Jamaica. Clin Infect Dis 34:1551-1557, 2002

41. Varma M, Mehta G: Incidence of HTLV-I in high-risk population in Delhi. J Commun Dis 31:237-240, 1999

42. Ureta-Vidal A, Angelin-Duclos C, Tortevoye P, et al: Mother-to-child transmission of human T-cell-leukemia/lymphoma virus type I: implication of high antiviral antibody titer and high proviral load in carrier mothers. Int J Cancer 82:832-836, 1999

43. Pombo-de-Oliveira MS, Carvalho SM, Borducchi D, et al: Adult T-cell leukemia/lymphoma and cluster of HTLV-I associated diseases in Brazilian settings. Leuk Lymphoma 42:135-144, 2001

44. Lal RB, Gongora-Biachi RA, Pardi D, et al: Evidence for mother-to-child transmission of human T lymphotropic virus type II. J Infect Dis 168:586-591, 1993

45. Numazaki K: Human cytomegalovirus infection of breast milk. FEMS Immunol Med Microbiol 18:91-98, 1997

46. Landolfo S, Gariglio M, Gribaudo G, et al: The human cytomegalovirus. Pharmacol Ther 98:269-297, 2003

47. Dworsky M, Yow M, Stagno S, et al: Cytomegalovirus infection of breast milk and transmission in infancy. Pediatrics 72:295-299, 1983

48. Hamprecht K, Maschmann J, Vochem M, et al: Epidemiology of transmission of cytomegalovirus from mother to preterm infant by breastfeeding. Lancet 357:513-518, 2001

49. Maschmann J, Hamprecht K, Dietz K, et al: Cytomegalovirus infection of extremely low-birth weight infants via breast milk. Clin Infect Dis 33:1998-2003, 2001

50. Yasuda A, Kimura H, Hayakawa M, et al: Evaluation of cytomegalovirus infections transmitted via breast milk in preterm infants with a real-time polymerase chain reaction assay. Pediatrics 111:1333-1336, 2003

51. van der Strate BW, Harmsen MC, Schafer P, et al: Viral load in breast milk correlates with transmission of human cytomegalovirus to preterm neonates, but lactoferrin concentrations do not. Clin Diagn Lab Immunol 8:818-821, 2001

52. Fowler KB, Stagno S, Pass RF: Maternal immunity and prevention of congenital cytomegalovirus infection. JAMA 289:1008-1011, 2003

53. Stiehm ER, Keller MA: Breast milk transmission of viral disease. Adv Nutr Res 10:105-122, 2001

54. Beasley RP, Stevens CE, Shiao IS, et al: Evidence against breast-feeding as a mechanism for vertical transmission of hepatitis B. Lancet 2:740-741, 1975

55. Woo D, Cummins M, Davies PA, et al: Vertical transmission of hepatitis B surface antigen in carrier mothers in two west London hospitals. Arch Dis Child 54:670-675, 1979

56. Henrot A: Mother-infant and indirect transmission of HSV infection: treatment and prevention. Ann Dermatol Venereol 129:533-549, 2002

57. Wang JS, Zhu QR, Wang XH: Breastfeeding does not pose any additional risk of immunoprophylaxis failure on infants of HBV carrier mothers. Int J Clin Pract 57:100-102, 2003

58. Lin HH, Kao JH, Hsu HY, et al: Absence of infection in breast-fed infants born to hepatitis C virus-infected mothers. J Pediatr 126:589-591, 1995

59. Polywka S, Schroter M, Feucht HH, et al: Low risk of vertical transmission of hepatitis C virus by breast milk. Clin Infect Dis 29:1327-1329, 1999

60. Zuccotti GV, Cucchi C, Torcoletti M, et al: Proposal of a step-wise follow-up for hepatitis C seropositive mothers and their infants. Pediatr Med Chir 25:6-11, 2003

61. Effects of mode of delivery and infant feeding on the risk of mother-to-child transmission of hepatitis C virus. European Paediatric Hepatitis C Virus Network. BJOG 108:371-377, 2001

62. Buimovici-Klein E, Hite RL, Byrne T, et al: Isolation of rubella virus in milk after postpartum immunization. J Pediatr 91:939-941, 1977

63. Klein EB, Byrne T, Cooper LZ: Neonatal rubella in a breast-fed infant after postpartum maternal infection. J Pediatr 97:774-775, 1980

64. Losonsky GA, Fishaut JM, Strussenberg J, et al: Effect of immunization against rubella on lactation products. II. Maternal-neonatal interactions. J Infect Dis 145:661-666, 1982

65. Losonsky GA, Fishaut JM, Strussenberg J, et al: Effect of immunization against rubella on lactation products. I. Development and characterization of specific immunologic reactivity in breast milk. J Infect Dis 145:654-660, 1982

66. Krogh V, Duffy LC, Wong D, et al: Postpartum immunization with rubella virus vaccine and antibody response in breast-feeding infants. J Lab Clin Med 113:695-699, 1989

67. Kusuhara K, Takabayashi A, Ueda K, et al: Breast milk is not a significant source for early Epstein-Barr virus or human herpesvirus 6 infection in infants: a seroepidemiologic study in 2 endemic areas of human T-cell lymphotropic virus type I in Japan. Microbiol Immunol 41:309-312, 1997

68. May JT: Microbial contaminants and antimicrobial properties of human milk. Microbiol Sci 5:42-46, 1988

8 Concluding Remarks

The mother, the baby, and science

After reading this book, it may be obvious that for mankind to have survived, very elaborate systems had to develop to protect against infections, especially in the newborn. The most dangerous period in a human's life is from delivery through the first year of life – even if the mother is healthy, well nourished, and has had a normal pregnancy. Unfortunately, for many women in the world, being healthy and well nourished, and having a normal pregnancy is not possible. Sadly, many newborns come into this world in a situation that is far from adequate.

From a global perspective, it is important to realize that currently about 30,000 infants die every day, most of them from infections. Our efforts to improve this situation have thus far been insufficient. However, we have learned how important it is to provide as optimal a situation as possible for the mother and the newborn. Even in the privileged areas of the world, a birth is still an event that is extremely important in every family. Obviously, everybody wants everything to be perfect when it comes to delivery and the handling of the newborn and the growing infant.

Today, we expect science to give us all the answers as how to do everything in the best way for the baby and the mother. As we look back through time, we see that each historical period has tried to do things correctly with the knowledge available at the time. From the perspective of current knowledge, we see how physicians and scientists in the past made mistakes because they did not have all the information required to make sound decisions and they were not sufficiently critical, questioning the data at hand. One of the mistakes people made was to believe that all bacteria were dangerous for the newborn. Certainly, it is true that the newborn is very sensitive to many of the bacteria which may be present in the mother's gut. But, based on this concept, various modes of hygienic measures were and still are taken at delivery preventing the normal bacterial colonization of the neonate with the mother's gut microflora. As you read in this text, this is not beneficial for the infant's developing immune system. In addition, physicians and scientists have only recently come to realize that the mother's breastmilk protects against her gut microbes because her milk contains SIgA antibodies against these bacteria.

The altered gut microflora in today's infants may, according to the "Hygiene hypothesis" discussed in Chapter 6, have another consequence: the immune system of the infant is not stimulated by the right bacteria and it does not develop its normal capacity to become immunologically tolerant to harmless non-microbial substances like food, pollen, mites, etc. This may be an important reason why allergies are now becoming so very common.

Another factor contributing to increased allergies is, presumably, based on the fact that we have changed the fat content of our diet such that the ratio of the essential fatty acids n-6/n-3 is too high. This not only contributes to more allergies, but also to a higher risk of obesity.

It is obvious that continued research is giving us answers that are very useful, but at the same time we have to remain cautious and skeptical until the answers have been totally scrutinized. Some decades ago, a prestigious pediatrician wrote that breastfeeding was probably not important for the defense against infections in the infant because milk antibodies were not found in the baby's blood as seen in the calf. At that time, it was not known that human milk had a totally different major system of defense, the secretory IgA (SIgA) antibodies, which are not taken up in the gut but remain there to stop infectious agents already at the mucosal level, preventing microbes from entering the infant's blood and tissues (Figure 10). Such a defense system is presumably much better for the baby because it protects efficiently without inducing the inflammatory symptoms obtained from the IgG antibodies the calf receives via the cow's milk. This illustrates how careful we have to be not to draw far reaching conclusions based on the current available data.

There is another example of how we took off in the wrong direction. We missed the normal physiological mechanisms which were there waiting to be used to optimize the initiation and continuation of breastfeeding. It took us a long time to discover what nature had arranged as a natural sequence of events directly after birth: the urge of the newborn to reach the mother's breast, massaging it to induce production of oxytocin, the "happiness hormone", that bonds the mother and the baby to each other and helps with the release of the milk. When babies are able to breastfeed right after birth while they are still active, awake and able to perform before their first nap, we have found that breastfeeding is more successful than if this early phase is missed.

White and black swans

A major problem in research is to bring information from the basic level into clinical reality. Today, we are all aware of the tough requirements of "evidence-based medicine". Unfortunately, it is very difficult to prove that a certain component from milk has a certain effect in a baby beyond any doubt. The philosopher Karl Popper taught us that "you may believe that it is proven that all swans in the world are white – till you one day see the first black one, that you did not know existed". Your hypothesis may seem correct and generally applicable until one day you meet an exception. This pushes us to be ready to reevaluate the concepts that we have relied on. This is why the word "research" can also be written "re-search".

In Chapter 5, you were exposed to a long list of components in human milk which have a number of effects that may be helpful for the baby in one way or another. But we really only have evidence for the SIgA milk antibodies, and this is not even irrefutable evidence, that these antibodies protect against a number of infectious agents like *Campylobacter*, etc. Many of the other milk factors can protect the baby and do so without inducing energy-costly, inflammation- and symptom-inducing effects. But, we don't know which components do what under different conditions. It seems to be a theme that human milk protects through non-inflammatory mechanisms.

This makes sense because in this way the baby can use all the nutrients in milk to grow and develop, not to fight infections. Research will have to continue to reveal to us how all these milk components function and what they do for the baby. It is obvious that much pressure during man's development has resulted in this complex array of factors in the milk with such a wide range of functions.

How useful is breastfeeding - what can we tell the parents?

When it comes to clinical research, there are only a few studies of the effects of breastfeeding that fulfill all of the criteria of evidence-based medicine. The reasons are not difficult to see - the most efficient method of study, that of randomization, is not really ethically possible. Still, one study randomized the program for promotion of breastfeeding, which gave helpful results. Also case-control studies can be helpful, but it is important to realize that confounding factors must be considered. This is not easy because so many factors may differ in the studied groups. Also, groups in other areas may differ so the results may not be fully applicable. Genetics, the presence of intermarriages in some regions, food quality and intake, climate, degree of exposure to infectious agents, etc. may vary and confound the results. When studying whether breastfeeding protects against certain diseases, it again becomes complicated. Many diseases are complex, like autoimmune and metabolic diseases. This makes it difficult to come up with definitive and clear-cut answers. But, that is still what parents are asking us to give them.

So what can we do? We must be able to talk to parents of many different backgrounds and we must be able to tailor our messages to fit their needs. In some regions, we have to compete with old traditions and convictions that are very difficult to overcome, especially since we cannot be equally definite. On the other hand, we can confidently explain how Nature has put tremendous effort into developing a very remarkable and complex system of components for the support and defense of the infant. The fact boxes in the text and the summaries included after each segment area can help you find the essence of what we can tell parents of today with reasonable accuracy.

Human milk provides optimal food. Furthermore, it contains a very large number of protective factors and signals from the mother to her baby, which seem to be involved in the immediate as well as the long-term effects of breastfeeding. The consequences of breastfeeding include enhanced protection against many different infections, from very dangerous conditions like neonatal septicemia to diarrhea, pneumonia, and, most likely, also upper respiratory infections. Breastfeeding reduces infant mortality not only in poor areas but also in rich ones, increases IQ, supports enhanced bonding between the mother and her infant, decreases the risk of developing certain complex diseases like symptomatic celiac disease, obesity, etc. The information to working parents that breastfeeding reduces respiratory infections in their baby for the next few years is also useful information. All of these positive factors when taken together defends breastfeeding as the optimal feeding method for the infant.

It is a sad problem that many Governments have not yet discovered the long-term advantages gained by breastfeeding not only for parents, but also for Society. To provide time for the mother to remain with her infant during the first year of life, or at least the first several months, is a very good investment in the future.

As I said in the introduction, after reading the book, you may agree with the saying: "Still confused, but at a higher level." I hope you are not so much confused but inspired to encourage all parents to breastfeed, to advocate for breastfeeding in your communities, and to encourage all Governments to promote, protect, and support breastfeeding!

Glossary

Adhesins	Structures on the surface of bacteria which make them able to adhere to the mucosal epithelium in the gut or the urinary tract. This attachment can be the first step in causing an infection. Adhesins are also called pili.
Aerobic bacteria	Bacteria that require oxygen to survive.
α–Lactalbumin	A major milk protein described in Chapter 5.
Allergen	Antigens which induce special IgE-mediated immune responses which cause allergic diseases. Normally, we should be immunologically tolerant to allergens and not react against them. Allergens may come from pollen, mites, foods, or other components that can induce allergic reactions.
Anaerobic bacteria	Bacteria that live and grow in the absence of oxygen.
Anti-antibodies	An antibody specific for the binding site of another antibody. Such anti-antibodies can either stimulate the production of the first antibody or inhibit its production.
Antigen	A protein or carbohydrate capable of stimulating an immune response. One kind of bacteria or virus may contain many structures which are recognized as antigens by the immune system. Viral antigens may be expressed on the surface of a virus-infected host cell.
Antigen-Presenting Cells (APCs)	Mostly dendritic cells which take up microbes, e.g. a bacterium, degrade it, and present its antigenic peptides to lymphocytes (Fig. 5).

Anti-secretory factor (AF) A component that can be induced in milk that helps prevent mastitis due to its anti-secretory and anti-inflammatory activities.

Atopic An individual that reacts to an allergen by producing IgE antibodies against it. When exposed to that allergen, symptoms of allergic disease may follow.

Auto-antibodies Antibodies produced against the body's own tissue constituents. Such antibodies against an individual's red cells may, for instance, cause autoimmune hemolytic anemia.

B lymphocytes An immunologically important lymphocyte that is produced by the bone marrow. B lymphocytes are the only cells capable of producing antibodies. These antibodies belong to various immunoglobulin classes.

Bacteroides Heterogenous group of rod-like Gram-negative bacteria which are common inhabitants in the intestinal flora. They are strict anaerobes.

Basophils A circulating granulocyte similar to mast cells. Basophils are inflammatory cells which are involved in reactions against parasites and which participate in allergic reactions.

Cathelicidin A peptide antibiotic that may be important for controlling normal bacterial flora and stopping infections.

Chemokines A class of pro-inflammatory cytokines. They serve as signals to bring in more phagocytic cells, like neutrophils or macrophages, to an infected or inflamed site.

Chemotaxis The migration of phagocytes to an inflamed site in response to chemokines.

Confidence interval (CI) A 95% confidence interval says that if the true unknown mean lies within this interval then the value is correct 95% of the time.

Cytokines Protein signals secreted by lymphocytes, monocytes, macrophages, neutrophils, and many other cells. The pro-inflammatory cytokines cause much of the inflammation at an infected site with typical symptoms of local pain and tenderness, swelling, redness, and increased temperature. Cytokines, like the chemokine IL-8, enhance these symptoms further by bringing in and activating many more phagocytic cells. This insures that the infecting agent is efficiently stopped. But there is increasing tissue damage and symptoms resulting from the inflammation and increased energy cost.

Cytotoxic T lymphocytes or Killer cells Derived in the bone marrow, they migrate to the thymus to mature. They are further divided into helper T cells and cytotoxic killer T cells. They are normally directed against microbes and will kill diseased cells infected by a specific virus expressing the viral antigen on its surface. If directed against the body's own cells, the body cells may be destroyed and auto-immune disease follows.

Danger signals Signals originating from our own tissues that indicate something untoward is taking place and defense actions may be needed. They are recognized by special receptors on phagocytes.

Dendritic cells The most efficient APCs. They are found in all mucosal membranes and most other tissues. They are readily activated when they receive cytokine signals from phagocytes which have taken up infecting microbes.

Dimer A molecule consisting of two similar but not necessarily identical subunits.

Entero-mammaric link Lactogenic hormones affecting the mammary glands toward the end of pregnancy that direct migration of lymphocytes (plasma cells) originating from the Peyer's patches in the gut to the mammary glands. In the mammary glands, these cells produce SIgA antibodies against the microbes they came in contact with in the gut. This entero-mammaric link explains why milk provides such good protection against a wide range of microbes which tend to infect the infant via its mucosal membranes. Milk SIgA antibodies cover not only pathogens in the gastrointestinal tract, but also in the respiratory tract, which is advantageous for the infant. This results from the mother swallowing aero-pathogens which activate the SIgA response in the gut via the Peyer's patches. Then, via the entero-mammaric link, this response reaches the mammary glands.

Eosinophils Leucocytes that use somewhat different killing mechanisms adapted to fighting certain infecting agents, like parasites. Their cytoplasmic granules contain toxic cationic protein. Eosinophils are associated with hypersensitivity and greatly increase the inflammatory response in allergic diseases because the chemotaxis in such states is specific for eosinophils (and basophils).

Facultative anaerobic bacteria Microorganisms which can survive without oxygen, but are not harmed by the presence of oxygen.

Fcn receptors, or Brambell receptors These receptors in the placenta very efficiently transfer the maternal IgG to the fetal circulation so that the full term newborn has a similar blood concentration of IgG antibodies as the mother. For unknown reasons, the transfer of antibodies of certain specificities and high binding capacity are favored.

Glycoconjugate A carbohydrate linked to a lipid or protein. Certain glycoconjugates act as blocking analogues to receptors of similar structure on mucosal epithelium and keep microbes and microbial toxins from attaching to the receptors as the first step in a mucosal attack.

Glycoprotein A carbohydrate linked to a protein. Certain glycoproteins block mucosal attachment by various microbes and toxins to mucosal receptors with a similar structure to the carbohydrate portion.

Gram-negative bacteria Bacteria which stain red with the Gram stain. The Gram stain is the classical method used to characterize bacteria. Gram negative bacteria are very common among the normal bacterial flora in the gut. Many are non pathogenic. Some are only able to cause disease if they reach very high numbers like many *Escherichia coli*. A few can cause severe disease in small numbers in the gut, like *Vibrio cholerae*, *Shigella dysenteriae*, *Salmonella typhi*, or when they reach blood and tissues, like *Klebsiella*.

Gram-positive bacteria Bacteria which stain blue with the Gram stain - the classical method used to characterize bacteria. Gram positive bacteria are often found in the respiratory tract like staphylococci and streptococci, but may also appear in the gut flora like enterococci. Some are non pathogenic in these sites. Others have more virulence factors and can cause severe disease like staphylococci infecting the umbilicus, or group B streptococci (GBS) in the mother's vagina.

Granulocyte Colony-Stimulating Factor (G-CSF) Cytokine that prevents apoptosis of neutrophils. It stimulates the growth and maturation of granulocytes.

Granulocyte-Macrophage Colony-Stimulating Factor (GM-CSF) Cytokines that stimulate the production of neutrophils from bone marrow cells. It can stimulate the formation of eosinophils.

Human Leucocyte Antigen (HLA) A preformed receptor consisting of that individual's tissue type on the cell surface. It is composed of proteins. These proteins are critical in activating the body's immune system since they function as receptors for antigenic peptides (e.g. from an infecting bacterium) when they are presented to the lymphocytes of the immune system (Fig. 5)

Hygiene hypothesis Claims that exposure, mainly during the first year of life, to certain microbes in the gut flora may help prevent allergic diseases by teaching the immune system to develop immunological tolerance to harmless structures like food, pollen, etc. The result of immunological tolerance is that no immune response appears against harmless antigens like allergens.

Immediate hypersensitivity reaction
In atopic individuals, control of IgE production has failed and IgE antibodies are directed against allergens like pollen. The individual is not tolerant to the pollen antigens as he/she should be. Such IgE antibodies attach to mast cells which have the capacity to release several active substances like histamine, leukotrienes, and Platelet Activating Factor (PAF). These mediators of the allergic symptoms are secreted by the mast cell when two close IgE antibodies attached to the mast cell bind to their specific allergen. Among the released active factors, some are chemotactic and bring in eosinophil and basophil leucocytes. In this way, many such cells appear at the site. They are activated and release further pro-inflammatory substances, normally aimed at destroying parasites. This inflammation is called an immediate hypersensitivity reaction and is what takes place in the lungs of a patient with asthma, in the skin of an eczematous patient, in the gut of a food allergic individual, etc. Other forms of inflammation may be added at later stages.

Immunoglobulin A (IgA)
Antibodies present in blood. Their significance is not quite clear.

Immunoglobulin G (IgG) Antibodies present in the blood and tissues that protect against many infections. They act on pathogens by agglutinating them and by activating complement which can kill some bacteria. Complement activation results in a cascade reaction enforcing chemotaxis for neutrophils and production of pro-inflammatory cytokines which enhance the inflammatory process and activation even further. The neutrophils engulf and kill bacteria while inducing cytokine production and inflammation. IgG antibodies can also neutralize microbial toxins. There are four subclasses of IgG. They cross the placenta with differing efficiency.

Immunoglobulin M (IgM) Antibodies present in blood and tissues. They are produced first in the immune response, followed by IgG. They are of lower specificity than IgG and can, therefore, react with a broader range of microbes, but bind and neutralize toxins less well than the better binding IgG antibodies. IgM also activate complement more efficiently than IgG.

Infant mortality rate (IMR) The number of infants per thousand dying during their first year of life.

Interferon-γ (IFN−γ) A cytokine that inhibits viral replication, inhibits cell proliferation, increases the lytic potential of natural killer cells, and modulates MHC molecule expression. It is an important signal in the immune system.

Interleukin-1β A pro-inflammatory cytokine usually produced in parallel with the other two main pro-inflammatory cytokines, TNF-α and IL-6. It is produced by lymphocytes, monocytes, and other cell types. It is released by cells in response to antigenic and non-antigenic stimuli.

Lactadherin A mucin-associated glycoprotein that binds to and inhibits rotavirus and blocks its replication. The lactadherin in milk may possibly help protect against rotavirus infection.

Lactational Amenorrhea Method (LAM) The strong contraceptive effect of breastfeeding that was suggested to prevent more births than all the family planning programs in Third World countries. For details see Chapter 6.

Lactoferrin A major milk protein that kills bacteria, viruses and fungi without inducing inflammation. It blocks the capacity of leucocytes to produce pro-inflammatory cytokines. It has been shown to reduce intestinal inflammation and prevent urinary tract infections in animal experiments. Milk lactoferrin and fragments thereof come out in the urine of breastfed infants.

Leptin Appetite-regulating hormone that reduces food intake and increases energy expenditure. Leptin is increased by pro-inflammatory cytokines which explains the infection-induced loss of appetite.

Leucocytes Generic name for white blood cell. The family consists of neutrophils, lymphocytes, eosinophils, and basophils.

Lipopolysaccharide (LPS) or endotoxin The component in the outer membrane of Gram negative bacteria. It binds to CD 14 and Toll-like receptor 4 activating innate immune mechanisms appearing as a stranger signal.

Lymphocytes White cells of the blood derived from stem cells. They are the only cells in the body capable of recognizing and distinguishing between different antigens. Lymphocytes originate in the bone marrow. Those which go on to mature in the thymus become T helper and T Killer cells providing cell-mediated immunity against intracellular parasites like viruses and certain bacteria like mycobacteria. The B lymphocytes which produce the antibodies found in blood and secretions originate in the bone marrow.

Lysozyme Milk protein which is a glycosidase. Lysozyme hydrolyses the bond between N acetyl muramic acid and N acetyl glucosamine, lysing the cell wall of many bacteria. It is also present in tears, saliva, and lysosomes of phagocytic cells. It may be helpful in antibacterial defense, particularly against gram-positive bacteria in cooperation with lactoferrin.

Macrophage / monocyte Long-lived phagocytic cells, the monocytes are circulating cells, whereas the macrophages are found in tissues. The macrophages can function as antigen-presenting cells, although the dendritic cells seem more efficient in that capacity. Both macrophages and monocytes respond to chemotactic signals and produce pro-inflammatory cytokines. Macrophages activated by IFN-γ kill microbes efficiently (Fig. 5).

Mast cell Resident cell of connective tissue. Mast cells are similar to the circulating basophil granulocytes. Like the basophilic granulocytes, mast cells release histamine and other mediators during allergic reactions.

Memory lymphocytes Lymphocytes with immunological memory that are specific for the antigen remaining after each primary immune response.

Natural killer (NK) cells A subset of lymphocytes found in blood and lymphoid tissues. NK cells are derived from the bone marrow. NK cells activated by IFN-γ possess the ability to kill certain tumor cells or normal cells infected by viruses. Such killing is not directed against any specific antigen and is part of the innate rather than the specific immune system.

Neutrophil A leucocyte with lobated nucleus and typical cytoplasmic granules on staining. They are the major responder in acute inflammations. Neutrophils can be activated by cytokines and are efficient phagocytes of bacteria.

Nucleotides Building blocks of DNA.

Odds ratio (OR) OR is used in case-control studies to determine the strength of association of a disease to a risk factor. It measures the ratio of the odds of exposure among the cases (diseased) to that among the controls (not diseased). If OR is 1.0, there is no association between the disease and the exposure. If OR is less than 1, then it indicates protection due to the exposure. If OR is greater than 1.0, there is an increased risk. An OR of 3 would therefore mean that those who are diseased were 3 times more likely to have been exposed compared to those who are not diseased. The OR is an estimate of Relative Risk (see this word) and is useful for rare diseases with long latency. In case control studies, several risk factors can be studied for one disease outcome. Both the disease and the exposure are studied at the same time.

Oligosaccharides Appear in tissues and tissue fluids in large numbers of combinations of five different monosaccharides - glucose, fucose, galactose, N-acetylamine and sialic acid. There are 3-10 monosaccharides in each oligosaccharide. Oligosaccharides also appear attached to proteins as glycoproteins and to lipids as glycolipids; these are called glycoconjugates. The many structures have numerous functions in various tissues.

Peyer's patches Organ in the gut covered by M cells which take in material from the gut content into the patches. Bacteria and other material are presented to the local immune system in the patches for processing. The responding lymphocytes present in the Peyer's patches then become committed to production of IgA dimer antibodies with J chain specific for the presenting material (bacteria, etc.). The lymphocytes then migrate and produce these antibodies in the gut, other mucosae, and also in remote exocrine glands like the mammary glands. Subsequently, the antibodies will then appear as secretory IgA (SIgA) in exocrine secretions like milk and on mucosal membranes in the gut, respiratory tract, etc. (Figs 8 and 10)

Phagocytes A cell that is capable of engulfing and killing bacteria. The main mammalian phagocytes are neutrophils and macrophages.

Pili See Adhesin.

PolyIgR The receptor on the basal surface of mucosal epithelium that binds locally produced IgA dimers with J chain and brings them through the epithelial cells so that they appear as SIgA antibodies on the mucosal surface (Fig. 8).

Probiotic bacteria Health-promoting bacteria. Their modes of functions have not been clarified yet. They may compete for space and nutrients with more pathogenic microbes.

Regulatory T lymphocytes (Treg) T lymphocytes which control other lymphocytes by production of the immunosuppressive cytokines IL-10 and TGF-β.

Relative Risk Used in cohort studies to determine the strength of association between an exposure and the disease outcome. It indicates the likelihood of developing the disease in the exposed group relative to those who are not exposed. It is particularly good for rare exposures. Since it is possible to calculate the incidence rates, the excess risk because of the exposure can also be calculated. RR is, hence, a ratio of the incidence of the disease in an exposed group to that of the incidence of the disease in an unexposed group. In cohort studies, several disease outcomes can be studied for one exposure/risk factor. The exposure is studied first and groups followed until the disease develops.

Secretory component (SC) A glycoprotein found in a variety of external secretions – tears, bile, colostrum. It is also the portion of the polyIgR which is present outside the basal portion of an epithelial cell (Figure 8) and attached to SIgA.

Secretory Immunoglobin A (SIgA) Protects the body's mucosal surfaces from infection. It is a main mechanism for providing local immunity against infections in the gut or respiratory tract and is the main antibody in human milk. SIgA is not found in blood (Figure 8).

Soluble CD14 This component binds to the surface structure lipopolysaccharide (LPS) of Gram negative bacteria. It supports the LPS to activate the Toll-like receptors on phagocytes which activates this phase of innate immunity. Soluble CD 14 also supports differentiation and expansion of B lymphocytes.

Stranger signals These signals serve to sound the alarm that a potentially dangerous stranger (microbe) is around by binding to the Toll-like and other receptors on cells of the innate immune system like monocytes, macrophages and neutrophils.

Sub-clinical mastitis There may be no obvious symptoms but milk production can be impaired. Sub-clinical mastitis is detected by the increase in the Na/K ratio in the milk. The increase relates to the content of IL-8. This cytokine is a strong chemokine signal for neutrophils. It reveals the presence of an inflammatory process in the mammary glands associated with neutrophils which probably promote the inflammation. It is relatively easy to demonstrate the presence of subclinical mastitis by determining the Na/K ratio in the mother's milk. It may be that sub-clinical mastitis is part of a more generalized inflammation. In two studies, dietary intake of vitamin E-rich sunflower oil was helpful in reducing this inflammation whereas postpartum vitamin A supplementation had no effect.

T cell receptor (TCR) Receptor on the surface of T cells that recognizes antigens.

T lymphocytes A major class of lymphocytes which are produced in the bone marrow and migrate to and mature in the thymus. T lymphocytes are subdivided into helper T cells and cytotoxic T cells. Helper and cytotoxic T lymphocytes recognize only peptide antigens that are attached to the host's HLA proteins expressed on the surface of accessory cells. T cells recognize and respond to cell surface-associated, but not soluble, antigens (Fig. 5).

Thymus The lymphoid organ found behind the breastbone next to the heart (Fig. 9). In this organ, T lymphocytes are educated, mature, and multiply. The thymus of an exclusively breastfed infant is twice as large as the thymus of a formula fed infant.

Toll-like receptors A special receptor that recognizes microbes or components from microbes. Upon recognizing the microbes, these cells are activated and produce a number of active components, especially cytokines. These components function by bringing in many more stimulated phagocytes to further support the defense. While acting in defense, the activated phagocytes and cytokines that are released cause tissue damage, clinical symptoms of infection, and an energy-consuming inflammation.

Transforming Growth Factor-β (TGF-β) A cytokine that stimulates growth of normal cells, but is also immunosuppressive. Some regulatory T lymphocytes function via this signal.

Tumor Necrosis Factor-α (TNF-α)	This cytokine has a wide range of pro-inflammatory actions and is responsible for many of the symptoms of an ongoing inflammation. The striking tiredness of many chronic inflammatory diseases seems to be primarily caused by this cytokine. When this cytokine is blocked, the tiredness vanishes as shown in patients with rheumatoid arthritis and Crohn's disease.
Type1 fimbriae	Thread-like structures present on bacteria like certain *E. coli*. They are used by bacteria to adhere to epithelial cells. Type 1 fimbria a form of pili or adhesins.
Virulence factors	Structures which make microbes able to infect a host and establish an infection. Examples are certain adhesins (pili), colonization factors, and toxins.

Index

Symbols

α-tocopherol 101
α–Lactalbumin 86
α1-antichymotrypsin 100, 101
α1-antitrypsin 93, 100, 101
β-carotene 101

A

Actinomyces 89
acute myeloblastic leukemia 162
adaptive immunity 34
adhesins 17
aerobic 14, 16, 19
aerobic bacteria 14–26
AF xi, 98, 99, 116, 220
allergens 144, 146, 147, 148, 149, 150, 152, 155
allergy 123, 142, 144, 145, 146, 147, 148, 149, 150, 152, 154, 155, 156, 173, 180, 181, 182, 183, 184, 185
anaerobic 14, 14–26, 15, 15–26, 16, 16–26, 17, 17–26, 18, 18–26, 19, 19–26, 20, 20–26, 21, 21–26, 23, 23–26, 196–212
anti-antibodies 140, 141, 164, 165, 167
anti-idiotypes 140, 164
anti-inflammatory components 99
anti-secretory factor 98, 99, 118, 196, 197, 199, 207, 220
antibodies 33, 36, 37, 39, 40, 41, 43, 45, 46, 77,78
antibody-mediated immunity 52
antigen 33, 34, 35, 36
antigen-presenting cells vi, xi, 33, 34, 36, 54
antigen-presenting dendritic cells 50
apoptosis 37
appendicitis 139, 178
ascorbic acid 101
asthma 143, 145, 148, 149, 150, 151, 152, 153, 154, 155, 156, 157, 180, 182, 183, 184, 185, 186
atopic 143, 144, 146, 147, 148, 150, 151, 152, 153, 154, 155, 156, 180, 181, 182, 184, 185, 186, 194
atopic dermatitis 143, 150, 151, 154, 155, 182, 184, 194
auto-antibodies 157
autoimmune 157, 159, 166, 168

B

bacteria 195
Bacteroides 15, 18, 19, 20
basophils 34, 41
BCG vaccine 43, 61, 62, 139
Bifidobacteria 84, 86
bifidobacteria 19, 20
Bifidobacterium 15
bile salt-stimulated lipase 90
biochemical compounds 29, 44
biochemical defense factors 50
BMI 154, 157, 159, 160
Body Mass Index 154
botulism 139, 178
Brambell receptors 71
breastfed 123, 126, 130, 131, 132, 133, 134, 135, 137, 139, 140, 141, 144, 146, 148, 149, 150, 151, 152, 153, 154, 158, 160, 161, 163, 165, 166, 167, 176, 189
breast cancer 163, 164, 192
bronchiolitis 135
B cell aggregates 56
B lymphocytes 49, 56, 58, 63

C

Campylobacter 20, 80, 82, 88, 107, 111

Campylobacter jejuni 88, , 111
Candida 28
carbohydrates 29
carbohydrate components 88
carcinoma 86
case-control studies 123, 172
catalase 101
cathelicidin 29
cats 147, 149, 152, 183
celiac disease 158, 159, 188
cell-mediated immunity 51
chemical defense factors 49
chemical factors 29, 44
chemokines 30, 32, 34, 35
child mortality 60, 69
chymotrypsin 83
cilia 29
cleft palate 133, 135, 175
clostridia 19, 20
Clostridium 15
coagulase-negative staphylococci 18
coagulation system 99
colitis 85, 86, 90, 109, 110, 118
colonization resistance 16
colostrum 77, 81, 82, 91, , 78, 106, 110, 114, 115, 118, 119, 121
complement factor 3 103
complement regulatory factors 101
complement system 99
congenital CMV 204
cow's milk 126, 146, 147, 152, 157, 158, 180, 181, 186, 190
Crohn's disease 158, 159, 188
croup 135
cryptopatches 93
cytokines 28, 31, 32, 33, 34, 35, 37, 40, 44, 45, 92, 116
Cytomegalovirus viii, xi, xi–xii, 203, 203–212, 210, 210–212
cytotoxic Killer T cells 56
cytotoxic T lymphocytes 33, 36, 37

D

danger signals 30, 46
defensins 29, 92
dendritic cells 33, 35
diabetes 157, 159, 186, 187
diarrhea 79, 88, 98, 107
diphtheria 139, 179
diphtheria toxoid 43
DNA 81, 91, 92, 108, 109
dysentery 79

E

E. coli 17, 18, 19, 20, 21, 23, 24
eczema 143, 145, 146, 148, 150, 151, 153, 154, 155, 156, 181, 182, 184, 185
elastase inhibitor 100, 101
endotoxin 30
Entamoeba histolytica 90
entero-mammaric link 79, 82
Enterobacter 15, 15–26, 20, 20–26, 21, 21–26
Enterobacteriaceae family 15, 15–26, 17, 17–26, 18, 18–26
Enterococcus faecalis 15, 15–26, 195–212
Enterococcus faecium 15, 15–26, 195–212
Enterococcus family 15, 15–26
enteropathogenic E. coli 84
enterotoxigenic E. coli 80
enzyme 81, 84, 87, 91
eosinophils 34, 41
eotaxin 94
Epidermal Growth Factor 100
erythropoietin 96
Escherichia coli 15, 15–26, 17, 17–26, 24, 24–26, 69–70, 106–122, 107–122, 109–122, 110–122, 111–122, 112–122, 113–122, 119–122, 172–194, 177–194, 192–194

evidence-based medicine 123, 131, 155
exclusive breastfeeding 199, 202
exocrine glands 58, 59, 60

F

facultative anaerobic 14, 15, 16, 17
fatty acids 86, 90
Fcn 71
Fc receptors 38, 71, 143
fibroblast growth factor 96
fibronectin 103
fish oil 154, 185
formula 88
fucose 88
fucosyloligosaccharides 88, 111
fungi 28

G

galactose 88
gastric lipase 90
gastroenteritis 80, 109, 112, 135, 142, 174, 183, 188
gastrointestinal tract 79, 96, 80, 121
germinal centers 56
Giardia lamblia 79, 80, 82, 107, 112, 113
glioblastoma 86
glucose 88
glutathione peroxidase 101
gluten 157, 158, 159, 189
glycan shield 200
glycoconjugates 29, 88, 89, 110
glycoprotein 29, 83, 87, 89
GM1 89
Granulocyte-Macrophage Colony-Stimulating Factor xi–xii, 52–70, 224–234
Granulocyte Colony-Stimulating Factor xi–xii, 52–70, 224–234
grass pollen 152
Group B (GBS) 15
Group B Streptococci xi, xi–xii, 20, 20–26
growth factors 95, 97, 98, 97, 116, 117
growth hormone 95, 96
gut epithelium 201
gut lumen 201

H

H. influenzae 57, 64
H. pylori 132, 139
Haemophilus influenzae 62, 69, 70
HAMLET xi–xii, 86, 86–122, 87–122, 86, 87, 110–122, 110, 163–194, 164–194
hay fever 145, 152, 154
Helicobacter pylori 89, 112
hemolytic-uremic syndrome 90
Hemophilus influenzae type b 97
hepatitis B virus 205
hepatitis C virus 205
hepatitis virus A 205
hepatocyte growth factor 96
hepatopathy 204
herpes viruses 206
histamine 144
HIV-1 88, 98, 103, 119
HLA antigens 47
Hodgkin's disease 162, 163
Hodgkin's lymphoma 163
hormones 95, 95, 116
host defense 27, 30, 34, 41, 44
Human Leucocyte Antigen xi–xii, 35, 35–46, 224–234
human T cell leukemia virus 202
human α-lactalbumin made lethal to tumor cells xi, xi–xii
hydroxyl radical formation 101
Hygiene hypothesis 22
hypertrophic pyloric stenosis 139
hypoglycemia 127
hypothalamus-pituitary-adrenal 95
hypothermia 127

I

IgA 33, 38, 39, 41, 42, 43
IgE 33, 36, 38, 41
IgG 36, 38, 39, 40, 41, 43, 45
IgM 33, 36, 38, 39, 40, 41, 43, 45
IL-10 32, 37, 44, 46, 84, 93, 97, 99, 100
IL-6 31, 32
IL-8 138, 146, 178
immune system 47, 49, 53, 54, 55, 56, 57, 58, 60, 61, 68
immunoglobulins 33, 39
Immunoglobulin A xi–xii, 225–234
Immunoglobulin G xi–xii, 226–234
Immunoglobulin M xi–xii, 226–234
Immunological memory 57
immunomodulatory cytokines 99
infant mortality rate 124, 129
inflammatory bowel disease 98, 99, 118
inflammatory reactivity 77, 99
innate defense mechanisms 49
insulin-like growth factor 96, 98, 116
Interferon-γ xi, xi–xii, 34, 36–46, 45–46, 226–234
Interleukin -1β xi, xi–xii, 32
Interleukin -6 xi, xi–xii
intestinal hypoxia 138
intestinal microflora 14–26, 20–26, 21–26, 24–26, 90–122, 136–194, 148–194, 182–194, 207–212
intraepithelial lymphocytes 93
intrauterine growth retardation 61
iron 83

J

joining (J) chain 38, 41

K

kallikrein-kininogen system 99
Killer cells 33, 37
Klebsiella 15–26, 18–26, 20–26, 21–26, 23–26, 28–46, 30–46, 88–122

L

L-histidine 101
L. crispatus 195
lactadherin 89, 112
lactalbumin 86, 87, 101, 110
Lactational Amenorrhea Method 124, 169
lactobacilli 19
Lactobacillus 15, 22, 23, 24
Lactobacillus gasseri 195
Lactobacillus rhamnosus 195
Lactococcus lactis 195
lactoferrin 83, 84, 85, 86, , 84, 100, 109
leptin 96, 97, 98, , 97, 117
leucocytes 28, 29, 102
Leuconostoc mesenteroides 195
leukemia 162, 163, 192
Leukemia Inhibiting Factor xi, xi–xii, 48–70, 96
leukotrienes 144
lipases 86, 113
lipids 90
lipid peroxidation 101
Lipopolysaccharide xi, xi–xii, 30, 35, 67–70, 101, 118, 228–234
lipoprotein lipase 90
Listeria 21
long chain polyunsaturated fatty acid 154
lower respiratory tract infections 133, 134, 135, 148, 176
luteinizing hormone-releasing hormone 96
lymphocytes 33, 34, 35, 36, 37, 39, 40, 41, 42, 44, 45
lymphoid aggregates 58
lymphoma 86
lysozyme 84, 87, 100, 101, 103, 108, 109

M

Mac-2 binding protein 89

macrophages 28, 31, 33, 37, 45
Macrophage Inhibiting Factor 104
mammary gland 88, 94, 98, 107, 114
mannose 30
mastitis 196, 197, 199
mature milk 77
mechanical defense mechanisms 28
memory lymphocytes 39, 40
meningitis 16, 18, 21, 127, 136, 142, 180
meningococci 57, 62, 64
micronutrients 60
mites 143, 144, 145, 149, 152, 156
monocytes 28, 30, 31, 45
Monocyte Chemotactic Factor 94, 104
monoglycerides 90
mucin 89
mucosal defense system 57
multiple sclerosis 158, 159, 187
mycobacteria 37, 43
Mycobacterium tuberculosis 61
M cells 58, 59, 201

N

N-acetylamine 88
natural killer cells xi–xii, 65–70
NEC vii–viii, xi–xii, 21–26, 49–70, 138–194
Necrotizing Enterocolitis xi, xi–xii, 21
neuro-endocrine system 95
neutropenia 204
neutrophils 28, 30, 31, 32, 40, 45
NK cells 33, 34, 36, 37, 47, 48, 54, 91, 92, 94, 96, 97, 103, 166, 202
NFκB 84, 85, 99
Nuclear Factor κB 84
nucleic acids 84, 91
Nucleotides 91, , 113

O

obesity 154, 157, 159, 160, 162, 168, 189, 190, 191
oleic acid 86, 87
oligosaccharides 88, 89, 110, 111
oral candidiasis 199, 200, 201
oxygen radicals 101

P

PAF-acetylhydrolase 138
parasites 206
partial breastfeeding 198
parvovirus 206
peptides 29, 33
Peyer's patches 58, 59
phagocytes 28, 31, 41
phagocytosis 50, 52, 56
pili 17
platelet activating factor 138, 144, 178
pneumococci 57, 62, 64
pneumonia 129, 134, 135, 176
polyIgR 38, 42, 43
polysaccharide 57, 62, 64, 69, 70, 80, 84, 107
polysaccharide-conjugate vaccine 139
pooled odds ratios 127
pregnancy 128, 141, 148, 154, 155, 160, 163, 182, 185, 186
premature infant 201
primary response 39, 44
pro-inflammatory 31, 32, 33
probiotic bacteria 22
programmed cell death 37
prostaglandins 1 and 2 100
protein/calorie malnutrition 60
proteins 83, 84, 86, 87, 99, 109, 114
protozoa 206

R

RANTES 94
regulatory T lymphocytes xi, 37, 44
respiratory tract 78, 79, 88, 89
rheumatoid arthritis 158, 159, 187, 188
ribonuclease 84
RNA 91
rotavirus 89, 109, 112
rubella 205, 206

S

S-fimbriae 89
salivary glands 58
Salmonella 20, 24
salt-stimulated lipase 90
SC 38, 42, 43, 60
schistosomes 206
secondary response 39
Secretory Component xi, xi–xii, 43, 60
Secretory IgA 19, 38, 41
septicemia 16, 18, 20, 21
Shigella 79, 80, 82, 85, 90, 107, 110
Shigella dysenteriae 90
Shigella Flexneri 85
sialic acid 88, 89
SIDS 128, 129, 171
SIgA 36, 38, 41, 42, 43, 45, 77, 78, 79, 80, 81, 82, 83, 84, 85, 87, 89, 90, 92, 99, 100, 103, 107
small for gestational age 61
smoking 123, 128, 129, 155, 160, 171, 176, 186, 188
Soluble CD14 101, 102, , 118
soluble Toll-Like Receptor 101, 102
Staph. epidermidis 195
staphylococci 18, 21
Staphylococcus aureus 15, 15–26, 18, 18–26, 20, 20–26, 24, 24–26, 148–194, 207–212
Staphylococcus epidermidis 15, 15–26, 18, 18–26, 20, 20–26
Staphylococcus family 15, 15–26
stool 79, 88
Strep. mitis 195
Strep. salivarius 195
streptococci 89, , 112
Streptococcus pneumoniae 88, 111
Streptococcus family 15, 15–26
sub-clinical mastitis 197, 198, 199, 200, 202
sudden infant death syndrome 128, 129, 171
sunflower oil 197, 207
superoxide 101
Systemic Lupus Erythematosus 48

T

tetanus 35, 43, 139, 141, 179
TGF-β 92, 99, 100
thrombocytopenia 204
thymus 35, 37, 55, 68
tolerant 22
Toll-like receptors xi–xii, 30, 30–46, 45, 45–46, 232–234, 234
tonsillectomies 139
toxins 79, 83, 88, 89, 90
transcription factor 99
Transforming Growth Factor-β xi, xi–xii, 32, 32–46, 44, 44–46, 100–122, 234
translocation 16, 21
triglycerides 86
trypanosomes 206
trypsin 83
Tumor Necrosis Factor-α xi, xi–xii, 32, 100–122, 234
type1 fimbriae 19
T helper cell 37
T lymphocytes 33, 35, 36, 37, 39, 44, 45, 48, 49, 51, 55, 56, 63, 93, 95, 97, 104, 118, 119, 120

U

Ureoplasma urealyticum 148
urinary tract infections 136, 137, 141, 144
urine 85, 86, 88

V

V. cholerae 89
vaccination 61, 62
Vibrio cholerae 80, 82, 111
virulence factors 17, 20

viruses 28, 197
vitamin A 60, 197

W

wheezing 134, 135, 142, 144, 147, 148, 150, 151, 152, 153, 155, 175, 180
World Health Organization 124, 179

Z

zinc 60

Ordering Information

Pharmasoft Publishing
1712 N. Forest St.
Amarillo, TX 79106
8:00 a.m. to 5:00 p.m. CST

Call.....806-376-9900
Sales...800-378-1317
FAX....806-376-9901

Online Web Orders...
http://www.iBreastfeeding.com